JOHN FORD

Wagon Master

JOHN FORD

Joseph McBride and Michael Wilmington

A DA CAPO PAPERBACK

Library of Congress Cataloging in Publication Data

McBride, Joseph.
    John Ford.

    (A Da Capo paperback)
    Filmography: p.
    Bibliography: p.
    1. Ford, John, 1895-1973. I. Wilmington,
Michael, joint author.
[PN1998.A3F59 1975b]   791.43'0233'0924 [B]   75-19179
ISBN 0-306-80016-0 pbk.

First paperback printing — July, 1975
Second paperback printing — November, 1980
Third paperback printing — December, 1988

John Ford by Joseph McBride and Michael Wilmington
first published in 1974 by Martin Secker & Warburg Limited.

First American Edition, 1975, by Da Capo Press, Inc.

Copyright © Secker & Warburg 1974

Published by Da Capo Press, Inc.
A Subsidiary of Plenum Publishing Corporation
233 Spring Street, New York, New York 10013

All Rights Reserved

Manufactured in the United States of America

Contents

1. Bringing in the Sheaves — 7
2. Half Genius, Half Irish — 17
3. Himself — 38
4. The Noble Outlaw: *Straight Shooting, Stagecoach, Wagon Master* — 48
5. Men at War: *They Were Expendable, My Darling Clementine, Fort Apache* — 75
6. Ireland: *The Quiet Man, The Rising of the Moon* — 110
7. Rebels: *The Sun Shines Bright, The Searchers* — 135
8. What Really Happened: *Sergeant Rutledge, The Man Who Shot Liberty Valance, The Civil War* — 164
9. The Last Place on Earth: *Seven Women* — 197
Filmography — 213
Bibliography — 227
Acknowledgments — 234

Ford on set, with John Wayne

1. Bringing in the Sheaves

by Joseph McBride

As the coffin was being lowered into position over the open grave, hanging on chains from the jaws of a bulldozer, one of the gravediggers lost his grip and took a flying pratfall into a bouquet of flowers. 'A bit of Fordian comedy,' whispered my companion as we watched John Ford's body sinking into its final resting place. His family, his military honour guard, the great names of the old Hollywood and the remnants of the Ford Stock Company had departed, leaving a dozen people, five of them gravediggers, to take part in his last funeral scene.

And just as in a Ford movie the mood may shift abruptly from comedy to sentiment, my eyes left the sprawling gravedigger and registered an unforgettable Fordian long-shot composition. On a distant hilltop overlooking the grave, silhouetted against the bright sky of early afternoon, were two tiny figures, a mother and son, standing between two large oak trees. The woman was Anna Lee, who had stood in a doorway waiting for her dead husband in *How Green Was My Valley*, had watched from a balcony as her husband rode to his death with the Cavalry in *Fort Apache*, and had occupied the place of honour at her husband's wake in *The Last Hurrah*. It was poetically fitting that the archetypal grieving widow of the Ford Stock Company should be the only member of his troupe watching him being committed to the earth.

John Ford died of cancer on 31 August 1973 at his home in Palm Desert, California, just five months after more than a thousand of his colleagues had gathered at a lavish nationally televised tribute in Beverly Hills to watch him receive the first Life Achievement Award from the American Film Institute. Although the nature of his illness was a well-guarded secret known only to his closest friends, it was apparent that Ford was slipping away, and the tribute was obviously arranged as his last hurrah. Maureen O'Hara sang a medley of songs from *The Quiet Man*, Jimmy Stewart spun his favourite yarns about 'Pappy', and John Wayne pushed Ford's wheelchair on to the stage so that he could receive the Medal of Freedom, the nation's highest civilian honour, from President Nixon, whose presence had caused Jane Fonda and several thousand other protesters to assemble outside.

Walking shakily but unassisted to the podium, Ford said, 'Mr President, I'm overcome with gratitude. I wish I had the words to express my feelings, but I don't. Tonight is a most important event – the first time a President has honoured a motion picture event with his presence.' His voice breaking, Ford thanked Nixon for bringing the prisoners home from Indochina (one can readily visualize that scene as Ford would film it), and concluded with, 'God bless Richard Nixon'. Touching as the event was, many admirers of Ford felt that it had deviously turned into a homage to Nixon; the television cameras lionized the President and all but ignored the painfully wasted old man in the wheelchair. Still, seeing Ford's pride at being honoured by the President made one's reservations seem churlish. When the band struck up 'Hail to the Chief' and Ford emerged from the wings, being pushed in his chair by his black chauffeur, with Nixon tagging along behind, it was as if Ford, the son of an Irish immigrant saloon-keeper, had become President for a night.

Luckily, 'God bless Richard Nixon' was not his final public statement. On May 28, Memorial Day, he was driven to the Motion Picture Country Home in Woodland Hills to give his annual address on the meaning of the holiday and to say farewell to the 94-year-old Donald Crisp, whose performance as Gwilym Morgan in *How Green Was My Valley* was modelled on Ford's memory of his father. My companion at the burial, Alex Ameripoor, a Persian-born film editor, went to Woodland Hills so that he could meet Ford at the reception following the ceremony. 'I said a few things to Ford,' he recalled, 'but of course he didn't hear me. I said, "I'm sitting in the presence of history." And he replied, "*What?* What do you mean?" After I repeated the statement twice, Ford finally got the point and looked at me as if saying to himself, "Big deal." ' Some of Ford's actors and crewmen, also sensing the 'presence of history', came to pay their respects, among them Anna Lee, Harry Carey Jr, Carleton Young, Wingate Smith, Ray Kellogg and James

Basevi. It was an emotional, tearful reunion and it had a classic Fordian ending. While the reception was still in progress, Ford walked out of the door on the arm of his chauffeur, nobody noticing that he had gone, like Ethan Edwards walking away from his family at the end of *The Searchers.*

In his final summer, Ford was visited regularly by old cronies, including Howard Hawks, who was with him two days before his death. On June 17, Hawks and Peter Bogdanovich paid him a Father's Day visit. Ford remained mentally alert until his last day, and one evening he called Wingate Smith, his brother-in-law and long-time assistant director, and asked, 'Are you ready to work?' Besides his cherished Revolutionary War project *April Morning*, Ford had been talking about three other films: an adaptation of Maxwell Anderson's play *Valley Forge*, with Frank Capra as co-director; an adaptation of Arthur Conan Doyle's novel *The White Company*, with John Wayne, Laurence Olivier and Alec Guinness; and *The Josh Clayton Story*, a Western about black cavalrymen to be shot in Monument Valley with Fred Williamson and Woody Strode. After hearing of Ford's death, Strode said, 'He should be buried in Monument Valley.'

Ford died in bed surrounded by his family and a few close friends, a scene he had so memorably imagined in *The Last Hurrah.* 'It was a beautiful death,' his sister Josephine Feeney told me in the Hollywood mortuary where his body was lying in state, the tattered flag from his headquarters at the Battle of Midway draped over the closed coffin. (Miss Feeney, a sprightly little woman of 81, was tenth in the Ford family of eleven children.) A Mass was celebrated every day at the foot of his bed, and when the Mass ended that day he growled, 'Now will somebody give me a cigar?' Those characteristic words were not his last, although when the report spread some of his friends thought they were; like Frank Skeffington in *The Last Hurrah,* Ford had two exit lines, one for the legend, the other more private. Josephine Feeney's account continued: 'Jack knew we were all there, and there was no suffering . . . He fell asleep about five o'clock and slept very quietly until the end.' Death came at 6.05 p.m., and scarcely an hour later the bulletin came over the Associated Press wire, hailing him as 'the greatest American director of the sound film era, as D. W. Griffith was acknowledged the master of the silent movie'. It was then that one could say of Ford, as Auden wrote of Yeats, 'He became his admirers.'

Four days later, after the coffin had been wheeled through the high bronze doors Ford had donated to Hollywood's Church of the Blessed Sacrament, his nephew Father John Feeney prefaced the rosary vigil with a further detail of those last moments: 'Stories of this man are legion, but I think the one

Ford on location for *Stagecoach*, with Tim Holt

which best sums up John Ford was what happened last Friday after he went into a coma. As we began saying the rosary, we heard his voice come out and say, "Holy Mary, mother of God . . ." This was a man who had dined with presidents and kings, and at the end it was his rosary beads clutched in his hands which gave him hope and consolation.' When the mourners filed out of the church, the organist played 'Bringing in the Sheaves', which Danny Borzage had played on his concertina just before the striking of the set at the end of every Ford picture.

The funeral Mass on September 5 and the burial service in Culver City's Holy Cross Cemetery were mostly bereft of Fordian 'touches' and outward show of sentiment. Ford's friends had lived with the anticipation of his death for many months, and to many of them his release from the illness came almost as a relief. During the Mass, Anna Lee had remembered the difficulty she once had in crying for a scene in one of Ford's movies: 'I told him, "Sean, I'll cry at your funeral," and, by God, I did.' Noticing white-bearded Danny Borzage talking with George Marshall, one of the few surviving directors of Ford's generation, I asked him if he might be planning to squeeze out a few staves of 'Shall We Gather at the River?' at graveside. Holding my hand tightly, his eyes filling, Borzage said, 'I couldn't take it.'

John Wayne, who joined George Cukor in escorting Ford's daughter Barbara into the church, seemed to be fighting for control of his emotions throughout the ceremonies. Standing on the steps of the church after the rosary, a cigar clenched between his teeth as he hailed his pals in a booming voice, Wayne seemed oddly alone, an ambulatory statue in the shadows whom few people dared approach. I mustered up the cheek to shake his hand and tell him I had once met Ford. As I started to say how much Ford meant to me, Wayne cut me off with, '*I* met him once.' Watching him stride back into the church, I knew I would never be able to capture the inflections he put on that line – half mean, half poignant, half gruff, half broken. Later, at the cemetery, he told a reporter thrusting a microphone into his car, 'It's rough to put a fellow away that you spent forty-five years of your life with, in close communication.'

Although, as the Los Angeles *Times* noted, 'the glossy, theatrical aura of some Hollywood funerals was conspicuously absent', one long-standing tradition was dutifully observed. Subdued pandemonium erupted as the big names – Wayne, Stewart, Henry Fonda, Charlton Heston, Loretta Young, Pat O'Brien, Gilbert Roland, George Murphy, Raymond Massey, Rod Taylor, Walter Pidgeon, Cesar Romero – picked their way through a sidewalk packed with spectators all too aware that today's Hollywood gives few such occasions for rubber-necking. Iron Eyes Cody, arriving in full tribal regalia, provoked near-hysteria among the television and press photographers, who persuaded him to go back down the steps and re-enact his entrance into the church. Of all the directors attending the funeral (among them Sam Fuller, William Wyler, Henry Hathaway, Robert Wise, Vincent Sherman), only Frank Capra received any attention from the *paparazzi*, probably because of his best-selling book.

The craftsmen and character actors who were closer to Ford than many of the famous players – second-unit director Cliff Lyons, stuntmen Chuck Roberson and Chuck Hayward, cinematographers William Clothier and Winton C. Hoch, actors George O'Brien, Woody Strode, Harry Carey Jr, Carleton Young, John Agar – enjoyed the luxury of public inattention as they chatted on the steps. Wingate Smith moved restlessly from group to group, making sure everyone was noticed and every detail was running smoothly, just as a good assistant director should do. Perhaps the remembrance that day which would have touched Ford most came from the Stuntmen's Association, which took out a full-page advertisement in *Daily Variety* reading, 'One of us and we'll miss him.'

Timothy Cardinal Manning of Los Angeles, officiating at the funeral Mass, offered in his eulogy an analysis of Fordian themes which lends an official imprimatur to critics who have argued that Catholic dogma is a crucial substratum of Ford's work. Describing Ford as 'the incomparable master of his trade', the Cardinal alluded to five of the six films for which Ford won Academy Awards. *The Quiet Man*: 'A skilled director will take the great themes of life – love and laughter – and will dramatize them against the green hills and fields of an island like Ireland.' *The Battle of Midway*: 'There will be war and peace. Men will see perhaps in some obscure atoll in the Pacific the destiny of mankind hanging in the balance.' *How Green Was My Valley* and *The Grapes of Wrath*: 'There will be great themes of human injustice, whether buried in the mines of Wales or in the sun-drenched grape fields of the San Joaquin Valley. There will be all the passion and the power and the pain of life.' And, finally, *The Informer*: 'Deep in the recesses of every heart there will be the sense of guilt, the possibility of betrayal. A great director will take this theme of guilt, the intercession of an informer, and we will all see ourselves.' A soloist sang 'The Battle Hymn of the Republic' when the coffin left the church, and John Wayne, marching behind with his eyes puffed up like a battered prizefighter's, could be heard crying on the words, 'He is trampling out the vintage where the grapes of wrath are stored . . .'

Ford was buried in a rolling green valley near the graves of his brothers Francis and Edward. Religion and militarism, so often commingled in his

John Ford's funeral: Ford's grandson gives the Midway flag to Mrs Ford

work, took equal place in the graveside ceremonies, with a Navy rifle squad firing salute and a bugler blowing taps. Dan Ford, the director's grandson, wore his Silver Star from Vietnam as he took the folded Midway flag from superior officers and handed it to the widow, Mary, whose eyes seemed to be looking far beyond the coffin – perhaps back to the St Patrick's Day dance where they had met more than 50 years ago. Not long before his death, Ford had been promoted from rear admiral to full admiral by President Nixon, who had said at the AFI tribute, 'Tonight I've heard Mr Ford referred to as "Boss", "Jack", and "Pappy", but I don't like to hear him referred to as "Rear Admiral". As commander in chief of the armed forces, I declare that for the remainder of the evening, John Ford is a full admiral.' Nixon later made the promotion permanent, sending Ford an admiral's hat, and one night in July he called Ford from the Maryland hospital where he was recuperating from pneumonia. 'I was lying here and I couldn't sleep, and I thought I'd call and chat with John,' the President said. In a telephone conversation earlier in the year, Nixon asked Ford what his reaction had been to the news of the POWs' return from Vietnam. 'Frankly, sir,' said Ford, 'I broke down and cried like a baby.' Places were reserved for the Nixons in the family section at the funeral, but they were unable to attend and sent a spray of red, white and blue flowers to the church; the spray was placed on the coffin at the cemetery, after the Midway flag was removed. The President's statement on Ford's death said that the director represented 'the best in American films and the best in America'. Not a man easily to forgive an insult, Nixon had apparently forgotten or chosen to overlook Ford's hilarious parody of his Checkers speech in *The Last Hurrah*. The strange metamorphosis of the relationship between politician and poet was vastly revealing of the deep ambivalences in Ford's view of America.

'The best things in movies happen by accident,' Ford once declared, and the best thing at the burial service also happened by accident. While taps were sounding, I heard a whooshing noise in the sky and looked up to see a jet streaking directly overhead as a flock of birds passed in the opposite direction, due West. Father Feeney closed his book, the flag was passed to the widow and there was an awkward silence. Everyone's eyes moved towards John Wayne, who was standing a few feet to my right. I was hoping he would recite Stevenson's 'Requiem', as he had at the funeral in *They Were Expendable*: 'Home is the sailor, home from the sea . . .' Wayne tensed, his big body started to move forward, then he froze and looked down at the ground, and people began to leave. The service was over. As with the burial in *The Searchers*, Wayne was the one who 'put an amen to it'.

The crowd splintered into small groups, most of the mourners reluctant to leave so quickly. Alex, quoting what Henry Fonda said at Grandpa Joad's burial in *The Grapes of Wrath*, expressed a feeling that must have been on many minds: 'Ain't none of our folks ever been buried without a few words.' Elizabeth Allen, leading lady of *Donovan's Reef* and one of Ford's special favourites, stood on the sloping hillside staring at the coffin out of the corner of her eye. Hank Worden held court to a group of youthful admirers, his spectral face beaming as they praised his performance in *The Searchers* (the fearsome-looking Henry Brandon, who played Chief Scar, was also at the cemetery). Somebody asked why Ben Johnson wasn't at the funeral, and Worden explained, 'If there's one thing Ben hates, it's going to funerals. When someone we knew died a few years ago, a stuntman, I called Ben and asked him to come, but he said, "I'd like to remember him as he was in life." ' Within half an hour, the cemetery was almost deserted.

It has always bothered me that burial services end before the body is placed in the grave; it's for a mistaken notion of 'decorum' that the mourners are expected not to witness the prosaic work of the gravediggers. But Alex and I felt that we had to supply what was missing in the service. The young chicanos busily preparing the grave worked with professional haste and

How Green Was My Valley (Donald Crisp, Sara Allgood)

unconcern (one of them smoking a cigarette), and their white foreman objected when I removed a pop bottle from the mound of earth, telling me, 'Leave it there, we'll throw it in.' Time was running short; the foreman turned on the hose for packing the earth tightly in place, and the bulldozer was roaring its engine and edging inexorably towards the grave like one of the caterpillar tractors getting ready to flatten Muley's home in *The Grapes of Wrath.* 'Ford is to me what Shakespeare is to the English,' said Alex, and the foreman, barely missing us with the hose, shouted, 'You better get out of the way.' I looked at the inscription on the casket cover, noticing that it said 'John A. Ford' (the initial, which he never used, was for his real middle name, Aloysius) and that it gave 1894 for the year of his birth, not 1895 as it has usually been given.

'Let's sing "Shall We Gather at the River?",' I said to Alex. 'I think he would have liked that.' Alex, who has an uncanny memory, later asked me, 'Did you realize you were repeating a line from the burial of the young soldier in *The Lost Patrol*? Victor McLaglen sticks the boy's sword in the ground over the grave and says, "I think he would have liked that." ' Grabbing handfuls of dirt from the mound next to the grave and each taking one of the President's roses, we stood close to the mouth of the grave and sang the hymn as the coffin was lowered into the ground. We waited for one of the gravediggers to climb out of the hole before we dropped the roses and the dirt on to the coffin, and seconds later it vanished from sight.

Three hours later, while sitting in the shade of a tree reminiscing about our favourite Ford scenes, we watched Anna Lee's son John Stafford, one of the young Australian sailors in *Donovan's Reef*, read the Bible over his godfather's grave as he played excerpts from the soundtrack of *How Green Was My Valley* on a portable tape recorder. We heard Beth Morgan's words, 'He came to me just now; Ivor was with him. He spoke to me and told me of the glory he had seen.' And the final words of the film: 'Men like my father cannot die. They are with me still, real in memory as they were in the flesh, loving and beloved for ever. How green was my valley then!' We watched Stafford go, lingered a while, and then ourselves walked away, leaving Ford alone.

2. Half Genius, Half Irish

John is half tyrant, half revolutionary; half saint, half Satan;
half possible, half impossible; half genius, half Irish...

FRANK CAPRA

John Ford always celebrated the simplest things – family, the land, justice, sacrifice – and he was always scornful of the hypocrisies of civilization. His acceptance of the traditional American ideals made him something of a rarity among modern artists; indeed, it even seems unfitting to call him a *modern* artist at all. A first generation American christened Sean Aloysius O'Fienne in 1894, he grew up speaking both English and Gaelic, and spent much of his childhood making visits to the family hearth.

Like the Italian-born Frank Capra, he nurtured a quizzical attitude towards America. He was an outsider in search of an allegiance, hearkening back to a simpler, purer existence even as a youngster. Judging from his work, he had the newcomer's compulsion to prove his love for his country, and the newcomer's anguish and disillusionment over the discovery of its flaws. When Ford wrote his touchingly ingenuous foreword to Capra's autobiography, he could have been writing about himself:

Frank Capra is an inspiration to those who believe in the American Dream ... For even in early youth he was no stranger to the work, the worry, and the long hours that went with being a poor immigrant boy in a dog-eat-dog society. If all this constituted a deprived childhood, Frank was too busy and too ambitious to notice. Humble beginnings have not deterred his rise to eminence in the arts, letters and sciences . . . He has served his country with distinction both in civil and military life. The famous and the notable seek his acquaintance . . . He has earned more awards than he would bother to count. Success has not dulled his wit, his wisdom, or his compassion.

When Ford was young, the American Irish were still climbing up the ladder to social acceptance. A matriarchal community, they were belligerent and chauvinistic, ruthless towards outsiders and exaggeratedly tender towards each other, much like the American black community today. The difference is, of course, that the Irish could eventually intermarry and become fully integrated into the fabric of American life; for them, the American Dream could become a reality. But Ford never stopped considering himself a rebel. When he barely failed to receive an appointment to the U.S. Naval Academy at the age of 19 (which goes a long way towards explaining his lifelong love–hate affair with the profession of arms), he made a brief attempt to start college at the University of Maine, became a cowboy, and then shocked his parents by entering a thoroughly disreputable trade – the movies.

Broke and needing a place to sleep, he wandered into Hollywood, where his older brother Francis, who had been an actor and assistant director for Georges Méliès, was directing and acting under the name of Ford. More than half a century later, Ford told Peter Bogdanovich, 'I certainly had no desire to go into pictures or have anything to do with them. Still haven't.' Asked how it happened, Ford replied: 'Hungry.' Changing his given name to Jack Ford – the more genteel 'John' came in 1923, when he entered the lace-curtain, or A-picture, category with *Cameo Kirby* – he began working as a labourer, property man, stuntman and assistant director for his brother and other directors, including Allan Dwan. In 1914 he rode with the Klan in D. W. Griffith's *The Birth of a Nation* ('I was riding with one hand holding the hood up so I could see because the damn thing kept slipping over my glasses'), but hit a low-slung branch the first day and spent the next three days, epochal days, watching Griffith direct. 'I wouldn't say we stole from him,' Ford once remarked. 'I'd say we copied from him outright.' When Ford graduated to director at the age of 23, because the regular director was missing after an all-night binge on the set, he demonstrated his rebelliousness by exiling himself into Westerns, making himself a pariah among pariahs.

Even late in his life, despite his professional honours and his admiral's brocade, he had, in the words of Orson Welles, 'chips on his shoulders like epaulets'. Though Ford sometimes chafed at being characterized as a Western director, he said in 1971, 'When I pass on, I want to be remembered as "John Ford – a guy that made Westerns".' He carried his outcast status proudly and defiantly, the way Ethan Edwards wears his tattered Confederate cape in *The Searchers*. And just as Ethan indicates his attitude towards his military medal with a transparent 'Doesn't amount to much,' Ford professed not to give a good damn about his Academy Awards. But if you mentioned that he won four Oscars, forgetting the two he won for Navy documentaries, he would snap: 'Six.'

Ford was a paradox. On the one hand, a profound popular poet, intuitively responsive to the deepest feelings of his people. And on the other, a 'hard-nosed' craftsman who shied away from ascribing any importance to his work and refused to call himself an artist. He liked to describe directing as 'just a job of work' and hated to talk about it. Nevertheless, it would be a mistake to take his comments at face value and see his films as the work of a primitive with 'a touch of the poet'. He was an extremely complex man who expressed extremely complex feelings and ideas with the utmost simplicity and directness.

His self-perpetuated image as an illiterate cowboy is belied by the testimony of his scriptwriters and actors, who report that Ford took a major part in the writing of his films. Scriptwriter Frank Nugent said that Ford exercised a 'whip hand' over every aspect of production, and Philip Dunne, who won an Oscar for the screenplay of *How Green Was My Valley*, said recently that the line he considers the best in the film was written by Ford on the set: when a half-blind man asks Barry Fitzgerald to join him on a rescue expedition into the mine pit, Fitzgerald replies, ' 'Tis a coward I am, but I will hold your coat.' On the set of *Seven Women*, Ford made a daily ritual of inspecting the script pages scheduled for shooting, then tearing them up and tossing out new lines for everyone in the cast.

Ford gained this 'whip hand' through his power at the box office, his efficiency as a craftsman (he finished *Fort Apache*, an epic of the Indian Wars, twenty-seven days *ahead* of schedule), and through his skilful bullying of producers. Stories of Ford's contempt for the higher echelons are legendary. During the making of *Wee Willie Winkie* he was told that he was four days behind schedule; Ford opened the script, tore out four pages, handed them to the producer and snarled, 'We're on schedule. Now beat it.' In 1971, when an old friend asked Ford what his grandson was doing, he said, 'He's playing piano in a whorehouse.' The friend stammered, 'He's *what*?', and Ford said, 'Well, dammit, you didn't want me to admit he was a producer, did you?' Tragedies occurred in Ford's career, such as the mutilation of *The Sun Shines Bright* and *Cheyenne Autumn*, but for the most part his degree of freedom within the Hollywood system bordered on the uncanny. Scriptwriter

The 'hard-nosed' craftsman: Ford with the Indians from *Stagecoach*

Alexander Jacobs probably had the best explanation: 'Choosing his Western world, and surrounding himself with this sort of Irish defence, as it were – you could never get a sane word out of him because he was a "mad Irishman" – was the absolutely marvellous decision he made about Hollywood. It allowed him to work in complete harmony and peace within his chosen world.'

Though his work, taken as a whole, is a vast complex of personal and national mythology, peopled with characteristic Fordian figures, echoing with familiar Fordian songs, and replete with visual and thematic cross-references, accident and inspiration played a great part in his working method. As his photographer Arthur C. Miller said: 'After working with him for some time, I realized what an impossible task it was to describe his work, because when John Ford made a picture, he could not be compared even to himself from one day to the next. He was one hundred per cent unpredictable and had no special method or formula. Only one thing is certain and that is that Ford made the pictures himself without any interference.' The bold photography of *She Wore a Yellow Ribbon* strikingly attests to Ford's knack for seizing the unexpected. One day in Monument Valley, the skies darkened with the signs of an approaching thunderstorm. The crew was getting ready to take shelter when Ford announced that they were going to film a sequence in which a wounded trooper is operated on in a moving wagon. It was shot in the midst of howling darkness, lightning flashes playing havoc with the exposure as the wagons rolled slowly along. When the film was developed, the results were magnificent. The feeling of the storm had been captured with hair-raising vividness. The film won the Oscar for best colour photography.

Ford was usually considered a conservative, but despite his nostalgia for traditional values, the term is misleading. Like Fenimore Cooper, he was impatient with the artificial harmony of organized society, as his fascination with the West and with all varieties of nomads, outlaws, outcasts and warriors makes abundantly clear. There was a strong streak of anarchy in his Irish temperament; his friend Robert Parrish described him as 'a cop hater by religion'. His characters are typically refugees from constricting societies (Europe, urbanized America) in which once vital traditions have hardened into inflexible dogmas, and they usually rebel against intolerant and unjust conditions in their own communities as well. As Philippe Haudiquet put it, Ford had 'an obsession with justice', and it is his odd synthesis of anarchism and authoritarianism which makes his work equally attractive to those on both extremes of the political spectrum.

The traditions he revered are the tribal traditions, and all of them came together in the image of the family, the purest form of society. This, to Ford, was beyond reason: when a French interviewer asked why the 'theme of family' is so important in his work, he replied, 'You have a mother, don't you?' But when tradition stultifies into a defence mechanism against life, as with the pious naïveté of the missionaries in *Seven Women*, he bitterly mocked it. The thread which unites Ford's work is what he described as the 'tragic moment', the crisis of an individual conscience which is also, by extension, the turning point of the society it represents: 'It enables me to make individuals aware of each other by bringing them face-to-face with something bigger than themselves. The situation, the tragic moment, forces men to reveal themselves, and to become aware of what they truly are. The device allows me to find the exceptional in the commonplace. I also like to discover humor in the midst of tragedy, for tragedy is never wholly tragic. Sometimes tragedy is ridiculous.'

Epics may be divided into two types: the pure epic, that of Homer, Virgil and Shakespeare; and the impure or subversive epic, that of Cervantes, Milton, Fielding, Melville and Joyce. The goal of the pure epic is to exalt the community by dramatizing the representative actions of its noblest character. The subversive epic, mistrustful of noble gestures but with an inchoate

The 'tragic moment': *The Grapes of Wrath, Cheyenne Autumn* and (*opposite*) *She Wore a Yellow Ribbon*

yearning for their purity, delights in reversals, perversity and double meanings. Ford stood midway between the two poles. Like his heroes, he often seemed torn between a love for the *idea* of the community and an estrangement from the *fact* of the community which could lead to contempt and even open revolt.

We are always acutely aware of a man's social position in Ford's work. We see him often in the past tense, with all his actions reverberating into the future and filtered through our modern perspective; often in a role of authority, in which his slightest decision affects the many; equally often in a challenging, rebellious posture; and frequently in all three at once. The opening reel of a Ford movie is typically a slow, methodical, mostly wordless development of atmosphere in which the audience is steeped in 'place' while the seeds of the crisis are being planted. In many contemporary movies the audience wastes half of the first hour trying to puzzle out who the characters are and what they are to each other; in a Ford movie the entire matrix of social relationships is laid out in the first few minutes. The opening of *The Searchers* is the consummate example. As John Wayne rides in from the desert towards the family homestead, the compositions and montage subtly delineate the hierarchy within the family, the spatial and emotional relationship of the outsider to the different members of the family, and the characters' varying relation to the land, while the dialogue concerns itself with essential information: 'Ethan?' – 'That's your Uncle Ethan!' – 'Welcome home, Ethan.'

Ford's style, in Andrew Sarris's words, 'evolved almost miraculously into a double vision of an event in all its vital immediacy and yet also in its ultimate memory image on the horizon of history'. Reality and legend, the actual and the ideal, memory and the moment of decision, are interwoven in a tense symbiotic correspondence. This, more than simple nostalgia or romanticism, accounts for the mysterious beauty of Ford's work. His films are documentary visions of an ideal world. Time and again in his interviews, Ford insisted that what he showed in his historical films 'really happened'. Of course it didn't, but it should have. There is no more thrilling depiction of courage in Ford's work, and few greater in all cinema, than the moment (which Ford himself photographed from a watchtower) in his documentary *The Battle of Midway* when the young sailors dash out in the middle of an aerial bombardment and run up the American flag, which billows out with a sudden gust of wind at the instant it reaches the top of the pole. 'The Star-Spangled Banner' dims briefly so that the narrator can whisper, incredulously, 'Yes, this really happened.'

Ford shows us human beings in moments of decision and times of revelation, but his characters are not always fully aware of the implications of

'Individuals blend into the landscape': *She Wore a Yellow Ribbon*

their actions. (His explanation of the sailors' act in *Midway*: 'Eight o'clock, time for the colors to go up ...') It remains for the director to fill in the context. The spontaneous humanizing touches which Ford encouraged his actors to work into archetypal characters comment on the 'foreground' and the 'background' of the action simultaneously. In the characteristic Fordian frame, individuals blend into the landscape as in a classical frieze, the camera discreetly distant, unobtrusively insisting on a predetermined pattern. The characters are shown in close-up only when the enormity of their actions presses in on them. And sometimes not even then. In *Three Godfathers*, near the end of the outlaws' trek across the Mohave Desert to take an orphaned child to safety, Pedro Armendariz breaks his leg in a fall and then shoots himself so that John Wayne can finish the journey. When Armendariz, off-camera, fires the shot, Wayne, holding the baby in his arms, halts in long-shot with his back to the camera. Almost any other director would cut to a close-up of Wayne's anguished face. Ford holds on the long shot as Wayne, after a pause, walks away. His emotional discretion and stylistic subtlety give the scene a remarkable intensity.

Arthur Miller recalled how, during the making of *How Green Was My*

Valley, Ford made a similar stylistic decision: 'The camera panned slightly to the left in a hardly noticeable manner to show the minister who had performed the wedding ceremony and who had consequently lost for ever the girl he loved. The minister was standing near the entrance to the church framed by a large oak tree, just a tiny figure in the distance. This was one of those rare occasions when Ford did his thinking out loud. Looking at the minister in the distance for a few seconds, he mumbled, "If I make a close-up, somebody will want to use it." Dismissing the thought, we moved to another location ...' The calm, smooth, even tempo of Ford's films (the famous 'invisible' editing style, as André Bazin defined it) shows life rolling on at its own pace. The characters' actions take their full meaning only when seen as part of an intricate moral, social and historical pattern in which character traits and communal movements are orchestrated and elaborated like tones in a fugue.

Ford would set up a precise, harmonious composition and then get the actors going before they were completely familiar with their lines, creating a freshness and rambunctiousness which stands in curious contrast with the rigour of the framing. This was more than a director's trick; it was a vital part of his outlook. He loved to seek out the common aspects of legendary characters and the heroic aspects of unknown characters (the 'common' cowboys and warriors whose names history has not recorded). His point of view is based on the recognition that while great events revolve round the smallest moments of individual decision, those very decisions are a response to inevitable social and historical forces. 'The idea of the picture,' Ford said of *Young Mr Lincoln*, 'was to give the feeling that even as a young man you could sense there was going to be something great about this man.' The way Henry Fonda's Lincoln awkwardly shifts his hands and legs while giving a backwoods speech, the way he cheats in a tug-of-war at a county fair, the way he delicately balances a pie in either hand and takes interminable samples while judging a baking contest, the way he plays 'Dixie' on his Jew's harp while riding his donkey along a river bank ... all of his actions are supercharged with our common knowledge of his destiny. As Sergei Eisenstein remarked, the film's 'informal plot, almost plotless or anecdotal, looks on closer inspection like a thoroughly composed image synthesizing all those qualities that shone in the historical–political role played by this American giant'.

The scenes have the magical intimacy of 'daguerrotypes come to life', as Eisenstein said, but Ford does not rely on our prior knowledge of the character to convey his point. If he did, the film would be little more than an elegant, witty charade. Instead, he gives a strange gravity to Lincoln's charac-

'A freshness and rambunctiousness': *The Quiet Man*

ter, a far-away look to his countenance, a self-absorbed equanimity to his bearing, and a feeling of inevitability and grace behind each image to keep us alert for the truth behind the appearance. Correspondingly, in dealing with the unknown heroes of *The Searchers* and *The Man Who Shot Liberty Valance*, he continually shows how complex events can be understood only by examining small, unheralded backstage gestures. It is this 'double vision' which has led to Ford being described as both 'the most Brechtian' of all film directors (by Jean-Marie Straub) and 'the least Brechtian' (by V. F. Perkins).

It often seemed, indeed, that there were two John Fords. He was both an iconographer and an iconoclast; his clear, unblinking scrutiny of history was balanced by his tendency to lyricize; his bumptious proletarianism contrasted oddly with his belief in that 'natural aristocracy among men' of which Thomas Jefferson wrote; and the vigour and directness of his visual style could not quite conceal what Philippe Haudiquet describes as his 'expressionist temptation'. In the opening sequences of *The Quiet Man*, for instance, Ford frames so smoothly and unobtrusively that we hardly feel the presence of a camera. Then, in Sean's first vision of Mary Kate, he shifts into a lavish romanticism reminiscent of a period painting; and later, in Sean's memory of

America, he moves completely into the expressionistic. Ford's admirers generally prefer the functional poetry of *Wagon Master, The Searchers* and *Seven Women* to the overt expressionism of such films as *The Informer, The Prisoner of Shark Island* and *The Long Voyage Home.* Yet the style of even a 'simple' Ford film such as *Wagon Master,* on further inspection, is revealed as a blend of forthrightly presented action and a highly sophisticated manipulation of foreground and background movements through a dazzling palette of shades.

Few of Ford's admirers, though, would build an elaborate case for his most expressionistic film, *The Fugitive,* despite the fact that the compositions are uniformly breathtaking. This may be because the nuances of Ford's temperament could not be expressed adequately through surface appearances alone. When he speaks primarily through light and decor, his films lack a vital dimension and remain as statically picturesque as his detractors claim they are. It is revealing that Ford drastically modified his normal working method on *The Fugitive*: 'We'd *wait* for the light,' he said, i.e., wait for it to fit his preconceived compositional patterns. Ford's visual artistry is at its height when its complexities are ingrained and apparently effortless, when his vision is elevated into the seamless fluidity of a dream.

Ford's favourite device for heightening the meaning of the commonplace was the ritual. Think of the endless ceremonial gestures which make up the fabric of his films – the dances, marches, births, deaths, drinking parties, brawls, courtships, funerals, wakes, weddings, church meetings, elections, speeches, trials, operations, dinners, riding contests, ceremonies of war and peace, arrivals, departures, more arrivals, more departures.... Bruce Beresford has remarked that in *The Searchers* 'the characters did nothing but arrive and leave again'. Think of the delight in colourful colloquialism which characterizes Ford's scripts, of the folk songs which call his images to mind long after the film has faded from the screen: 'Red River Valley' in *The Grapes of Wrath*; 'The Isle of Innisfree' in *The Quiet Man*; 'Harbour Lights' in *The Long Voyage Home*; 'My Old Kentucky Home' in *The Sun Shines Bright*; 'The Minstrel Boy' in *The Informer*; 'Come, Come, Ye Saints' in *Wagon Master*; 'My Darling Clementine' and 'She Wore a Yellow Ribbon' and 'The Rising of the Moon' in the films of the same names; and 'Garry Owen' (*née* 'The Daughters of Erin'), 'Bringing in the Sheaves' and 'Shall We Gather at the River?' in film after film.

The feeling of community so vital to Ford's work found natural expression in his development of a theatrical troupe, the John Ford Stock Company. All major directors have favourite actors, of course, but few have created such an elaborate system of role-playing (Ford's mentor, Griffith, was one, and his admirer, Bergman, is another). Ford was once asked how an audience should watch a movie. 'Look at the eyes,' he said. The small gestures back and forth, the communal interplay, this is where the meaning is localized. As James Stewart inimitably put it in an interview with Peter Bogdanovich:

Everybody's always talkin' about the Ford stock players, y'know ... I think it's a helluva good *idea*! Wish everybody'd do it. The people know how to work together. They don't have to ... each film doesn't have to be the first time. And a lotta directors ... y'know ... it's a barrel a laughs on the set and ya have fun and ... and then you see the picture and you say, 'Where is it? Where's the ...' But Ford *gets* it on the screen.

Yet it is remarkable, for all the communalizing in Ford's films, what a great sense of loneliness his characters convey. Unlike Howard Hawks' characters, for example, Ford's seldom *touch* each other except in formal situations; each is locked irretrievably in his own conscience, and there is an edge of desperation in their communal urge.

A person involved in ritual is celebrating the solemnity of his own actions, and at the same time is bowing to something greater than himself. The ritual becomes most vital when we sense that the characters are improvising it in reaction to a crisis. This is perhaps the most moving aspect of Ford's work. For example, in most war films the transfer of command from one officer to another calls for a stock flurry of salutes and tight-lipped smiles which fades from the mind as quickly as it is accomplished. But when Robert Montgomery transfers command of the squadron to Ward Bond in *They Were Expendable* by taking the binoculars from around his neck and placing them around Bond's, the image is indelible. The sons' farewell to their parents in *How Green Was My Valley* is instinctively performed as a family cere-mony. The mother lighting a fire, the sons entering the room, leading her to a rocking chair; one kneeling at her feet, the other rocking her as the father reads the 23rd Psalm; then the oldest son closing her eyes, both of them walking silently away, the father pausing from his book and looking up as they leave, returning to the book and reading '... My cup runneth over', and then the sons walking down the hill from the valley as the sun sets behind them. The spontaneity of the gestures draws us into the characters' emotions, but our awareness of the ritual's balletic beauty also keeps us subtly distanced and able to comprehend its deepest meanings.

By making a ritual improvisatory, Ford flouts convention and conveys a sense of tribal understanding. A political convention (in *Liberty Valance*), a trial (in *Three Godfathers*) and an operation (in *My Darling Clementine*), are held in saloons, and the urgency of each ritual in the life of the community is

'A sense of loneliness': Lt Kirby York (John Wayne) in *Rio Grande*

heightened by its informality. The wedding in *Steamboat Round the Bend* (held in a jail) and the birth in *Seven Women* (in a tool shed) gain in solemnity through the baseness of their surroundings; and, conversely, the dance in *Clementine* (held at the dedication of a church) and the political meeting in *The Last Hurrah* (held at a wake), far from profaning their settings, make them more precious. To Ford, a tradition is only as valuable as the people who carry it out, its meaning only what the people make it. Edwin O'Connor put a majestic analysis of this kind of ritual into the mouth of Mayor Skeffington in *The Last Hurrah*:

... Life wasn't exactly a picnic for our people in those days. They were a sociable people but they didn't get much chance for sociability. They were poor, they worked hard, and they didn't have much in the way of diversion. Actually, the only place people got together was at the wake. Everybody knew everybody else; when somebody died, the others went to pay their respects and also to see and talk to each other. It was all part of the pattern. They were sorry for the family of the deceased, to be sure, but while they were being sorry they took advantage of the opportunity to have a drink and chat with the others who were being sorry, too. It was a change, an outlet for people who led back-breaking, dreary and monotonous lives. And if, once in a while, someone took a few too many and wanted to set fire to the widow or play steamroller in the kitchen, it was possibly deplorable but it was also slightly understandable. All in all, I've always thought the wake was a grand custom, and I still do.

Ford's irreverent sense of humour, though it tends to offend the guardians of respectable art, is one of his strongest trumps. In his greatest works, the plot line oscillates freely between the tragic and the ridiculous, with the comic elements providing a continuous commentary on the meaning of the drama. When asked once why he hadn't made more comedies, Ford replied, 'I feel I'm essentially a comedy director, but they won't give me a comedy to do.' His comedy, broad and idiosyncratic and self-conscious as it may seem, is the rough prose to the exalted visual verse. Just as his few actual comedies have had notably grim undertones (such as *The Quiet Man*, which is about the romantic fantasies of a guilt-ridden boxer), his tragedies usually have undertones of giddiness. The critic who finds the situations of *The Searchers* or *Seven Women* ridiculous is ignoring or choosing to ignore the fact that Ford finds the situations ridiculous as well. His view of human drama embraces the conviction that what is most noble, most poignant and most terrifying in life is frequently a hair's-breadth away from howling absurdity. What makes films such as *The Searchers* and *Seven Women* great is the striking manner in which they reconcile the noble with the absurd, the way in which their seemingly straightforward situations are shaped to encompass the maddest perversities and still retain a sense of order. Like so many other Catholic artists – Chesterton, Greene, Joyce, Buñuel, Hitchcock – Ford expresses himself through paradox, which Chesterton defined as 'a truth standing on its head to attract attention'. When Ford fails, his sense of humour is usually the first casualty.

Because of their sense of the awful finality of human behaviour, Ford's films always seem to be taking place in the eye of eternity. Moments of failure or victory or fateful indecision will be re-enacted in the mind for ever. Abe Lincoln strolling beside a river with Ann Rutledge, Tom Joad dancing with his mother in *The Grapes of Wrath*, Bronwen meeting her new family in *How Green Was My Valley*, Wyatt Earp leading his lady to an open-air dance in *Clementine*, Sean and Mary Kate sighting each other on a hillside in *The Quiet Man*, Ethan presenting his niece with his medal in *The Searchers*, Spig Wead tumbling down the staircase in *The Wings of Eagles*, Hallie accepting Tom's cactus rose in *Liberty Valance*, the chief shooting the wild young brave in *Cheyenne Autumn*, Dr Cartwright drinking the poisoned tea in *Seven Women* ... these moments will reverberate for ever, like the circles which spread slowly from the stone the young Lincoln tosses casually into the river.

When Ford began to immerse himself in the landscape of the American past in his *annus mirabilis*, 1939, he became increasingly preoccupied with the tortures and consolations of memory. The vague melancholia which plays round the edges of the luminous images in *Stagecoach*, *Lincoln* and *Drums Along the Mohawk* reflects a Sisyphean desire to push past an unbreachable boundary – the boundary of time. The cherishing of a momentary image, immutable in its delicacy and precision of framing, begins to assume obsessive proportions as shot after shot rolls inexorably away. It is as if the very perfection of the image is the cause of its transience. Nostalgia is not an adequate word to describe the feeling called up by such an image; it is something more urgent, more desperate, almost like the feverish sense of being trapped in a maze. Henry Nash Smith, analysing the mythic West in his classic *Virgin Land* (a virtual textbook for understanding Ford's world), speaks of the 'static, dreamlike' quality of the symbols employed by Western novelists. The seductiveness, and the terror, of a dream lies in its feeling of stasis, its sense of illusory possibilities. A dream is a dead-end disguised as an escape, and if Ford's visual style tends towards the static, it does so for a purpose.

There is a strange irony involved in Ford's visual metaphors for Ireland, the land of his ancestors, and for the West, the land of his dreams. The rocky, starved soil which so many people fled is seen as a lush, green, endlessly fertile valley, and the American Dream to which they escaped is a desert valley slashed intermittently by rivers which serve only to emphasize its

John Ford

The landscape of the American past: *Wagon Master*

'Monument Valley is a moral battleground': *Fort Apache*

essential aridity. Yet the America of Ford's stories is presumably a land of fertility and opportunity, or why did the immigrants leave home in the first place? The Irish characters of *The Quiet Man* and *The Rising of the Moon* (one of whom actually lives in a national monument) are hemmed in on all sides by centuries-old traditions to which they must accommodate themselves. But in primitive America, every man is his own master. The pioneers are thrown into a testing ground whose only landmarks are the million-year-old mesas of Monument Valley, the vast expanse of land on the Navajo Reservation which Ford first used as a location in *Stagecoach*. D. H. Lawrence could have been describing Monument Valley when he wrote: 'White men have probably never felt so bitter anywhere, as here in America, where the very landscape, in its very beauty, seems a bit devilish and grinning, opposed to us.' Yet Ford, perversely, considered Monument Valley 'the most complete, beautiful, and peaceful place on earth'.

A reviewer of *The Searchers*, attempting to demonstrate Ford's abuse of 'realism', observed that the story ranges all over the West, up into Canada and down into Mexico, but the players never seem to leave Monument Valley. Precisely. Monument Valley is more than a real place to Ford. It is a state of mind. Its beauty is reminiscent of the decadent poets' theories about the aesthetics of uselessness, for it is both a dead end and an ultimate value, the perfect setting for the *acte gratuit.* Its weird, gargantuan panoramas resemble nothing so much as an extra-terrestrial landscape (Kubrick used it for the star-gate sequence in *2001*), and to the Navajos themselves it is spirit-land. Monument Valley is a moral battleground, stripped down and rendered more perfect by the absence of organic life within its boundaries. In Ford's 'dream' Ireland, a man returns to his past. In the American Dream, his every move reverberates into the future. The horizons of Monument Valley, both primeval and beyond society, point towards eternity.

Lindsay Anderson, whose *Sequence* articles on *They Were Expendable* and *She Wore a Yellow Ribbon* were the pioneering work in Ford criticism, wrote:

His work can be enjoyed by anyone, regardless of cultural level, who has retained his sensitivity and subscribes to values primarily humane . . . Rich in phrasing, simple in structure, it is a style which expresses a sure, affirmative response to life – the equivalent to that Biblical prose which, today, it takes greatness of spirit to sustain.

Certain key words, without amplification, crop up again and again in de- rogatory references to Ford – 'sentimentality', 'chauvinism', 'vulgarity' – and each has a measure of validity. A popular artist is bound to reflect many traits of his culture, the bad as well as the good, but this is what gives popular art a value and a resonance which is often denied to more self-enclosed work. Why is it that Ford's sentimentality, for instance, is so often denigrated and that of D. W. Griffith (which is in every way more extreme) so widely accepted? Perhaps it is because the world of Griffith is so far removed from us that it has become exotic and aesthetically distanced.

In Europe, where Ford's world has always been exotic, his artistry has always been appreciated, and among mass audiences at home (who are, at least, usually honest about what they like), it has always been enjoyed. Perhaps the real argument against Ford is simply that he was popular; that he refused to play down to his audience or play the cynical entrepreneur; that he understood what moved and touched and amused them, and was honestly moved by much of it himself; that by understanding the ideals and conven- tions of his culture he was able to reflect it with an uncommon degree of richness and fidelity.

3. Himself

by Joseph McBride

Knowing Ford's fabled disdain for interviewers, I decided to play the professional Irishman in approaching him. My letter had gone unanswered, so I phoned his office in Beverly Hills. Ford walked in as I was talking to his secretary. 'Mr McBride,' he said. 'Mr Ford,' I replied, and told him we were writing a book about him. 'My God! What for?' he growled. 'You certainly picked a dull subject.' He picked up my letter and said he hadn't looked at his mail for a month. I had added 'County Mayo' after my name and Ford read the words aloud, accenting the last syllable as the natives do. Warming up, he told me his people had come from a neighbouring county, Galway, and that his wife was a McBryde. So I was practically a relative.

Then I really laid it on, mentioning that one of my ancestors had come to America after deserting from the British Army. When Ford told me about *his* ancestor who had deserted from the British Army and come to America, I knew I had it made – even though my little stunt was, as Dylan Thomas used to say, 'very lepricorny'. It developed that Ford's ancestor had beaten mine over by thirty years, arriving during the Revolutionary War, and had received a personal letter from George Washington, which Ford had in his possession. I was about to mention that I had attended the same high school as Spencer Tracy and Pat O'Brien when Ford said again, rather archly now, that he had 'led a dull life'. I muttered something about how many movies he had made. But then he said I could have the interview since I had 'the proper ethnic background', and added, 'Otherwise I'd tell you to go to hell.'

I arrived at his office on 19 August, 1970. Talking to Ford was like squatting beside the chuck wagon with one of the Earp brothers for a chaw and a swig of coffee from a tin cup. As Colin Young wrote of his Ford interview, Ford 'was likely to want to talk about his socks more than about his work'. There was a hum of activity inside the office. People were being ushered in and out, phones were ringing, letters were being thrust into his hands, and the bustle had a melancholy cast; this was a director who hadn't been able to make a feature for nearly five years. The office was surprisingly spartan. I had expected to find it crammed with memorabilia, like the office of 'John Dodge' in *The Wings of Eagles*, but Ford had most of that in his home. A few items did stand out: paintings of Monument Valley and of Ford in his admiral's uniform; a photograph of the USS *Columbus*, inscribed to 'John Ford, from your friend and shipmate' by Johnny Bulkeley, whose story Ford told in *They Were Expendable*; portraits of James Cagney and Will Rogers. But no Oscars and no spittoon.

Dour and unruly, Ford was wearing tennis shoes, baggy off-white trousers and a blue shirt with his belly poking through the buttons. His eyepatch hung askew over his left eye, and his remaining eye fixed you with a basilisk stare – when he looked at you, which was mainly when he was irritated. The session began on a cordial note. After showing me snapshots of his wife and himself at their fiftieth anniversary celebration, he pulled open a drawer and proferred a cigar. Stupidly, I said I already had one, then tried to make up for my *faux pas* by saying, 'Mine's only a nickel cigar.' To which he replied, 'Well, these are seven-and-a-half cent cigars.' He spat bits of his cigar into a waste-basket next to his desk, and when he took a pill ('My wife's gonna call and say, "Be sure that Mr Ford takes his pill" '), he stuck out his tongue and gargled in mock disgust.

I knew, of course, what a hard case he was going to be. I knew that behind his cowboy pose lurked a shrewd, sophisticated man, ready to pounce on any foolishness. Bill Libby, who extracted an eloquent interview from Ford in 1964 by asking him to defend the Western, had written: 'It is easy to be fooled by such a man. His outer senses are dulled and he is no longer young. He has been making movies for ever. When you ask him a question, you must wait against a long silence for a reply, until you begin to wonder if he has forgotten or even heard you in the first place. But when he has considered your question carefully, he will give you your answer, and if it has been a foolish question, his answer will mock you and make you seem a fool, and if it

Memorabilia: Ward Bond as 'John Dodge', with John Wayne; and (*opposite*) Ford himself, with Dudley Nichols

has been a good question, his answer will be good and make you feel good.' Or as John Wayne put it, more bluntly, 'You ask a question of Ford, and he looks at you as if you were the stupidest dope in the world.'

Although my Irish trick got me the interview, it also backfired on me. After the initial pleasantries, Ford asked what *village* I was from in Mayo. Mortified, I confessed that I didn't remember. Ford looked at me as if I were the reincarnation of Cromwell himself. It wasn't until I saw Denis Sanders' CBS–TV special *The American West of John Ford* more than a year later that I discovered Ford had been under the impression that I was a *native* Irishman. In that show he told Henry Fonda: 'I had a kid come out the other day, came in fear and trembling . . . to interview me. So I put him right at ease, I says, "I don't like to be interviewed, I've never liked to be interviewed." '. . . But he said he was from County Mayo, so we got along fine until I found out he *wasn't* from County Mayo, he was from IOWA!' (Well, actually, Wisconsin.) Fonda commented, 'The result, I gathered, satisfied him, but didn't give the writer much material to work with.' And Ford cut in, 'I didn't tell him *anything*.'

Ford used his partial deafness as a ploy to avoid answering questions he didn't feel like answering. Perversely, he had me sit on his deaf – and blind –

side, and made me shout questions several times ('I'm deef as hell in this ear, you know'), even spelling out words, to get them across. We began by talking about the documentary of the Vietnam War, *Vietnam! Vietnam!*, he was currently producing (but not directing) for the United States Information Agency.* Ford showed little interest in talking about the film, and I was reluctant to risk his wrath by pressing him: 'What I did is generally went out there and said, "That'd be a good thing to shoot, let's shoot that." I say, "This would be a good thing to shoot," then I go up into the boondocks ... I had one very happy experience. I went up there and decorated my grandson, Daniel, my son's boy. He got the Silver Star and several Purple Hearts. He can do without the Purple Hearts, we've got enough of those in the family, but the Silver Star is a pretty high decoration for a kid up there, and they don't come up with the rations.'

Is that the only film you've worked on since Seven Women?
No, I'm doing a documentary, I just finished it, on a very dear friend of

* An ill-conceived project which I discussed in an article in *Sight and Sound*, Autumn, 1972.

mine, Lt-Gen. Chesty Puller, who was the most decorated Marine in history. I just did a one-reeler on his life, for television.

What company?

A private group. We had no sponsor. It isn't placed yet.*

What does it consist of?

Interviews with his friends, newsreel stuff, taking him all the way from World War I through Nicaragua and Haiti and through World War II and Korea. I was with him in Korea quite a while. I was his tentmate and we were very close friends, so they asked me to do this thing, and out of friendship for Chesty I did it.

Who were some of the people you interviewed?

Well, the only one you'd know ... a lot of names I forget, Marine officers ... I'm not good at names. John Wayne narrated the thing. He was a great friend of Chesty's.

Were you happy with the way it came out?

Well, as a matter of fact, it's too long. We had to pad it too much. The first three-quarters are great, then we have to pad it a little bit. The finish is really good. I'm very pleased with it, yes.

What about April Morning, *the Revolutionary War story? How's that coming?*

Well, it's still coming. No company wants to do it. It's a great script. It's the best script I've ever read.

It's about a young boy, isn't it?

A boy and a man, a boy and his father. His mother. It's not really a battle story, it's a character sketch. The only historical character we use is Paul Revere.

Not George Washington?

No, he was unknown then.

Didn't you mention once that Frank Capra always wanted to do a film about George Washington, and wasn't able to?†

Yeah, he's got a great story about Valley Forge, but nobody would go for it.

Why?

These are an ignorant lot of bastards.

* And still hasn't been.

† In his autobiography, *The Name Above the Title*, published in 1971, Capra said that Harry Cohn had bought the rights to Maxwell Anderson's play *Valley Forge* for him in the 1930s, but he decided not to direct it because it was 'beyond my competency. I wanted a story closer to our times; about people that I knew'. In an interview with Vernon Scott of the Associated Press in November 1971, Ford said that he and Capra were planning to co-direct a film based on *Valley Forge*, but nothing ever came of it.

Did they think the public wouldn't buy it?

No, they say, who the hell's interested in George Washington? I heard one producer say that to him. I says, 'I am, for one, and I know millions of other people are.' He says, 'Ah, that's dead fish, nobody's interested in the American Revolution.' I said, 'You ever read the *history* of the American Revolution?' He says, 'Hell no, I had better things to do.' I says, 'They didn't teach you in the sixth grade, when you graduated?' He says, 'What do you mean, I went through to the *eighth* grade.'

What do you think the chances are of persuading them to let you make April Morning*?*

Very slim.

I wanted to tell you that I saw Judge Priest *recently in a theatre in Chicago, and the audience gave it a big cheer at the end.*

Good. I'd like to see it again. I don't know where the hell I can get a print of it.

I heard that something was cut out of the remake of Judge Priest, The Sun Shines Bright*?*

Oh yeah, they ruined that. Well, they didn't ruin it, they *couldn't* ruin it. But they cut a lot out of it. You're working with a stupid lot of people, the executive producers, so what the hell, you've got to expect it. In this case a fella named Herbert Yates.

What exactly was cut out?

He cut out a lot of the black stuff, the Negro stuff. Not a lot of it, but there were climactic scenes and he cut 'em out and it hurt the picture.*

Could I ask you about Seven Women*?*

Sure, go ahead. It's one of my favourite pictures. See that plaque up there? The London Film Festival gave me that for *Seven Women*. It's the British equivalent of an Oscar.

Were you surprised when it didn't do well with the American audience?

Unh-unh. It was over their heads.

You made it knowing that the Americans wouldn't like it, then.

No, I didn't give a God damn whether they liked it or not. I thought it was a swell story and a good script, so I did it.

Did it intrigue you to direct a film about women for a change?

No, it was just a job of work. I've directed women before. Who else are you interviewing out here?

Jean Renoir.

---

* Prints of the film circulating today are complete, but when the film was first shown it was cut by more than twenty minutes. Ford was so outraged by Yates' decision to cut the film that he refused an offer to become head of production at Republic Studios.

Cheyenne Autumn

Oh, is Jean here? Give him my best, will you? Jean and I are very good friends. He's a very fine director.

What are some of his movies that you like?

I like all of them.

Are there any favourites you have?

No, I don't have any favourite pictures. I mean, what the hell, that's a waste of time. I look at 'em and enjoy 'em. I can't say I like that better than so-and-so.

You gave an unusual treatment of the Cavalry in Fort Apache.

I don't remember what the hell it's all about.

It's kind of a Custer's Last Stand. With Henry Fonda.

Oh, that's right, yeah. Yeah, it's all right.

I understand that John Wayne felt uneasy about being in Fort Apache *because he thinks Custer was a disgrace to the Cavalry.*

Oh, that's a lot of crap. I don't think he's ever heard of Custer.

Cheyenne Autumn *sort of questioned what the Cavalry was doing, didn't it?*

I don't know. Did it? The Cavalry weren't all-American boys, you know.

They made a lot of mistakes. You just mentioned Custer, that was a pretty silly goddamn expedition.

Some people thought The Man Who Shot Liberty Valance *was a summing-up of your attitudes about the West.*

I don't know.

Why did you wait ten years to make your first sound Western, Stagecoach*? Weren't they trying to get you to make Westerns in the 1930s?*

No. Westerns were a sort of ... people said they were a drug on the market. Nobody was making Westerns. This was a good story, so I went out and made it. I'm considered a Western director, but I haven't directed so many Westerns as all that, you know.*

[In desperation] *Do you like* The Searchers*?*

I enjoyed *doing* it. Yeah, *The Searchers* is a good picture. It made a lot of money, and that's the ultimate end.

When you first started directing John Wayne, was he a natural actor?

Umh-hmm. He still is.

How much do you have to talk to somebody like him after you've directed him ten or twenty times? Do you have to discuss the role much with him?

They read the script, they know what you want, they get out in front of the camera and say 'What do we do?' and I tell 'em, and they do it, usually in the first take.

You don't like to shoot more than a couple of takes?

No, because then the actors'll get tired.

Do you like the sort of nervousness that they have?

Yes, I do. I like that sort of ... that spirit of uncertainty. It makes it more real. I mean when a thing is glib and everybody answers and picks up their cues, you know ... they lose a certain amount of spontaneity.

What did you think of Wayne finally getting the Oscar after so many years?

Isn't that rather a useless question?

Well, did you see True Grit*?*

Unh-unh. I was *delighted* when he won it. I went out and pioneered, campaigned for him and everything else. Come on, Mac, for Chrissake, those are stupid questions. For a man from Mayo, whose forbears are from Mayo, to ask.... the people from Mayo are noted for their shrewdness and smartness. We're a smart, shrewd, poor race. Proud as hell. You don't say 'County Mayo', say 'County Mayo, God help us.'

When you're planning a film, do you draw the shots in advance?

No.

* Ford made fifty-four Westerns.

John Ford

'I tell 'em, and they do it': Ford shooting *Stagecoach*, with John Wayne and Andy Devine

How do you go about planning the shots?
Walk on the set, look at the set, look at the locations. You do it by instinct. You tell the cameraman to place the camera here and get in so-and-so and so-and-so, so he does it. That's all there is to it.
You don't like to move the camera much, do you?
No, because it throws the audience off. It says, 'This is a motion picture. This isn't real.' I like to have the audience feel that this is the real thing. I don't like to have the audience interested in the camera. The camera movement disturbs them.
When do you think the camera should be moved?
When there's a cause for it.
When you started your career, why did you direct only Westerns?
Because the pay was good. I still enjoy doing a Western. If a story came along, I'd go out and do it now, but hell, they're not coming. I get two or three scripts a week, but they're remakes or rewrites of pictures I've already done. Or they're all filthy or sexy, and that would be against my nature, my religion and my natural inclinations to do those things.
Are you still working on O.S.S., about Wild Bill Donovan?
Yeah.
How's it coming?
Not very well. It's hard to get a writer out here, you know. I mean, I don't know any of the writers.
Are there any other projects you'd like to make?
No.
I'm sorry I asked some silly questions.
Well, it isn't that, but everybody asks the same questions, all you people, and I'm sick and tired of trying to answer them, because I don't know the answers. I'm just a hard-nosed, hard-working ... ex-director, and I'm trying to retire gracefully.
So you don't like people asking you about your old movies?
No, I've forgotten them, I don't know what they're about. I'm just trying to live out my life in peace and comfort and quiet. So I'm going to say *au revoir*, God bless you, County Mayo *guide* ...
Erin gu bragh.
County Mayo *gu bragh.*

4. The Noble Outlaw: *Straight Shooting* (1917), *Stagecoach* (1939), *Wagon Master* (1950)

Straight Shooting

The hardest thing to comprehend about *Straight Shooting* is the fact that Ford was once 23 years old. As Ethan says of Mose Harper in *The Searchers*, Ford seems to have been 'born old'. Seeing his first feature is like taking a trip in a time machine back to a dimly remembered, vaguely chronicled, almost legendary past. Ford directed four short Westerns in 1917 – *The Tornado* and *The Scrapper*, starring himself; *The Soul Herder* and *Cheyenne's Pal*, starring Harry Carey – before he and Carey made *Straight Shooting*, which grew into a five-reel feature. Universal was 'very upset' about the extra length, until Carl Laemmle intervened with a perfectly logical argument derived from the occupation which spawned so many early movie moguls: 'If I order a suit of clothes and the fellow gives me an extra pair of pants free, what am I going to do – throw them back in his face?'

The survival of *Straight Shooting* is a fluke. It was discovered in the Czechoslovak Film Archive in 1966 and restored to circulation by the American Film Institute in 1971. A dozen or so of Ford's sixty-one silent films are now known to survive (the negatives of his first thirty-three films were destroyed in a fire at Universal around 1922, but there is always a chance that more prints will surface in archives), and other long-lost Ford silents are being circulated again, including *Just Pals, Cameo Kirby, Three Bad Men* and *Hangman's House*. Until quite recently, Ford scholars have lacked access not only to the silents but also to the bulk of his fascinatingly diverse work between 1929 and 1938, which includes at least four major films – *Pilgrimage, Judge Priest, Steamboat Round the Bend* and *The Prisoner of Shark Island*. Because of this problem, and because of the need for a manageable scope, we have limited this study to Ford's work since the watershed year of 1939. However, we have included *Straight Shooting* because of the invaluable and unexpected light it throws on Ford's evolution.

From guesswork and from Ford's descriptions, it had been possible to formulate a mental composite of his early Westerns which went like this: Carey, rugged, candid and unaffected, plays a 'saddle tramp' akin to William S. Hart's 'good bad man', but more volatile, more human, the precursor of the John Wayne–James Stewart line rather than the laconic Gary Cooper–Randolph Scott model. His picaresque ramblings bring him in contact with an increasingly interesting gallery of Ford character actors, the villains probably less flamboyant than their descendants, the girls probably more a plot necessity than the individualized, strong-willed ladies of Ford's maturity. But as Ford told Peter Bogdanovich: 'They weren't shoot-'em-ups, they were character stories. Carey was a great actor, and we didn't dress him up like the cowboys you see on TV – all dolled up ... Carey was sort of a bum, a saddle tramp, instead of a great, bold, gun-fighting hero. All this was fifty per cent Carey and fifty per cent me. He always wore a dirty blue shirt and an old vest, patched overalls, very seldom carried a gun – and he didn't own a hat.' Plot synopses indicate that these early Westerns clung doggedly to the theme of moral reformation – Harry is repeatedly brought out of his aimless frontier solitude into conflict with social injustice, and forced to opt for the home-steaders against the outlaws. Later Ford Westerns, such as *My Darling Clementine* and *Wagon Master*, also fit this pattern, and it was only in his 1950s and 1960s Westerns, like *The Searchers* and *Liberty Valance*, that Ford settled firmly on an entirely unidealized view of the civilized order. There, both the wilderness *and* civilization are seen as dead-ends, and the hero's dilemma becomes tragically insoluble.

From the hindsight of fifty-seven years and 137 films, the most interesting section of *Straight Shooting* is the long dénouement in which Cheyenne Harry, after marshalling his outlaw friends to save the homesteaders from the ranchers, is forced to choose between civilization and the wilderness. The entire film foreshadows *The Searchers*: the obsessive framing of characters through doorways (the introductory shot of Danny Morgan is identical to that of Martin Pawley in *The Searchers* – jumping off his horse, seen through the doorway of the home), the attack on the isolated family, the girl's vacillation between the rootless Harry and the tame, domesticated Danny (a very young Hoot Gibson). And John Wayne revealed recently that the moving gesture he makes at the end of *The Searchers*, grasping his arm protectively as Olive Carey and her family vanish into the home, was a conscious echo of a Harry Carey gesture which occurs near the end of *Straight Shooting*. (Wayne said he imitated Carey because he thought the gesture made him seem lonely and also because 'his widow was on the other side of that door, and he was the man Pappy said taught him his trade.') Ethan rides away from the homestead into the desert at the end of *The Searchers*; Harry stays with the girl at the end of *Straight Shooting*. But it would be misleading to see this as a simple affirmation of the civilized order Ford would later come to reject.

Straight Shooting begins with a title indicating that Harry is to be seen as a romantic, fighting for an ideal against the inevitable: 'The ranchers' empire, a vast grazing land. A once endless territory now divided and cut by farmers' fences.' The frontier after the Fall, ripe for internecine war. And the first shot identifies the nature of the Evil fallen on this former paradise: the camera irises out to reveal a man (the boss rancher, 'Thunder' Flint) sitting on horseback, high on a hill, with cattle visible as a swarm of specks below. The iris opens further on to the full intricacy of the composition: below Flint on the hill, facing in the opposite direction, are two other men on horseback, and far below is the large herd, arranged in a formalized winding pattern. Everything is organized in the New Order, everything fits into a coldly elegant diagram. Harry, the last romantic, is part of the natural order; we first see him emerging from his hiding-place inside a hollowed-out tree. Since he is an individualist, he naturally gravitates towards an outlaw life. But in the New Order, even the outlaws are organized, and he finds himself working for the ranch interests – who represent selfish individualism gone rampant.

Against this, Ford poses an ideal of selflessness: the family, represented by the widower farmer Sims, his daughter Joan and his son Ted. Later Ford will bring his families alive with intricate rituals, and will bring his villains alive with colourful bursts of anarchic violence, but at this early stage, the family and the villains are equally banal. The characters he *does* understand are the two outsiders, Harry and Danny, who like Harry works for the ranchers but is emotionally drawn to the family. The family and the villains are both abstractions, and as a result the early scenes of the film are sluggish and unfocused. *Straight Shooting* ceases to be a museum piece and begins to assume dramatic life when the two abstractions come into open conflict –

Straight Shooting

plot exposition gives way to action poetry – and when the abstractions cause conflict within Harry, between Harry and Danny over Joan, and within Joan.

The turning point is Harry's discovery of the family (including Danny) grieving over Ted's death at the hands of the ranchers. In plot terms, the sequence is simple enough. Harry sees the father prostrate on the son's grave, is moved to sympathy, and throws in with them. But in visual terms, it is as complex as anything in Ford's maturity. First there is a moment of foreboding: Harry dismounting near a river to stand in the flickering shadows of rustling branches, the ripples of light and shade across his face indicating his confusion and inner turbulence. His sudden appearance from the dark forest terrifies the family, who group tightly together. (Until the father confronts Harry, Ford keeps Harry in individual shots and the family always in a full shot – never a shot of a single member, always the three as a unit.) Cut to a magnificent close-up of Harry, his eyes completely shadowed by the brim of his hat, conveying his solitude, his withdrawal, his estrangement from society at the moment before his acknowledgment of social responsibility. Ford later used similar shots in showing Brickley's farewell to his men in *They Were*

Expendable and Ethan's return home at the beginning of *The Searchers*, moments of both longing and loneliness.

An odd device follows, evidence against Lindsay Anderson's contention that Ford was seduced into expressionism by Dudley Nichols in the 1930s. We see a point-of-view shot of the family clustered round the grave and its cross, bathed in unnatural brilliance. Cut back to Harry removing his hat and wiping his eyes. Crude as this device is (a title later has Harry explaining, rather superfluously, that the family 'opened his eyes'), it at least makes obvious the fact that Ford has *always* been willing to break the bonds of naturalism if it suits his purpose. The way, for example, that he habitually shoots horse riding sequences in fast, daring jump cuts over a wide variety of terrain, or the way he nonchalantly breaks the rules of screen direction in chase sequences: it is all here in this early film. (Further examples might be the Indian battle in *The Iron Horse*, shown in shadow on the side of a train, or the shot of the 'ghost riders in the sky' which ends *Three Bad Men*.)

When Harry's outlaw friends come to the rescue of the besieged farmers, there is a series of staccato cuts of horsemen riding into the frame from behind the camera, culminating in a quick reverse angle of an enemy rider plummeting off his horse in front of the camera as one of the outlaw band shoots from his horse in the background. This sequence manifests an instinctive grasp of directing, as clearly as the structure – and many of the shots – of the rescue sequence show the influence of Griffith. The aftermath of the rescue also contains a deliciously protracted bit of Fordian whimsy. A black outlaw in a sombrero discovers a pot of jam in the cupboard, surreptitiously takes a taste, takes several more, then hides the pot in his shirt and saunters out of the door.

Exciting as the rescue is, *Straight Shooting's* real moment of truth is Harry's enigmatic embrace of Joan (i.e., family, civilization, posterity, tradition) at the very end. The last few minutes of the film are, paradoxically, an elegy of farewell, with Harry gazing wistfully from the doorway and throwing down his tobacco pouch as his outlaw pals ride off, waving to him; Joan leaning against the doorway in a passionate, moodily lit close-up as her adolescent face becomes a mask of womanly anguish; Danny waving goodbye to Harry as he, not Harry, goes to claim Joan; a heartbreaking shot of Joan coyly opening the door to find Danny in Harry's place; and Ford's trademark final shot of a sunset horizon . . . but without the solitary rider we expect to see vanishing over the hill. Instead, Joan intercepts Harry and begs him to stay. He removes his hat and draws her against him in a protective embrace more like an uncle's than a lover's. That is the fade-out, but it is as melancholy as the opening shot of the ranch baron on the hill. The girl may expect Harry to stay – she has thrown away the security of Danny on the chance – but we do not. We know it is only an early episode in the Fordian hero's long voyage away from home.

Stagecoach

Stagecoach was Ford's triumphant return to the Western after a thirteen-year hiatus. Since *Three Bad Men* in 1926, he had been working in a variety of genres, honing his style, developing a greater facility with actors, and proving his credentials as a versatile and 'hard-nosed' craftsman. In the 1920s at Fox, Ford was often forced to do films in which he had little interest. When he branched out to other studios in the 1930s, he began to win back some of the creative freedom he had enjoyed in the early silent days at Universal. With this went a growing desire for critical recognition, a desire evidently springing more from a need to keep his new-found freedom than from simple pride, because after World War II, when his status in the industry was secure, he again began making films primarily for his own amusement.

But in 1939, when he returned to the genre which had preoccupied him at the beginning of his career, it was with a story of Balzacian scope and gusto. *Stagecoach* revolutionized the Western. Nowadays it is fashionable to speak of it as 'the Western which created the clichés,' but *Stagecoach* did not create clichés nor even sustain them. It defined Western archetypes and created a new frame of reference rich in irony and sophistication. It was not a new realism which Ford introduced to the genre, as reviewers of the day claimed (one could argue that the Western is innately fantastic), but a new sense of tradition and a new dramatic flexibility.

The effect of the film has been mixed. On the one hand, the self-consciousness it brought to the form has enabled the Western to continually transform itself, chameleon-like, to pressures in the society which produces it. Before *Stagecoach*, the Western seemed to be dying; after *Stagecoach*, it became the one permanently popular film genre. Fritz Lang was not exaggerating when he said that the Western is to America what the Niebelungen Saga is to Germany, for the traditions to which Ford gave definitive shape have proved capable of sustaining the most extreme inflections. On the other hand, Dudley Nichols' schematic and overtly allegorical screenplay has encouraged the misconception that the Western form is worthy of discussion only when it is used to teach a moral lesson. Making it possible for 'prestige' directors to make Westerns without having it seem that they were slumming, *Stagecoach* has left a long trail of bastard children, 'Westerns for people who don't like Westerns', of which *High Noon* is the most typical. Ford has not helped matters by claiming that *Stagecoach* 'sort of blazed a trail for the adult Western', as if his early classics and those of William S. Hart were insignificant.

Stagecoach: the stage in Monument Valley

What makes *Stagecoach* so durable, however, is not its historical signifi-cance but the vividness with which it creates a dream landscape from the American past and peoples it with simple and striking characters who, despite their reincarnation in countless 'A' and 'B' Westerns, still retain a believable ambivalence and depth. *Stagecoach* bears a family resemblance to the popular omnibus films of the 1930s (*Grand Hotel, Shanghai Express, Lost Horizon, The Lady Vanishes*, and the Ford–Nichols collaboration of 1934, *The Lost Patrol*) in which a colourful collection of characters from different social strata are thrown together in dangerous or exotic circumstances. The 'chance' society of these films is typically treated as a microcosm, with the characters acting out among themselves the social tensions which interest the writer and director; what seemed to delight Ford most in *Stagecoach* was the possibility of glorifying disrepute by plunging a group of pariahs into danger and having the most apparently abject of them emerge as heroes. (If Ford had not suffered from the critical neglect of his later Westerns, he might be able to savour a delicious irony. A film which exalts outcasts over the members of 'respectable' society made the Western respectable.)

The passengers on the stage are not so much a social microcosm as a counter-society, like the Irish revolutionaries in *The Informer*. They include a drunken doctor, a former Confederate officer turned cardsharp, a timid whisky drummer who is constantly mistaken for a clergyman, a prostitute, an escaped convict, a bank embezzler and the pregnant wife of a Cavalry lieutenant, whose child is born during the journey. Just before he made the film, Ford gleefully announced, 'There isn't a single respectable character in the cast.' He would seem to have overlooked the young mother, but an Army wife has little social currency back East and, besides, she guards her respectability so starchily (refusing to sit with the prostitute) that she makes it a mockery of decency. The other characters have all been thrown out of or are fleeing from the straightlaced town of Tonto, ruled by the dour Ladies' Law and Order League, who march to Ford's favourite hymn, 'Shall We Gather at the River?' (Critics who complain of Ford's 'orthodoxy' should be required to account for moments like this.)

Although Ford and Nichols adapted the movie from an Ernest Haycox story, *Stage to Lordsburg,* Ford has speculated that Haycox actually took his idea from Guy de Maupassant's *Boule de Suif,* the story of a prostitute and prominent members of the bourgeoisie travelling in a carriage through wartorn France. It would be fairly easy to work out a symbolic reading of the plot and characters of *Stagecoach.* The coach is America, a nation of exiles, riven with warring and contradictory factions; the Indians are the wild forces of nature; the pregnant woman is Liberty; the banker is the corrupt Republican Establishment, the spokesman for selfish individualism; the benevolent sheriff riding shotgun is Roosevelt; the Plummer Gang are the Axis powers; Buck, the driver, and his Mexican wife 'Hoolietta' are the ethnic mixtures which give the country its democratic character.

But like all good fables, *Stagecoach* has a universal application. It is the idea of the noble outlaw, the 'good bad man' represented most concretely by John Wayne as the Ringo Kid, which provides the film's centre. Outlaws (and outcasts in general) have always fascinated Ford not so much for their rebellion as for the subtle ways they are linked to the society which scorns them. They act *for* society in ways society cannot see, and they understand society better than society understands itself. Their rebellion (even at its most complex level, that of Ethan in *The Searchers*) is as much a matter of circumstance as of temperament. As Ringo puts it, 'I guess you can't break out of jail and into society the same week.' His vendetta is a family matter – he is trying to avenge the murder of his father and brother. In the process, he symbolically ensures the continuance of the forces of order, by saving the Cavalryman's wife and child, and the destruction of the forces of anarchy, by

Stagecoach: the Ladies' Law and Order League

outlasting the Indians and killing the corrupt Plummer family. At the end, with the sheriff's acquiescence, he rides towards the Mexican border to start his own family with Dallas, the prostitute (Claire Trevor).

The ending is a paean to primitivism, but it is important to realize that the film is endorsing primitivism as an *ideal* rather than as a viable reality. Ringo, the Rousseau noble savage, takes the law into his own hands, but he ultimately brings about the very Law and Order which the film attacks in its caricature of the overcivilized ladies of Tonto, described by Dallas as 'worse than Apaches'. *Stagecoach* leaves the question of American imperialism, the Cavalry vs. the Indians, tantalizingly unresolved. The Indians are totally one-dimensional here, but Ford's attitude to the role of the Cavalry, which will undergo complex metamorphoses in his later work as his interest in the Indians grows, is strangely ambiguous: he has the corrupt, hypocritical banker continually abuse the Cavalry, and the priggish young mother defend it. Ringo, the prime mover in the tale, more or less ignores the threat of the Indians and the authority of the Cavalry, relying purely on his own resources. The gambler views the Indian threat with a Griffith-like Aryan rectitude. The barrel of his pistol protrudes into the close-up of the mother praying fran-

Stagecoach: Ringo joins the stage

Stagecoach: fording a river and (*opposite*) the chase

tically in the last moments of the attack, and he is saved from firing his last bullet into her head (a copy of a scene in Griffith's 1913 Western *The Battle at Elderbush Gulch*, with Lillian Gish) only by being shot himself seconds before we hear the Cavalry bugle.

Ringo's showdown with the Plummers has been regarded by some critics as an anticlimax, coming as it does after the legendary chase across the Monument Valley salt flats and the Cavalry rescue. But it is only through his heroic action in the chase that Ringo wins the sheriff's respect and with it the right to bypass civilized law and carry out primitive justice. And the attack, which significantly occurs just before the stage reaches its destination, is the final test of the group's ability to survive. In the end their salvation depends on the appearance of a *deus ex machina*. But the Indians are just as much a part of the machinery of chance as the Cavalry, and as Ford has pointed out, if the chase had been staged realistically, with the Indians shooting the lead horses of the coach instead of firing madly into the air, 'it would have been the end of the picture'. Both the challenge and the salvation are metaphorical. What was it, after all, that threw the outcasts together but the rupture of order in their own lives? The war-ravaged desert through which the stage passes

Stagecoach: the Cavalry officer's wife, the gambler and the prostitute (Louise Platt, John Carradine, Claire Trevor)

(the curtains on the windows for ever whipping in the wind) becomes a metaphor for the instability of this archetypal primitive community, thrown together of necessity and chance and forced to rediscover the meaning of society. The passengers' vindication or condemnation is sealed by the time they enter anarchic, wide-open Lordsburg (a puckishly American diminution of 'Heaven'). Their real destination is within themselves.

Since the group in *Stagecoach* is an inversion of a stable community, it is poetically logical that the most disreputable characters – the drunken doctor, the prostitute and the convict – perform best in the two major crises (the childbirth and the Indian attack, life and death). As Jean Renoir (who has called this his favourite Ford film) did in *La Règle du Jeu* the same year, Ford develops his social thesis by minutely examining the tensions which threaten to shatter the group's order. The rules of Ford's game are simplicity and direct attack. At one extreme, there are the community's rhetoricians: the gambler Hatfield (John Carradine) and the banker Gatewood (Berton Churchill). Hatfield, glacial and stiff, is decked out impeccably. The rote nature of his chivalry is emphasized by his corpse-like attenuation and his deep, over-cultivated voice; his is the nobility of the suicide, the passing-on of

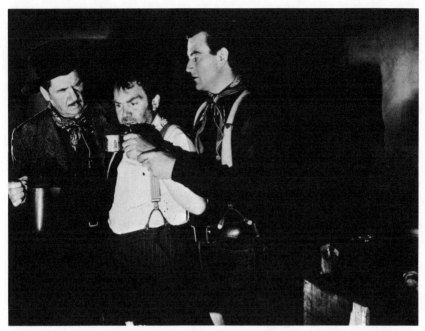

Stagecoach: Doc Boone sobers up (George Bancroft, Thomas Mitchell, John Wayne)

dead forms and lifeless ideals. Gatewood, who spends most of the journey fulminating against big government and taxes, clutches the briefcase containing his embezzlement. Against these two figures, the simple, instinctual gallantry of Ringo and Dallas takes on great eloquence. It is an eloquence expressed not in rhetoric but in action: when the pregnant woman sits piously aloof from Dallas at the dinner table, Ringo nonchalantly helps Dallas with her chair and sits next to her; when the woman enters labour, Dallas acts as midwife and then sits up all night holding the baby.

Somewhere in between these extremes of fraud and candour is Doc Boone (Thomas Mitchell), whose flushed, unruly features and comic versifying mask an intense privacy of emotion. The poet of the community, he alone is able to see the situation from the outside and articulate its meaning. His is a natural nobility which accepts its own limitations and absurdity, and he often acts as Ford's spokesman, both verbally and through reaction shots in the moments of crisis. When a vote is taken on whether the journey should continue in the face of imminent attack, Boone comments, 'I am not only a philosopher, I am also a fatalist. Somewhere, some time, there may be the right bullet or the wrong bottle waiting for Josiah Boone. Why worry when or where?'

Simultaneously Hatfield cuts a deck of cards and comes up with the ace of spades. But he casts his 'aye' with the doctor. This note of fatalism is picked up at the end, when the brutish Luke Plummer, waiting in the El Dorado saloon for the showdown with Ringo, is dealt the 'dead man's hand' of aces and eights. The idea is not quite predestination, but rather a stoic, almost comic awareness of individual responsibility. What happens to a man, no matter what the extenuating circumstances, is finally determined by what he *is* – by what he demonstrates of himself in the face of circumstances.

Boone does not let his alcoholism destroy his ability to function. Religious and military men in Ford's films are often frustrated in their pursuit of transient or illusory goals, but doctors have a simple and concrete function, the preservation and transmission of life, and their alcoholism is often a result of this awful responsibility. It is no accident that the whisky drummer who keeps Boone supplied is thought to be a minister: the bag from which he produces his bottles resembles a doctor's instrument kit or the valise in which a priest carries his wine for the sacrament of Communion. The physical agony which Boone undergoes in sobering up for the delivery of the child is a metaphor for the mental and moral agony of the doctor's role. Like the noble outlaw, he is both the saviour and the cynosure of society.

As Dallas and Ringo disappear from the dark, boisterous streets of Lordsburg, Boone comments, 'Well, they're saved from the blessings of civilization.' The sheriff, removing his badge, offers him a drink, and the doctor replies, after a grand moment of protraction, 'Just one.' This exchange (not in the script, which ended on a last bit of exposition about the murder plot) adds the perfect note of irony to the film's portrait of society. The primitive couple's flight into the freedom of the wilderness is seen through the eyes of society's watchdogs, the lawman and the doctor-poet. It is as if they are watching their own dream being realized at a distance – a dream whose beauty lies in its contrivance and improbability. This is Ford's vision of primitivism and the American past. We can feel it, watch it and cherish it, but we cannot quite touch or recapture it.

Wagon Master

> A hundred years have come and gone since 1849
> But the ghostly wagons rolling West
> Are ever brought to mind . . .

Wagon Master was the director's personal favourite among all his Westerns. Like his early Harry Carey Westerns, it was a low-pressure project, shot on a minimal budget far from civilization and producers. Ford himself wrote the

Wagon Master: a quest for the Promised Land

original story, and his son Patrick collaborated with Frank Nugent on the screenplay. *Wagon Master* details a series of episodes, alternately epic and picaresque, in the Westward trek of a Mormon wagon train. Lindsay Anderson, who described it as an 'avant-garde Western', remarked of the film: 'Ford often abandons his narrative completely, to dwell on the wide and airy vistas, on riders and wagons overcoming the most formidable natural obstacles, on bowed and weary figures stumbling persistently through the dust.' Superficially the most straightforward of films (Andrew Sarris, in calling it Ford's masterpiece, said that there are 'no moral shadings'), *Wagon Master* is actually a deeply ambiguous, almost perverse moral fable.

As the film begins, the Mormons are preparing to leave their inhospitable Midlands town under force of arms. A community of outcasts – like the communities in *The Outcasts of Poker Flat*, *Stagecoach*, *The Grapes of Wrath* and *Cheyenne Autumn* – they set out on a perilous quest for the Promised Land. It is the mingling of outlaw and pilgrim in these groups which so engages Ford. Symbolically, the Mormons represent all the American pioneers, and it is a typical Ford irony to express American ideals through a group of pariahs. The Mormons' spiritual ideal, like that of the

Wagon Master: Elder Wiggs and the Cleggs (Ward Bond, Charles Kemper)

Pilgrim colony, is identical with their physical ideal – to found a community in which freedom of belief means the same as freedom of movement. It is not enough, for Ford, that the Mormons face the dangers of intolerance; they must also face hunger, thirst and the mountains, all the hazards of an indifferent nature. Yet even this is not enough. They are kidnapped by a reptilian band of outlaws, the Clegg family, who act without a shred of reason or decency, like Furies avenging an uncommitted sin.

It is the extent to which Ford feels free to chide the Mormons' piety, to play a little roguishly with their travail and martyrdom, which makes *Wagon Master* such a rich and exhilarating work, particularly in comparison with the overbearing rhetoric of *The Grapes of Wrath* and *Cheyenne Autumn*. Ford makes them face facts by confronting them not only with the villainous Cleggs but also with a pair of amoral young horse traders and a *déclassé* medicine show troupe. To reach their Promised Land, the Mormons must come to terms with the real world; to survive, they must expose their ideals as well as their bodies. The perils facing the Mormons on their quest are terrible,

Wagon Master: the Mormon family (Jane Darwell, Russell Simpson, Kathleen O'Malley)

but even more terrible is the resolution of that quest: the Cleggs must be killed before the mountain leading to the Promised Land can be crossed.

The film is conceived as a series of threats, increasingly ominous, to the Mormons' group unity. At the outset, their solidarity is absolute. Elder Wiggs (Ward Bond) makes a brief speech ('It looks like we've got a trial ahead of us ...'), and Ford shows the community breaking camp in a magnificent tableau of shuffling figures moving silently through the frame, each to his own business, but all moving as harmoniously as in a ballet. It is the Cleggs we see first, though, appearing out of their own wanted poster; Uncle Shiloh Clegg (Charles Kemper) shoots down a man before the credits appear. Under the credits, a long line of wagons moves past the camera, Ford panning up to each as it approaches, family by family. Then he introduces the pragmatists who will be the Mormons' ultimate salvation: the horse traders, Sandy Owen (Harry Carey Jr) and Travis Blue (Ben Johnson), who eventually becomes wagon master. The Elder urges the young men to 'give the Lord a hand' by joining the wagon train. But Travis is not convinced until the local sheriff, during a card game, makes a disparaging reference to the Mormons, calling them 'horse traders'. Ford shows Travis' decision through a physical gesture. Earlier the Elder had chided the young men for 'gambling with cards . . . and a hundred people gambling their lives on us'. So when Travis hears the sheriff's remark, he looks down at his hand of cards, glances contemptuously towards the sheriff and flips a coin into a cup in the foreground of the frame with an off-hand remark: 'I'm in.' Ford dissolves to the Mormons preparing to depart, the sheriff and his posse riding up to watch them go, and then, at the last moment, Travis and Sandy joining them.

Along the way, the Mormon 'family' will be challenged by three other 'families' – the Cleggs, the show troupe and a tribe of peaceful but wary Indians. What holds the Mormons together during their long trial is the moral flexibility of their leader, Wiggs. Like any other Ford community, however noble, they have internal tensions. Wiggs is a typical Ford hero: he represents all that is most vital and valuable in his group, yet he stands aloof, and is sometimes in open conflict with the others. When the actors are found in the middle of nowhere, drunk, with no destination and no known origin, the other Mormons are hostile to them. 'Don't think we ought to take up with their kind of people,' says the deacon (Russell Simpson). Here Ford employs one of his infrequent tracking shots as Wiggs takes the deacon away from the others – who are standing in the background, watching but unable to hear – and points out the absurdity of such a reaction in light of their own situation. He adds, with beautiful irony, 'The way I see it, the Lord went to an awful lot of trouble to put these people in our way . . . and if I were Him, I wouldn't want anybody messing up *my* plans.' 'Well,' the deacon admits, 'putting it that way . . .', but Wiggs is already marching back to join the group. Ford's staging of the confrontation is a graphic illustration of how a leader exerts his power: by singling out an antagonist and conquering him in a showdown which is half public and half private. The element of mystery in the off-stage manipulation of power enables the leader to demonstrate his authority without having to enforce it, just as Judge Priest in *The Sun Shines Bright* stops a lynch mob by calling the bluff of its leader.

The Elder alone realizes the moral necessity of letting the actors join the wagon train, just as earlier he had realized the practical necessity of hiring the horse traders as scout and wagon master. If he had yielded to the group's tendency to irrational self-sufficiency, they might have become too rigid to adapt to later threats, such as the kidnapping by the Cleggs. Similarly, when one of the Cleggs rapes an Indian woman while the Mormons and the Indians are joining in a communal dance, the Elder quickly orders the man to be whipped. He risks the anger of the Cleggs to forestall a greater danger; a moment's hesitation, and the Indians would have opened fire (Ford shows a long row of rifles instantly protruding from beneath their blankets). And it was the Elder's example which had prevented bloodshed when the Indians appeared on the trail. Ordering Travis and Sandy to drop their guns and follow him, he walks up to the Indians and exchanges friendly greetings, while the Cleggs wait for an excuse to fire (Hank Worden chortles, 'Never did kill me a Navajo,' just as Ken Curtis will murmur 'I sure would like to kill me a Injun' before blasting a hungry Cheyenne off his horse in *Cheyenne Autumn*). The Indians' response is sublime. They tell the Elder that the Mormons are their brothers – not big thieves, like most white men, 'just little thieves'. The bond of kinship shared by the two groups of American outcasts is celebrated metaphorically in their circular dance round the fire, with the great Jim Thorpe arm-in-arm with Jane Darwell and Wiggs sitting in a place of honour among the tribal elders.

It is fascinating to see Ward Bond at the centre of a Ford film, because his screen personality seems so close to that of the director himself. Bond is the authority figure in Ford's stock company – he is the one who explodes with joy and runs the first Stars and Stripes up the flagpole at the end of *Drums Along the Mohawk* – and in his penultimate Ford appearance, in *The Wings of Eagles*, he actually becomes Ford, playing 'John Dodge', the gruff maker of sea stories and Westerns. It is a clue to Ford's moral stance that Bond's three fullest roles (*Wagon Master*, *The Quiet Man* and *The Searchers*) all have him playing clerics who are also secular leaders, and even, in the latter two cases, warriors (in *The Quiet Man* he is involved in an IRA cell, in *The Searchers* he is a Texas Ranger). Because both roles are necessary for the survival of a primitive community, the Bond character is able to sacrifice the purity of one to satisfy the demands of the other. The most pragmatic of Ford's characters, he is a representative of the civilized order who has won his position by restraining an innate primitivism.

Ford discovered Bond, along with John Wayne, in the University of Southern California football team, and gave him his screen debut in the 1929 *Salute*. He played mostly heavies at the start of his career, and his early roles for Ford usually had him playing a yahoo – sometimes, as in *Young Mr Lincoln*, a villainous one. Bond's morality is a matter of personal integrity rather than an inflexible adherence to an ideal. In *The Quiet Man*, his priest lies to save a marriage, and in *The Searchers* his minister averts his eyes on witnessing a moment of marital infidelity, acknowledging the tissue of tactful evasions which enables a struggling society to stabilize itself. But there is nothing more revelatory of Bond's character than that glorious moment during the fight scene in *The Quiet Man* when his boyish assistant asks him if they should take some action to stop it. 'Ah yes, we should, lad,' he replies, eyes glowing, fists jabbing in the air. 'We should. It's our duty. Yes, our duty.'

In *Wagon Master*, as befitting a story with a 'mass hero', Ford gives us a central character whose contradictions are held in perfect harmony rather than an individual hero (Henry Fonda, John Wayne) whose interior drama determines the course of events. Ford makes sport of the Elder's dual nature. Wherever Wiggs goes, he is trailed by the deacon, who stops him from frequent temptations to cursing (or, as the deacon quaintly puts it, 'using the words of wrath') with a brusque 'Elder!' and a firm shake of the head. When the Elder dickers with the horse traders, he is wearing his formal ministerial garb but leaning back against a fence post and whittling like a cowboy. When the wagon train heads West, he discards the frock coat – and some of his ministerial restraints – for rough frontier clothes, but he only enhances his authority by doing so. (In Bond's long-running *Wagon Train* television series, which was inspired by *Wagon Master*, his character is a virtual duplication of Wiggs, and there he is not a Mormon but a retired Civil War officer.)

It is the Elder's worldliness which, paradoxically, allows him to be more Christian in his attitude towards the theatre people than the other Mormons are. Their distaste is a moralistic reaction against the actors' drunkenness and loose sexual habits, yet their moral leader accepts the troupe because he remembers his 'sinnin' days' and can see what a 'dad-blamed fine figure of a woman' the actor's mistress is. Like Judge Priest, the Elder is without direct lineage. He makes a wry joke about his solitude when he explains to the young cowboys why he is being run out of town: 'Why, I got more wives than Solomon hisself!' We are told nothing of his past; his life is the life of the community. The Mormons are, in a very real sense, his family.

What makes the film's celebration of the simple virtues so convincing is its recognition of the shrewd calculation and pragmatic nature needed to maintain generosity, decency and tolerance. It is typical of Ford that while the Elder's humanism is expressed in action, not in rhetoric, the nihilism of Shiloh Clegg is cloaked in religiosity. Clegg expresses his cynicism towards the Mormons' hospitality by telling them that their meeting shows how the Lord 'marks the sparrow's fall'. The dance the Cleggs interrupt is being held to celebrate the finding of water in the desert; their entrance, surly and silent, causing the music to stop, provides a metaphor for their spiritual aridity.

Ford abruptly shifts from flowing group shots of the dance to a series of ominous close-ups of the Cleggs, the Elder, Travis and Sandy: the communal feeling is graphically disrupted in a clash of individual wills. Clegg's double-edged remark, 'Wherever there's music you can be sure there's good Christian folk – never did know a bad man had any music in him,' under-

Wagon Master: the show troupe (Ruth Clifford, Alan Mowbray, Joanne Dru)

scores the almost sacrilegious overtones of the outlaws' disruption of the group. Uncle Shiloh, like Pa Clanton in *Clementine*, is a perverted father figure, letting his boys act out their wildest impulses and the next moment whipping them for their stupidity. He is the brute in man, callous, self-centred and avaricious. When Andrew Sarris remarks that there are no 'moral shadings' in *Wagon Master*, what he is really saying is that it is less a drama than a lyric poem. One value is set against its opposite; the poetry comes from the clash of absolutes, and the way the absolutes overlap each other. The Clegg family is an inversion of the Mormon family; the juxtaposition throws the moral conflict in relief, brings out all its contradictory overtones, and deepens the force of the poetry of sacrifice and suffering.

Keeping this scheme in mind, we can more readily appreciate the role that the show troupe plays in the film. Seemingly an arbitrary inclusion, the actors represent that side of the Mormons, and specifically of the Elder, which has had to be restrained for the sake of religious duty – the casual, spontaneous, free response to life. Like all theatre people, they live only for the moment;

Wagon Master: the drive across the mountains

when Dr A. Locksley Hall (Alan Mowbray, another carry-over from *Clementine*) rises from a drunken stupor to find a couple of horses staring him in the face, he mutters 'Horses!' and puts on his top hat, ever ready to resume his professional duty. Paradoxically, the function of the show people in the drama is to serve as an audience for the moral conflict which the Mormons and the Cleggs are acting out on the bare stage of the desert.

Far from criticizing the actors' aimless vagabondage, Ford portrays it with affection, just as he does the nomadic life of the Navajos: their independence is a difficult but healthy alternative to the hypocrisy of the civilization which expelled the Mormons (and the Indians). Ford even draws an explicit connection between the Indians and the actors in a stunningly inventive shot showing Denver (Joanne Dru) preparing herself for the dance in a series of ritualistic gestures syncopated to the beat of tom-toms. And far from being corrupted by the actors, as the deacon feared, the Mormons are made more alive and cohesive by their presence. By the end, the actors have been fully integrated into the community: Dr Hall makes a courageous wagon drive across the mountain (his mistress comments, 'You big ham!'), and Denver links up with the wagon master. The film celebrates the Mormon community, but it does so in the context of a folk tradition which Sarris aptly describes as 'free adventure and compelling adaptability'.

Just surviving the journey is not enough; it is the quality of the group which survives that interests Ford. And the climactic action of the film – the wagon master's shooting of Shiloh Clegg – is the finishing touch on Ford's moral canvas. The Mormons, who consider themselves the Lord's 'chosen people', can only be saved through an act of killing (albeit in self-defence). The man who pulls the trigger is the man whom the Elder asked to 'give the Lord a hand'. This climax is strikingly similar to that of a later journey to the Promised Land, that of the Indians in *Cheyenne Autumn* from the reservation back to their homeland. To achieve a final peace, the source of anarchy within the tribe must be destroyed: in *Cheyenne Autumn* the chief shoots the trouble-making young brave who threatens the life of the entire tribe, and in *Wagon Master* the most antagonistic of the Mormons, a nameless character who continually provokes trouble with the horse traders and the Cleggs, is killed by Shiloh.

When Travis kills Shiloh, he hurls his gun into the desert, just as the chief in *Cheyenne Autumn* smashes his rifle after killing the brave. A necessary action, but a bitter one. Ford's recognition of the impotence of religious idealism in the face of hard facts is as clear in *Wagon Master* as it is in *Seven Women*. Curiously, Ford does not seem very interested in the Mormons as Mormons. He does not delve into their religion, or any customs

Wagon Master: 'Shall We Gather at the River?' (Ben Johnson, Ward Bond)

which set them apart from other pioneers, and he does not bother to isolate more than a handful of the group for dramatic attention. Even Jane Darwell, mouthpiece for the downtrodden in *The Grapes of Wrath*, appears in the Mormon entourage mainly to cackle at jokes and blow the meeting-horn. Ford devotes much more time to Travis and Sandy, the actors, and the Cleggs. This is not the limitation it might seem. For all his interest in disparate communities, Ford is less interested in what sets them apart than in what effect they have on society as a whole, and what effect society has on them. He gives us only enough details of the Mormons' communal life to let us share their feeling of exclusion, then jettisons any notion that they are 'different'.

The religious element of *Wagon Master*, the unshakeably affirmative response to life, is made concrete in the characters' relationship to the land around them. Time and again the tiny wagon train is picked out in vast long shot against the implacable desert terrain, and in one fantastic image the train becomes an almost invisible speck threading its way across the mountain pass to the strains of 'Shall We Gather at the River?'. The film is mostly set in flatland, away from Monument Valley's configurations and mesas (once, though, a distant spire is sighted, and Sandy compares it to the tower of a cathedral); the people are the monuments in *Wagon Master*. At the most wearing part of the journey, when the water is lowest, Ford shows the Mormons marching in procession through a fixed frame in mid-shot, then shows their feet in close-shot walking through a fixed frame, and then retreats to a full view as they march past the still immobile camera. The landscape, until the sighting of the verdant Promised Land in the valley beyond the mountains, is unusually stark for a Ford Western. The only reassurance of a harmony between man and nature is the robust folk-song commentary, which, as Lindsay Anderson puts it, almost seems to 'summon up the images'. Otherwise, Ford's settings are strictly in keeping with the progression in the Mormons' quest. There is a sacramental effect in the movement from a baptism of water (the river crossing) to a baptism of fire (in the desert), to images of fruition (the fertile valley); but the elements are neither benign nor malevolent, simply a reflection of the characters.

After the mountain is crossed, Ford ends the story, but not the film, which continues with a poetic reprise of earlier scenes. The last of these is the river crossing, an image repeated from the beginning of the journey. From the bank of the river, as discreet and aloof as the perspective of history, we watch the wagons floundering along in mid-stream. Dream and documentary modes are magically fused as the camera makes a jerking movement to follow a moment of action. 'The End' appears on the screen, and dissolves off. But the film remains alive with a glorious image: a glistening colt trotting up the river bank, horses and wagons following in his path. Ford fades out on this image of the eternal renewal of life.

5. Men at War: *They Were Expendable* (1945), *My Darling Clementine* (1946), *Fort Apache* (1948)

They Were Expendable

They Were Expendable was shot in late 1944. The war in Europe was ending, but the Allied forces in the Pacific were steeling themselves for an invasion of Japan. The odds were strongly on their side; the principal question was how much the victory would cost. Ford, whose credit carries the legend 'Captain U.S.N.R.', was under orders, along with members of his cast and crew, to make the film as a document for the American people. It is reported that he chafed at the order, because it would take him out of actual combat, but accepted with the stipulation that his salary, $225,000, would go to build a shelter home, The Farm, endowed in perpetuity for the men of his Navy Field Photographic Unit, with whom he had been filming war documentaries since Pearl Harbor.

It is characteristic of Ford that *They Were Expendable* did not attempt to offer an upbeat, jingoistic view of the war, but dwelt instead on its most hopeless moments – the crushing defeat in the Philippines after the bombing of Pearl Harbor. It was at this point, this 'tragic moment', that the human meaning of the war could be most clearly and deeply felt. Ford was not alone in his approach, as Leif Furhammar and Folke Isaksson point out in their *Politics and Film*:

When victory was near, it was no longer necessary to maintain the encouraging and dishonest wishful image of the war. Nor was it desired by war-weary audiences; the reality had become so intense that war was no longer a subject for escapism. Towards the end, despair, exhaustion, and reality break through the mythical treatment in films like Raoul Walsh's *Objective Burma*, in which even Errol Flynn loses his romantic aura, Milestone's *A Walk in the Sun*, and William Wellman's *The Story of G.I. Joe* – all from the last six months of the conflict.

Ford's view of the war in *They Were Expendable* is little changed, however, from that in his two Academy Award-winning documentaries, *The Battle of Midway* (1942) and *December 7th* (co-directed with Gregg Toland in 1943). *December 7th* also concentrates on a military disaster, and in *Midway*, as Andrew Sarris points out, 'It is not the battle itself that intrigues Ford, but the weary faces of rescued fliers plucked out of the Pacific after days of privation.'

Based on the experiences of Ford's shipmate Lt John Bulkeley (played by Cmdr Robert Montgomery, 'Brickley' in the film), *They Were Expendable* tells of a handful of men, a Motor Torpedo Boat Squadron, whose mission is simply to buy time, with whatever means possible, for the crippled American forces in the Pacific. One of Bulkeley's men explained the situation in the book by W. L. White, published in 1942, from which Cmdr Frank Wead's script derives:

Suppose you're a sergeant machine-gunner, and your army is retreating and the enemy advancing. The captain takes you to a machine gun covering the road. 'You're to stay here and hold this position,' he tells you. 'For how long?' you ask. 'Never mind,' he answers, 'just hold it.' Then you know you're expendable ... You don't mind it until you come back here where people waste hours and days and sometimes weeks, when you've seen your friends give their lives to save minutes.

The hopelessness of the squadron's position is everywhere underlined; they cannot hope to win the battle, only to lessen the degree of the catastrophe. No other war film has so subtly and movingly explored the idea of sacrifice. As Lindsay Anderson wrote: 'Its characters are shown in the light of their sacrifice, ennobled by it – not through words, but through image after image of conscious dignity.'

Yet in later years Ford did not much care for the film, and, looking at his later war films, such as *Fort Apache* and *The Civil War*, it is easy to see why. The nobility of the characters in *They Were Expendable* seems to spring not so much from their human qualities as from their superhuman possibilities, from their sublimation of fear and pain and loneliness into a virtual mystique of heroism. The most powerful drama in *Fort Apache* and *The Civil War* comes from the men's struggle to reconcile their sacrifices with the necessities

They Were Expendable

'Dream images of military glory': battle scenes from *They Were Expendable*

of history. But the historical perspective which would later allow Ford to bring out this conflict was a luxury unavailable in *They Were Expendable*. He made the film immediately after witnessing the kind of events he is depicting, and observation of suffering at close quarters tends to breed an oblique, abstracted response as a means of defence.

It is revealing that White's book contains many passages which in hindsight seem perfect Ford material but which were not used in the film – intimate glimpses of the men in moments of doubt and indecision and even some raucously humorous episodes. For example, the long, suspenseful account of the ferrying of General Douglas MacArthur through enemy waters, as gripping as a Hemingway short story, includes hilarious descriptions of the admirals and generals lying in the hold of the boat too seasick to care that enlisted men are stepping all over them in the dark. Ford entirely omits the details of the journey, concentrating instead on the Homeric panoramas of leave-taking and arrival. The general climbs aboard ship aloof and erect, silently greeting the awe-inspired men to the strains of 'The Battle Hymn of the Republic'. There *is* a wry moment when a hero-worshipping young ensign

holds out his cap for MacArthur to autograph, and Mulcahey (Ward Bond) throws up his arms in disbelief, but this only serves to emphasize the solemn context of the scene.

They Were Expendable is probably unique for a war film of the period in that it contains not a shred of enemy-baiting. In fact, we never even *see* an enemy soldier or sailor. This can be attributed in part to Ford's professionalism – the warrior's instinctive respect for his enemy's ability – and partly to his respect for the integrity of separate cultures. The bombing of Pearl Harbor is announced over a protracted shot of an anguished Oriental woman interrupted in her knitting; a Filipino girl tearfully sings 'My Country, 'Tis of Thee' as the squadron files out of the night-club; and there is a large close-up of another Oriental woman dazedly watching her man leaving on an ambulance boat at the fade-out on the first air raid. In *December 7th*, as the Japanese bombers are leaving Pearl Harbor, there are shots of a crying Oriental child pointing to the sky and of a grieving old Oriental couple. Though this is certainly propaganda (good Orientals mourning the acts of bad Orientals), it is propaganda of the noblest sort, reminding the audience that the enemy is not from an inhuman, unsuffering race. But what the invisibility of enemy troops gives *They Were Expendable*, most of all, is a pervasive sense of fatalism. As in *The Lost Patrol* – Ford's story of a British desert squadron picked off one by one by an unseen Arab enemy – death is everywhere, absurd and inevitable. As Russell Campbell pointed out in discussing *Fort Apache*, 'It is remarkable even in *They Were Expendable* how little sense there is of a *cause* for combat.'

This gives the film a strange kind of grace, but it also tends to lessen our involvement in the drama. Although Ford lavishes great attention on the physical details of warfare, often interrupting his narrative to show the men replenishing their ships' supplies of fuel and ammunition or performing mundane repair jobs, there is little feeling of what it is actually like to be in combat. The battle sequences are dream images of military glory. The battles are not so much tests as spectacles, with bombs streaking through the night sky to cast eerie silhouettes around the boats as they sweep and reel to avoid being hit; day-time bombs shattering in kaleidoscopic smoke patterns; enemy cruisers (invariably seen in long-shot) exploding in fiery cadenzas, like Fourth of July fireworks; and downed planes tracing endless arcs before they crash (off-screen). There is an irony in the narrative line too: though the tide of the war is running against the United States, most of the underdog squadron's missions are in themselves phenomenally successful, suggesting the eventual outcome of the war. Even when they fail (as when one of the boats explodes on a beach), Ford presents the action in an idealized manner which gives the impression of predetermination. In his late films, Ford presents combat in brief, inglorious spurts and flurries. Here the action is whole and incongruously beautiful, an end in itself.

In this context, the interdisciplinary conflict between Brickley and his second-in-command Rusty Ryan (John Wayne) counts for relatively little. Ryan's impetuousness and his desire for a Navy reputation, set against Brickley's self-sacrificial insistence on 'playing for the team', interestingly prefigures the Thursday–York conflict in *Fort Apache*, but with a vital modification: in *Fort Apache* it is the more easygoing and adaptable Wayne who emerges as the ideal soldier – the team player – and it is the stiff, disciplined commander (Henry Fonda) who winds up playing against the team for personal glory, finally leading his men into a massacre. Despite Robert Montgomery's superb performance (cited by James Agee as 'the one perfection to turn up in movies during the year'), Ford's development of Brickley's character registers as somewhat evasive. He is too perfect, too disciplined, too selfless to be entirely convincing as a foil to Ryan. Although the extremity of the situation dictates that the commander exercise such self-

They Were Expendable: stern father and prodigal son (Robert Montgomery, John Wayne)

control – the crippling of Ryan's right hand occurs when the wheel of his boat metaphorically spins out of control during an air raid – one feels that Ford is holding back on some of Brickley's emotions to make the point about team-work. The hint of jealousy in Ryan's attitude towards Brickley is left merely a hint, and Ford seems unwilling to explore the possibility that Brickley's self-conscious sacrifice may be a form of self-aggrandizement more subtle than Ryan's. After all, it was John Bulkeley who became a national hero, not his second-in-command.

For the most part, to invert Ford's comment about his *April Morning* project, *They Were Expendable* is not really a character sketch, it's a battle story. The most convincing dramatic relationship in the film is that between Ryan and the Navy nurse Sandy (Donna Reed), brought briefly together and then forced apart by the vicissitudes of war. Our memory of Sandy's remarkable composure in the makeshift operating theatre during the siege of Corregidor doubles the impact of her breakdown in Ryan's arms after the dinner with the squadron. As John Baxter points out, Ryan's interlude with Sandy – a dance, a few moments alone on a hammock, the dinner – 'becomes

They Were Expendable: Sandy (Donna Reed) in the operating theatre

increasingly important as the film progresses, recalling another set of traditions, those of American home life, to preserve which the war is being fought'. The love affair is as tantalizingly brief for the audience as it is for the participants, and its anticlimactic ending, with Sandy and Ryan interrupted in their last conversation when their telephone line goes dead during an invasion, is one of the most crushing moments in any Ford film. It is worth noting here that Frank Wead apparently based this incident on an event in his own life; for in *The Wings of Eagles*, Ford's film biography of his old friend and scriptwriter, Wead's last chance of reconciliation with his wife ends when their telephone conversation is interrupted by a radio announcing the invasion of Pearl Harbor.

Ford's use of the family as a metaphor for national solidarity governs all the relationships in *They Were Expendable*. The squadron is representative of the national 'family', Brickley the stern but understanding father, and Ryan the prodigal son. Ford places great emphasis on the touching callowness of the ensigns – most memorably in the shot of a very young sailor drinking a glass of milk as the men toast their retiring doctor – and on the paternal overtones of Brickley's authority. When the admiral initially rejects the PT boats as not

They Were Expendable: interrupted conversation

'substantial' enough for combat, it is the headstrong Ryan who wants to quit the squadron for a destroyer and Brickley who walks over to the command boat and, in close-up, regards it with a serene expression of confidence. The commander constantly calls the ensigns 'son', and when he challenges Ryan's resignation, the younger man snaps, 'Look, Brick, for years I've been taking your fatherly advice, and it's never been very good. From here on in I'm a one-man band.' Ford comments by cutting to a comic ritual of 'team-work', four sailors cutting in on each other as they dance with a delighted girl; but it takes the announcement of the Pearl Harbor bombing to make Ryan change his mind. Brickley and several other officers group accusingly round Ryan, who looks into Brickley's eyes, says 'Let's go', and tosses away his resignation papers. The film's ending, with Ryan and Brickley ordered back to America to help develop PT boats, is a brilliant twist on the conventional heroic war film finale; for as Gerald Peary points out, 'One of the great ironies of *They Were Expendable* is that the heroic sacrifice at the end is for Ryan and Brickley to agree to be *saved* and leave their men behind, probably to die.'

Ford shows the squadron as a group of ghostly shadows on the ground as

They Were Expendable

Brickley leaves his command post and, eyes shadowed by the brim of his hat, gives his last order: 'You older men ... take care of the kids.' Two dogfaces are seen grinning at the ensigns with avuncular pride, and the ensigns sheepishly return the affection. Then Ford cuts back to Brickley, who says, almost to himself, 'Maybe ... That's all.' The only time rebelliousness threatens Brickley's paternal stability occurs when the admiral (who calls *him* 'son') cites team-work as his reason for relegating the squadron to inglorious messenger duty: 'Listen, son. You and I are professionals. If the manager says "sacrifice", we lay down a bunt and let somebody else hit the home runs ... Our job is to lay down that sacrifice. That's what we were trained for, and that's what we'll do.' As Brickley leaves the admiral's bomb-shattered headquarters, he pauses for a long moment under a jagged piece of roofing, which casts a deep shadow over his face, as if to suggest the buried ambition which he has trained himself to suppress. Clearing his mind of the thought, he says 'Thank you' to the admiral, salutes, and leaves for duty.

The thematic climax to which the whole film moves is Ryan putting his arm around Brickley, finally accepting the idea of team-work, in the troop plane at the end. But one of the most revealing methods of finding clues to a director's attitude is to examine what he puts in the corners and backgrounds of his shots, or what he does in seemingly irrelevant moments, 'privileged moments', as François Truffaut calls them. One of the privileged moments in *They Were Expendable* comes as MacArthur, in long-shot, is thanking the men for their service to him. It was perhaps Ford's submerged doubts about the kind of authority Brickley represents which made him show MacArthur giving a long hand-clasp to John Wayne's Ryan after only a perfunctory farewell to Brickley.

My Darling Clementine
After the end of the war, Ford worked on two projects which for various reasons never came to fruition: a long compilation of documentary footage to be used as evidence in the Nuremberg Trials; and a remake of his 1919 Western *The Last Outlaw*, with his old star Harry Carey (who *wasn't* in the original) in the role of an outlaw released from prison after ten years' confinement (is it too fanciful to see this in terms of Ford's wartime 'confinement' overseas?) and returning home to find his town and family situation drastically altered. Any film made by Ford immediately after the war could hardly have escaped the influence of the military mystique. The film he eventually made was *My Darling Clementine* which, despite the fact that he made seven films about the US Cavalry, is probably his most wholeheartedly

My Darling Clementine: saloon government (Henry Fonda, Ward Bond, Victor Mature, Alan Mowbray)

militarist Western. None of the Cavalry films comes as close to an unambiguous endorsement of militarism as a social principle. Freely based on the career of Wyatt Earp, *Clementine* celebrates the coming of law and order to the West. Earp, the cowboy who brings civilization to Tombstone in the course of settling a personal score with the anarchic Clanton family, is the kind of lawman even an old cop hater like Ford could admire: cool and loose, motivated by family ties and a sense of justice, a man who influences others more by example than by force.

The allegorical nature of the plot makes us feel that a battle is something sublimely over and above its human elements. The collision of moral absolutes (Earps and Clantons, civilization and barbarism) is seen as both inevitable and entirely beneficial to society, despite the sacrifice of life which it entails. This may be why Ford regarded *Clementine*, one of his most visually adventurous films, as essentially a film for children, and why critics who regard Ford as a 'primitive poet' with a naïve moral sense consider it one of his masterpieces.

It is, indeed, a child's world which *Clementine* presents: noble knight rides

My Darling Clementine: dandyism: Wyatt Earp at the barber's

into town, resists the temptation of the shady seductress, vanquishes dragon, and rides out with the love of the virginal heroine. The town is so removed from civilization that it does not seem to have a working mayor (fulfilment of the military's desire for absolute authority?); governmental affairs are conducted either in the saloon or on Main Street. Adolescent boys would be especially attracted to the theme because the Earp brothers run the town as if it were their clubhouse, protecting it against the incursions of the rival boys' gang, the Clantons, a bunch of overgrown bullies given licence by their irresponsible father. Now it could be objected that this account of the plot misrepresents the film as childish, when it should be seen as child*like*. However, Ford treats the law-and-order theme (though not Earp himself) with uncharacteristic solemnity, and suppresses his characteristic impulse to idealize nomadic primitivism. This makes for a stirring, beautiful film, but it is a film of far less complexity, nuance and moral subtlety than a later work such as *The Man Who Shot Liberty Valance*, which takes the same archetypal situation and emphasizes all the ironies and tragic ambiguities in the collision between primitivism and civilization.

Henry Fonda's Earp was a new kind of hero for Ford, however much he might owe to Fonda's previous incarnations of Lincoln, Gil Martin and Tom Joad. The performance presents Earp as a pawn of his own heroism. He is repeatedly found staring at himself in mirrors and shop windows. When we first see him on the cattle trail, he is bearded and scruffy, but the almost unconscious undercurrent of dandyism in his character urges him to make the fateful entrance into Tombstone – so that he can go to the Bon Ton Tonsorial Parlor.

Fonda's Earp stands at the turning point of his curious evolution in the Ford Stock Company. He began his career with Ford as the quintessential American common man: the populist future president, the farmer turned Revolutionary War soldier, the dispossessed American of the Depression. Fonda's qualities as an actor make him uncommonly suitable for charismatic roles; his face has a kind of sculptural, boiled-off purity, and the most notable aspect of his style is his restraint – he is one of those actors who is interesting largely for what he does not say. Yet it is this very purity which makes his impersonations of fanatics and weaklings equally convincing. Fonda can be said to stand for history's foreground, and John Wayne for a hidden vital force (Wayne seldom played common or famous men for Ford). It is interesting to note that Wayne, who eventually evolved into *the* Ford hero, played an outlaw in his first starring role for Ford (*Stagecoach*), and Fonda, who began by playing a future president, wound up as a cowardly priest (*The Fugitive*) and a pathological martinet (*Fort Apache*) before ending his association with Ford because of a fistfight with the director during the making of *Mr. Roberts.*

Earp is halfway between the fanatic and the common man: rigid and gentle, taciturn and forceful, demonstrative and aloof, keeping all his conflicting facets in perfect harmony. His dandyism (always a danger sign for a Ford character) hints of his latent impulse towards civilization; and if we look a little deeper, we can begin to discern the hints of arrogance which Fonda's *Fort Apache* role brought out into the open. In the magnificent dance sequence in the half-erected church, Earp whirls in a rigid mechanical waltz like a figure magically sprung to life from an old tintype. When Lincoln danced with Mary Todd, we laughed at his clumsiness and saw it as the common man shining ineradicably through his ambition; here, though, we are in awe, with the townspeople, of Earp's magical grace. The flowing camera-work in *Young Mr Lincoln's* dance sequence, counterpointed with Lincoln's awkwardness, emphasizes the contrary pulls in the character; but the hieratic long-shots and low angles of *Clementine's* dance elevate the dancer *above* the common man, and the mathematical precision of the montage is the breathless formulation of a myth.

One of Lincoln's foremost traits is generosity, but Earp has an unpleasant streak of puritanism, particularly in the way he handles the Mexican dance-hall girl, Chihuahua (Linda Darnell). Their snappish confrontations are played largely for humour, but it is a humour oddly lacking in Ford's customary chivalry and respect for the outcast. Ford often teases his female characters for their prudery, but here he seems to be mocking Chihuahua for her sensuality. (As Robin Wood has observed: '[Ford] can only tolerate Chihuahua when she is shot and dying, whereupon he promptly sentimen-talizes her.') At one point, the girl berates Earp for his condescension as he sits on the boardwalk, chair tilted and hat shading his eyes. Without answer-ing her, he gives an elaborate yawn and begins a slow bicycle-pedalling motion with his feet. Amusing as it is, the scene strikes a sour note for a director who in *Stagecoach* had defended Dallas, the prostitute, against the puritanism of an entire town. The joke about the honeysuckle perfume – when Clementine Carter (Cathy Downs) takes a deep breath of 'pure' Western air and remarks on 'the scent of the desert flower', Wyatt confides, 'That's me – barber' – is another example of this note of affectation, the curious and subtle playing with Earp's dignity which seems to find Ford caught between his best and worst impulses. (When James Stewart takes over the Earp role for Ford in *Cheyenne Autumn*, Earp has become a jaded, effete *poseur* who epitomizes the decadence of the Old West.)

Although *Clementine's* Tombstone is one of the most lovingly and painstakingly reconstructed of all cinematic Western towns, and though the situations are played with a keen eye for verisimilitude, Ford has taken an unusual degree of licence with history to satisfy the demands of his allegory. The source material for the film was Stuart N. Lake's anecdotal biography, *Wyatt Earp, Frontier Marshal*, based on the ageing lawman's own reminiscences. Ford himself knew Earp (who died in 1929), as he recalled recently:

When Wyatt Earp retired as a lawman, he went to some little town north of Pasadena. Now his wife was a very devout religious woman, and a couple times a year she'd go to these religious conventions in Utah and Eastern Arizona, and Wyatt would get on the streetcar and go up to Universal City and join us. We became quite friendly . . . Wyatt would sneak into town and get drunk with my cowboys. Along about noon, they'd sneak away and come back about 1.15 swacked to the gills – all my cowboys *and* Wyatt – and I'd have to change the schedule around . . . I didn't know anything about the O.K. Corral at the time, but Harry Carey knew about it, and he asked Wyatt and Wyatt described it fully . . . As a matter of fact, he drew it out on paper, a sketch of the entire thing. Wyatt said, 'I was not a good shot, I had to get close to a man.' . . . So in *My Darling Clementine*, we did it exactly the way it had been. They didn't just walk up the street and start banging away at each other; it was a clever military maneuver.

But the rest of the film is far from 'what really happened', and it was these deviations from history which probably bothered Ford most in retrospect. As did the fact that the studio changed the ending: 'It was so long ago I've forgotten, but it wasn't that way at all. I think I wanted the girl to stay there and teach school, and I wanted Wyatt to stay there and become permanent marshal – which he did.'

The structure of the film is simple and symmetrical, beginning with the Earp brothers' ominous meeting with the Clantons outside Tombstone; continuing through Wyatt's assumption of the marshal's office and his jockeying for power with Doc Holliday; and ending with the gunfight and Wyatt leaving town, half-promising to return. All this seems to take place in about three days. In fact, Wyatt knew Doc Holliday in Dodge City, and Doc tagged along when he went to Tombstone; Holliday did not die in the gunfight, as he does in the film, but of tuberculosis eighteen months later; Old Man Clanton was killed before the gunfight occurred; the feud between the Earps and the Clantons lasted over a long period and had nothing to do with the Earps' cattle; and Virgil Earp was marshal, Wyatt only a deputy, on 26 October 1881, the day of the gunfight. Once again, the objection is not to Ford's mythification but to his sacrificing of moral and historical nuances for the sake of a singleminded allegory. Appropriately enough, it is the ambiguous figures in the middle-ground of the conflict, such as Chihuahua and Victor Mature's Holliday, who suffer most from the concentration on moral extremes.

In fact, when one considers *Clementine* in the light of its 'remake', *Liberty Valance*, it becomes apparent how easily Holliday could have been the central character in the drama. Ford's sympathy in *Liberty Valance* is divided between the historical necessity of Stewart's role and the self-destructive heroism of John Wayne's ambiguous, Holliday-like Tom Doniphon, one of Ford's most complex characters. Holliday's two women, Chihuahua and Clementine, are the classic dark and fair women of the American romantic imagination. Like Wayne's characters in *The Searchers* and *Liberty Valance*, Holliday is tragically torn between primitivism (Chihuahua) and civilization (Clementine). Unlike Earp, he has failed to find a way to reconcile his contradictions, and wastes himself in bitterness. His dissipated, alcoholic personality is powerfully visualized in the shot of his anguished face reflected in his framed doctor's licence – he is a physician in the film, not a dentist – as he contemptuously mutters, '*Doctor* John Holliday!' and shatters the frame with his whisky glass. When Chihuahua dies under his hands on an improvised operating table (the only known instance in Ford of a drunken doctor being unable to perform his duty), the family woman passes over to Wyatt.

The sacrificial deaths of Holliday and Chihuahua in the Earp cause seem to be dictated by the Puritan ethos, by the desire to expunge every trace of moral ambiguity, even the most attractive, from the nascent society. Earp's vendetta springs from the violation of taboo. In the opening sequence, Ford plunges into the clash of moral absolutes in a succession of low-angled close-ups of the Earps and Clantons looming against a sky of deep neutral grey. The pattern of action and reaction is set up immediately. After Wyatt refuses Old Man Clanton's offer to buy the herd, the Clantons kill young James Earp and make off with the cattle. The disintegration of family was the dominant theme of the films Ford made just before the war; here the family is literally being killed off. The Clantons, a vicious parody of blood devotion, seal their violation by stealing a gold cross from the corpse of the youngest Earp, a cross he was taking to his sweetheart, Carrie Sue. In this bleak environment, the simplest totem assumes momentous proportions, symbolizing (like the medal in *The Searchers*, the gold cross in *Sergeant Rutledge*, and the widow's brooch in *Liberty Valance*) all the solaces of tribe and tradition which the outlaws' anarchy is threatening.

The unalloyed viciousness of Old Man Clanton's sneak attack is what determines the severity of Wyatt's response and gives him a moral justifi-

My Darling Clementine: Olympian detachment: Tombstone's marshal

cation for using the marshal's office to settle a personal wrong. The key to the film's method is the feeling it creates of the subtle power of small actions against brutish shows of force, i.e., the superiority of moral righteousness. It is finally the *crudeness* of the Clantons (in the gunfight) which makes them fall under the Earps' shrewd calculation. Wyatt has powers which verge on the magical; he seldom carries a gun and seems to be performing his peace-keeping duties by remote control, slouched in his chair and issuing languid remarks. By the time of *Cheyenne Autumn*, this Olympian detachment has turned him into a clown.

The effectiveness of Earp's *sang-froid* in *Clementine* is enhanced by Old Man Clanton's bizarre switches from courtliness to unrestrained savagery, most of them presented in single takes to emphasize their irrationality. Walter Brennan as Clanton is one of the classic Ford villains, and like his counter-parts Charles Kemper (*Wagon Master*) and Lee Marvin (*Liberty Valance*), he is given to ruling his cretinous gang/family with a whip. He sits at his son Billy's deathbed in a model pose of stony paternal grief and then, when Virgil Earp turns to leave, shoots him in the back. When his sons are wiped out in the gunfight at the O.K. Corral, he cries 'My boys! Ike . . . Sam . . . Phin . . . Billy . . .' like a sagebrush Medea, and then tries to pick off a few more Earps before Ward Bond mows him down with a righteous blast from the hip. The situation and the dialogue are virtually identical with Kemper's end in *Wagon Master*; in both films Ford is using the nihilism of the bandit family as a counterpoint to the fragile unity of the idealized family, here the Earps, there the wagon train.

Tombstone, which the three surviving Earps enter beneath a turbulent El Greco sky, is like the painter's *View of Toledo* – an isolate, throbbing citadel of light nestled in a pall of chaos and darkness. Yet the town, when seen at close range, is almost as chaotic as the void which surrounds it. Wyatt's shave is disrupted by gunshots shattering the barber-shop mirror, outraging both his narcissism and his sense of law and order. 'What kind of town is this?' he demands several times as he heads into the street, still wreathed in towel and lather, to pacify a drunken Indian in a saloon. It is typical of the film's Grecian discretion that the Indian is dispatched off-stage, as the townspeople watch in the street. Robin Wood comments: 'Earp knocks him around a bit and wants to know why he's been let out of the reservation; in racial terms the scene is obviously very unpleasant, but in mythic terms very meaningful, civilization conceived as demanding the rigorous suppression of the untamed forces Indian Joe represents.'

Later, after Wyatt and his brothers have taken it over, the town is seen almost entirely in sunlight, the streets stretching out in the hazy brilliance of

My Darling Clementine: the dance in the half-built church (Cathy Downs, Henry Fonda)

high noon. The film's moral schematization is echoed in the town's topography. Tombstone seems to be divided into squares and planes, like a chessboard or a map of a battlefield (or that sketch Earp drew for Ford). The framing continually emphasizes horizontal planes stretching into the distance (the boardwalk and the long bar), and horizontals slicing the image in two (especially the use of fences in the gunfight), creating a sense of theatrical detachment through background–foreground tension. The soundtrack during the gunfight is similarly stylized, through the unnatural absence of background music. We hear only the measured beat of laconic conversation, the crack of gunfire, and the crisp staccato of hoofbeats; an interesting contrast to the tidal waves of Dimitri Tiomkin music needed to disguise the chaotic direction of the gunfight in *High Noon*.

The most spacious, relaxed sequence is the dance in the embryonic church, which stands at the far end of the town's main street, like a skeletal monument at the boundary between civilization and desert. As the church bells ring and 'Shall We Gather at the River?' plays softly on the soundtrack, Wyatt gravely squires Clementine to church, the steady tracking shot and the music imbuing their courtship with a sense of eternity. The barber, symbolic high priest of civilization, salutes them as they pass and then stands back to admire his handiwork. The dance on the floor of God's house under the cool, luminous sky has a vigour and a sweetness which speak volumes about the nobility of the communal impulse; seldom has Ford found a more felicitous yoking of idea and image.

As Wyatt and his lady move into the crowd, it parts deferentially around them as they whirl into a waltz pattern which grows in grace and speed, like the sustained variation of a sonata. Their ecstatic pirouettes, the way their bodies speak what their faces cannot quite express, the entire scene, with its complex undercurrent of themes and associations, recalls Whitman's classic description of the mythical American: 'Their manners speech dress friendships – the freshness and candor of their physiognomy – the picturesque looseness of their carriage . . . their deathless attachment to freedom . . . the air they have of persons who never knew how it felt to stand in the presence of superiors . . . their delight in music, the sure symptom of manly tenderness and native elegance of soul . . .' In this glorious moment, the infant civilization draws its first pure breath of optimism. Without quite realizing what he has done, Wyatt Earp has hewn a garden out of the wilderness. The darker implications of his triumph lie beneath the surface, like rocks beneath a lush meadow. The name of the town, remember, is Tombstone – and if we remember Ford's anecdote about Earp's old age, we may even have second thoughts about the church sequence.

Fort Apache

> Does it ever matter who fires the first shot?
>
> The schoolteacher in *Cheyenne Autumn*

With the appearance of *Cheyenne Autumn* in 1964, it became a critical commonplace to speak of Ford's 'disillusionment' with the United States Cavalry he had once celebrated. Ford has described the film as if it were a penitential exercise ('I've killed more Indians than Custer, Beecher, and Chivington put together'), but to see *Cheyenne Autumn* as a simple reversal of a typical Cavalry Western – with the Indians as 'good guys' and the soldiers as 'bad guys' – is as misleading as viewing the heroic Cavalry trilogy of 1948–50 as a glorification of war.

Ford's films about the Cavalry operate on two levels: as adventure sagas about the heroism and group conflicts of beleaguered outposts, like *The Lost Patrol* or *They Were Expendable*; and as essays on the politics and history of America. His Indians are often destructive, but they are seldom simply 'bad guys'. Even Chief Scar in *The Searchers*, his most brutal Indian, is motivated by the highest of Fordian values, family devotion. His Cavalrymen, with the exception of certain aberrant individuals (Henry Fonda's glory-seeking martinet in *Fort Apache*, Karl Malden's 'orders are orders' Prussian in *Cheyenne Autumn*), are presented with romance and affection, as chivalrous professionals trying to preserve an uneasy peace with a minimum of bloodshed on either side. What tips the scales in *Cheyenne Autumn*, making the Cavalry ride against a band of helpless nomadic Indians, is, significantly, not any fundamental change in the Cavalry ethos but a change in politics – the remote and vindictive government in Washington is forcing the Cavalry into an inhuman role. It requires a representative of that government, the Secretary of the Interior, to right the wrong; the Cavalry is trapped in its role. The vindication, and the tragedy, of Ford's military is that it represents, as Richard Thompson has pointed out, 'a distinct and limited society unto itself'.

All three films of the loosely connected Cavalry trilogy revolve round a crisis of leadership, played out against the timeless backdrop of Monument Valley and the immediate danger of Indian attack. All three take place long after the die of war has been cast between white and red. *Fort Apache* dramatizes the climactic event in the Indian Wars, Custer's Last Stand, which galvanized the United States for its final thrust against the Indian nations. *She Wore a Yellow Ribbon* begins with the words 'Custer is dead' and tells of the last week in the career of an ageing, war-weary captain. In *Rio Grande*, John Wayne plays the same character he played in *Fort Apache*, Kirby York, but

Fort Apache: life at a Cavalry fort (Shirley Temple, John Wayne, Henry Fonda)

now middle-aged and hardened under pressure, a flawed professional on the verge of becoming a martinet himself.

Wayne is present in all three films, providing the focal point in Ford's scrutiny of the Cavalry's tradition even when, in *Fort Apache*, Fonda plays the dramatically central role. The Wayne character stands for the ideal Cavalryman. When he defies Fonda's orders (*Fort Apache*), performs a secret peace-keeping mission without informing his superiors (*She Wore a Yellow Ribbon*), or breaks a government treaty by making a sortie into Mexico (*Rio Grande*), he is putting the spirit of the Cavalry ahead of the rulebook and ahead of the government itself. Anticipating the ending of *The Man Who Shot Liberty Valance*, Wayne lies to cover up Fonda's misdeeds at the end of *Fort Apache* because the greater truth, known only to the men themselves, is their loyalty to each other and to their country. It is, as Russell Campbell has commented, 'the noble lie of Plato's philosopher king', but it is also, more simply, an expression of camaraderie, a protective action towards an erring member of the family.

Frank Nugent, who worked on the scripts for the first two films in the trilogy, recalled what Ford told him when outlining the subject of *Fort*

Apache: 'In all Westerns, the Cavalry rides in to the rescue of the beleaguered wagon train or whatever, and then it rides off again. I've been thinking about it – what it was like at a Cavalry post, remote, people with their own personal problems, over everything the threat of Indians, of death . . .' Shortly after making *Cheyenne Autumn*, Ford spoke of it in similar terms: 'I've long wanted to do a story that tells the truth about [the Indians] and not just a picture in which they're chased by the Cavalry' (ironically, though, that is just what the picture is about).

The Cavalry trilogy is a family tragedy about the birth of a nation, with the Indians as estranged brothers and the Cavalry as the better part of white culture – the people, not the government. It is important to remember that at the time of the Indian Wars the Cavalry, like the Indians themselves, was a group of outcasts. They were a motley bunch of debtors, outlaws, misfits and immigrants (largely Irish) who did the dirty work for a 'respectable' society which scorned and ostracized them (no wonder Ford romanticizes them), until the explosion of national piety and outrage over the death of Custer, which suddenly turned the Cavalry into gallant knights. When an ambitious officer in a Ford film exploits the Cavalry and the Indians for his own purposes, he becomes one with 'every big-wig in Washington' (*Cheyenne Autumn*) who callously sits back and plays politics with other people's lives.

Ford is not willing to indict the white race as a whole by blaming the government's policies on the people: a sentimental populism, perhaps, but no less forceful in its sense of outrage and injustice than a film like *Little Big Man*. There are no monsters in Ford's Cavalry films, just people. It is revealing that his film about the Indians contains a tragic conflict of authority among the Indians themselves. The survival and tribal unity of the Cheyenne is constantly threatened by the impetuous acts of a young hot-head, Red Shirt, who is killed by the chief at the end. Like Fonda in *Fort Apache* and the war-mongering brave in *She Wore a Yellow Ribbon* (also named Red Shirt), he is working only for himself – during the peace parley guaranteeing the remaining Cheyenne the right to their tribal land, he almost succeeds in assassinating the Secretary of the Interior – and he pays for his selfishness with his life, as Fonda does.

Fort Apache sets up an opposition between the egomaniac (Fonda's Lt-Col. Owen Thursday) and the 'team-player' (York), between the play-actor and the man. Locked into an arrogance which has made the Cavalry a vehicle for his own bitterness and conceit, Thursday behaves gracelessly towards his men and foolishly towards the Indians, finally precipitating a pointless massacre. When he berates his casually dressed officers for their 'individual,

Fort Apache: distinctions of rank: the colonel's daughter and the sergeant-major's son

whimsical expression', it may seem that he is asking them to live up to a tradition, but he is actually trying to remake them in his own sterile West Point image. Russell Campbell has pointed out that the 'sloppy morality' of Grant Withers' villainous Indian agent 'is mirrored in his sloppy appearance'. But it should also be noted that Thursday's similarly villainous morality is mirrored in his excessively refined dress and deportment. Ideal behaviour, Ford suggests, lies somewhere in between the extremes of laxity and punctiliousness, in the individualized orderliness of York and his fellows, and a detail of uniform is a key metaphorical element in the film's complex dénouement.

Thursday's mania for the textbook extends to his battle philosophy. Before moving out on a patrol, he makes a pompous allusion to the tactics described in 'the paper that Captain Robert E. Lee wrote when he was at the Point . . . that paper impressed me – particularly the manoeuvre that Genghis Khan employed in the Battle of Khin Sha in 1221'. He is met with incredulous silence from York. Just before the massacre, York says, 'They outnumber us four to one. Do we talk or fight?' Thursday's reply is quixotic: 'You seem easily impressed by numbers, Captain.'

Behind the credits, Ford quickly sketches in some of the aspects of fort life which will be seen later in more detail: a marching line, a solitary horseman against the horizon, a 'Grand March' dance and a long procession of Indians. The next sequence contrasts our own appreciation of the natural beauty of Monument Valley with Thursday's waxen self-absorption. As a tiny stagecoach emerges from the brush, approaching a huge rock formation, the camera tilts up from the stage to frame the rock (asserting eternity over the momentary), and then descends to the coach. Inside, Thursday is grumbling to his excited daughter about the time the journey is taking, and about the humiliation of being sent to such a 'God-forsaken outpost'. His gaze never wanders outside. Thursday's arrival at the fort is slyly satirized – he disrupts a dance which he assumes is being held in his honour, forgetting that it is George Washington's birthday. Dialogue between two troopers when the coach arrives: 'Who goes there?' – 'The new commanding officer.' – 'Holy *Moses!*' – 'No, the new commanding officer.'

Thursday's isolation, even from his own daughter, is criticized repeatedly in the film through Ford's intricate delineation of the fort's communal structure. As Russell Campbell has described it:

Ford's depiction of existence at a Cavalry outpost is a devoted attempt to realize an ideal: the organic community. It is an ideal at odds with the main current both of the American Dream and of the American experience; its closest approximation in practice was probably in the early religious settlements – and among the Indians ... The hierarchy of command is not equivalent to stratification in a feudal sense, and relates only to military affairs; beyond this, there is a natural unspoken equality between men of whatever status. (To appeal to this equality in words is, however, suspicious.) Thus by arrogantly insisting on distinctions of rank in refusing to allow his daughter to be courted by O'Rourke, Thursday subverts the natural communal order and is clearly in the wrong. Here insubordination is justified, and Mrs O'Rourke ridicules her menfolk's hesitation in defying the colonel. There are certain things which must be done whatever the orders to the contrary: as Mulcahy and his colleagues drink a crate of liquor rather than destroy it, so Michael O'Rourke continues, with his mother's urging, to court Philadelphia.

Thursday is portrayed as a tragic figure, however, not a mere villain, and one of the ways Ford humanizes him is by placing such importance on his relationship with his daughter. His refusal to let Lt Michael O'Rourke (John Agar) court her is motivated not only by his snobbery – O'Rourke's father (Ward Bond) is only a sergeant-major – but also by young O'Rourke's recklessness in taking her riding during a war alert. Philadelphia is played by the adolescent Shirley Temple, whose ostentatious coyness in the part is a throwback to the golden days of Griffith and Lillian Gish. Perhaps we

Fort Apache: the NCOs' dance

should consider Ford's fatherly indulgence of Philadelphia as a compensatory reaction to her own father's boorishness. And since we always judge a Ford character in relation to his family situation, we realize that Thursday's coldness may well be due to the disruption of his marriage (the death of his wife). There is a sad glimpse into his character during the Noncommissioned Officers' Dance, when Thursday is expected to lead Mrs O'Rourke on to the floor for the fort commander's traditional dance with the wife of the sergeant-major. As she holds out her arms to him, the other couples waiting, he stands paralysed with social unease, momentarily unable to join in the ritual. When he snaps out of it, he proves himself a marvellously graceful dancer (recalling Fonda's Wyatt Earp), but an utterly formal one, unlike Captain York, who spins Philadelphia round the floor with broad, lumbering flourishes and an uninhibited grin.

Fort Apache was not very well received by contemporary reviewers; it is too impure, perhaps, for people who like a film to stay within its genre. The main objection was that the young romance is irrelevant to the issues of the plot. The emphasis Ford places on the youngsters at the most important points of the story belies that assumption. Take, for instance, the key moments before, during and after the massacre. On the night before the march, when Thursday orders a halt to the dance, Michael O'Rourke and Philadelphia are dancing by themselves on the verandah. The camera swings gently back and forth with them in rhythm to 'Good Night, Ladies', and they are clinging together as Ford fades to the bugler blowing troop assembly. Moments before the final charge, Thursday drops his icy façade long enough to order his future son-in-law to take shelter with York, much against the boy's wishes. Far from considering this favouritism, the other troopers recognize it for the communal gesture it is and cheer as York rides down the line (two breathless panning shots) to pull O'Rourke out. And during the catastrophe itself, there are two electrifying moments of prescience: York sends the lieutenant for help (but more to save the boy's life, since rescue is virtually impossible), shouting 'And marry that girl!' as O'Rourke rides away; and when Thursday, mortally wounded, offers his apologies to Sgt-Maj. O'Rourke, he replies, 'You can save them, sir, for our grandchildren.' Just as the Cavalry survives its dead, so the ideal of family persists.

But the full force of the family motif comes home only at the very end of the film, when the men are about to ride out for another mission, possibly as futile as the last. Philadelphia stands demurely beside her husband, holding their infant son, Michael Thursday York O'Rourke, a living echo of the past like the infants named after the bandits in *Three Bad Men* (Stanley Costigan Allen O'Malley) and *Three Godfathers* (Robert William Pedro Hightower). After a wordless farewell, she, the child and the child's grandmother stand watching the troop ride away, just as the women did on the morning of Thursday's fateful march. The hopefulness, the urge for a tradition embodied in the child (he seems to stand for the future of the country itself) contrasts bitterly with the likelihood of his young father's death – and with the implication that the child may grow up only to meet the same fate as his forefathers. The child points uncomprehendingly after his father, and Ford cuts to the final shot of the film, the long line of troops entering Monument Valley. The metamorphosis of the wide-eyed girl of the beginning into the grave young mother of the end is deeply fatalistic.

The scene directly preceding the appearance of Michael Thursday York O'Rourke, York's encounter with the newspapermen, has provoked a good deal of critical controversy. Robin Wood has claimed that York's whitewashing of Thursday 'does violence to the previous development of the Wayne character and to the whole drift of the preceding narrative'. The path Wood traces to reach this over-simplified conclusion is a misleading one, based on a cursory synopsis of the scene itself, a too schematic comparison with

The truth of the legend: the massacre sequence in *Fort Apache*

Cheyenne Autumn, and a simplistic statement by Ford himself that the men were right in obeying Thursday because 'he was the colonel, and what he says goes'. Russell Campbell reaches a similar conclusion, contending that the film 'celebrates' the massacre 'simply because that was the official order', and also clinching his case with a Ford statement – that 'it's good for the country to have heroes [i.e., even like Thursday] to look up to'.

Beyond the skeleton of plot, the fact that Thursday is whitewashed before history and York takes his place as commander, what exactly happens in this scene? In the eyes of the nation, the incompetent Thursday has become a legendary hero, 'the idol of every schoolboy in America', complete with iconography of portrait and relic of sword, dutifully caressed by one of the newspapermen. York holds court in front of the portrait, listening to naïve blather about the 'magnificent work', hanging in Washington, which depicts Thursday's Charge. 'Correct in every detail,' he replies, and the irony in his look and tone of voice goes unnoticed, as does his basilisk glance when the same reporter refers to Captain Collingwood as 'Collingworth'. Like the editor in *The Man Who Shot Liberty Valance*, who decides to 'print the legend' after hearing Senator Stoddard confess that his heroism was a sham, York decides to let history's error go uncorrected. His reasons are simple on a personal level and problematic on a historical level. 'No man died more gallantly, nor won more honour for his regiment,' he says of Thursday, and it is an accurate statement as far as it goes. What York does not admit (or does not *allow* himself to admit) is that Thursday's men died for nothing. Like Senator Stoddard and the editor in *Liberty Valance*, he covers up a personal injustice for the sake of what he considers a higher necessity, the future of the country.

Other critics have drawn this parallel with *Liberty Valance*, but there is an even more explicit point of contact between the two films which has gone unnoticed; it occurs at the exact moment of climax in Thursday's tragedy. Conferring with his officers on what to do about Cochise's flight from the reservation, Thursday murmurs to himself, 'The Man Who Brought Cochise Back'. Ford underscores the legendary and megalomaniac implications of the phrase by having Collingwood remove his pipe from his mouth and stare at Thursday in shock, realizing that from then on the commander will be working for his own posterior glory at the expense of his men's lives. It is instructive, in this context of individualism vs. community, to contrast Ford's handling of the massacre itself – the group bunched tightly together waiting for the Indians, and dying as one in long-shot under a cloud of dust from the Indians' charge – with the massacres in two other superb films about the Custer legend, Arthur Penn's *Little Big Man* and Raoul

Fort Apache: the massacre from a distance (John Wayne, John Agar)

Walsh's *They Died With Their Boots On*, both of which show the troopers deployed at distances from each other, dying not *en masse* but one by one, as individuals.

Wood's contention that York's lie falsifies the character is amply refuted by Campbell's analysis of York: 'He is a fervid opponent of the official line. Yet he does not once disobey a command ... York is the obedient rebel ... Despite all evidence to the contrary, the captain continues to place his trust in the ultimate virtue of the system to which he belongs. He questions, but he does not defy.' The fact that Ford recognizes this contradiction in York's character is not indicated by anything spoken in the film, but it is made crystal-clear in *visual* terms (unfortunately the terms most often overlooked by film critics). When York takes leave of the newspapermen, he first introduces them to Michael Thursday York O'Rourke and then picks up the same kind of grandiose, archaic commander's cap which Thursday affected and puts it on. He is no longer wearing the slouch hat which Thursday characterized as 'individual, whimsical expression'. It is impossible to put too much stress on this gesture; it implies nothing less than York's tragic submission to Thursday's vainglory and, through this 'obedient rebel', the submission of the Cavalry itself. Jean-Marie Straub cited York's gesture to illustrate his contention that Ford is 'the most Brechtian of all film-makers, because he shows things that make people think ... by [making] the audience collaborate on the film'. After the gesture occurs, there are further, and one would think unmistakable, tragic implications in Ford's depiction of the march out of the fort: fatalistically, Ford repeats the same camera set-ups he had used when Thursday led the men to massacre, while on the soundtrack he reprises 'The Girl I Left Behind Me', the anthem of doom.

What makes the ending so complex and powerful, and so difficult to reduce to a simple statement, is that Ford, as Straub put it, forces the audience's collaboration. He does this by using the Brechtian distancing device of the hat, by forcing us to see through York's lie, and perhaps most disturbing of all, by forcing us to realize that we are sympathizing with men who are following a suicidal course. Ford has not only exposed the danger of Thursday's play-acting at legend, he has given that play-acting the same glorification – in his romantic, 'magnificent' depiction of Thursday's Charge – that he ridicules through the reporter's naïve description of the painting. And, daringly, he repeats that glorification moments after ridiculing it: he has York stand at a window eulogizing the Cavalry while an image of marching men is romantically superimposed on the glass. York's tribute to men who 'fight over cards or rotgut whisky but share the last drop in their canteens' (delivered to the tune of 'The Battle Hymn of the Republic') is identical in spirit with the closing narration of *She Wore a Yellow Ribbon*, which perhaps expresses his feeling more forcefully:

From Fort Reno to Fort Apache, from Sheridan to Starke, they were all the same – men in dirty-shirt blue and only a cold page in the history books to mark their passing. But wherever they rode, and whatever they fought for, that place became the United States.

The remarkable achievement of *Fort Apache* is that it enables us to see with Brechtian clarity that an insane system may be perpetuated by noble men, and indeed, that it *needs* noble and dedicated men to perpetuate itself. Whether this will shock or intrigue a viewer probably depends upon his devotion, or lack of it, to an ideological system. It is comforting to think that evil is done by beasts, monsters or 'pigs', but profoundly disturbing to realize that it is done by human beings.

6. Ireland: *The Quiet Man* (1952), *The Rising of the Moon* (1957)

The Quiet Man

O Innisfree, my island, I'm returning
From wasted years across the wintry sea . . .

War had become almost an obsession with Ford by the time he made *The Quiet Man*. Since Pearl Harbor, he had made fifteen films, eleven of them set in World Wars I and II, the Indian Wars or Korea. Of the exceptions, only the religious allegory *Three Godfathers* completely escaped the pattern. *Clementine* presented the Earp–Clanton feud in militarist terms; *The Fugitive* was about a police state; and *Wagon Master* was about a community tyrannized by outlaws. A bucolic Irish comedy, *The Quiet Man* seemed finally to break the spell of combat – Ford described it as 'the first love story I've ever tried, a mature love story', and, in a looser moment, as 'the sexiest picture ever made' – but it is no less haunted by violence and social disruption than the films which preceded it.

Sean Thornton (John Wayne), an Irish–American boxer who has killed a man in the ring, returns to his birthplace in County Galway, which he remembers only from his mother's stories. Her voice, musical and sad,

The Quiet Man: the courting of Mary Kate (Maureen O'Hara, Victor McLaglen, John Wayne, Barry Fitzgerald)

appears on the soundtrack at his first sight of the cottage: 'Ah, don't you *remember*, Seaneen, and how it was . . .' He is fleeing into a dream country of peace and primitive simplicity, leaving behind his painful immigrant past and his assumed identity as 'Trooper Thorn'. Filmed in colour through a veil of diffusing mist, rural Ireland has, as Manny Farber put it, 'the sunless, remembered look of a surrealist painting'. *The Quiet Man* is a ballad of the warrior's rest, and it is not coincidental that Sean's birthplace is in the very county which the parents of another Sean, Ford himself, once deserted for America. Sean is making an exile's return, but, in a peculiarly Fordian paradox, he is, in the same act, exiling himself from the only homeland he has ever actually known, the United States.

The distance between Ford and Wayne, by now his principal protagonist, has never been smaller, both in the external details (Ford is back to being Sean O'Fienne, as 'Trooper Thorn' is back to being Sean Thornton), and in the deepest motivations of the character. Robin Wood points out that in his 1960s films Ford expressed his revulsion at modern America by making a 'flight from his own country – I think in artistic terms it amounts

The Quiet Man: a gesture made . . .

to that – to the Pacific, to China, or back to Ireland . . . interrupted only by
his account of the desperate trek of the Cheyenne back to their native
country'. In fact, this process of mental exile began with *The Quiet Man*. And
as Anthony Burgess remarked of another expatriate Irishman, James Joyce,
'Exile was the artist's stepping back to see more clearly and so draw more
accurately; it was the only means of objectifying an obsessive subject-
matter.' Ford had to leave America to rediscover himself, and in a curious
coincidence it was during the making of *The Quiet Man*, his exorcism of the
demon of battle, that he received his highest military honour, being named
an admiral. John Wayne celebrated the event by pushing Ford into Galway
Bay.

The Quiet Man is probably Ford's best-loved film, but it is often
misconstrued by critics who fail to perceive the tensions beneath its dreamlike surface. Donald S. Connery writes in *The Irish*, his study of modern
Ireland:

The popular image of the natives is a kind of gummy Irish stew of comedians,
colleens, characters out of *The Quiet Man*, drunk poets, IRA gunmen, censorious

... a gesture returned (John Wayne, Victor McLaglen)

priests, and cantankerous old farmers who sleep with their boots on. It is as if time had stood still in the Ould Sod while other nations had moved on ...

But of course it is the very essence of Sean's dream that time has stood still, that the fairytale illusion of his childhood innocence can be recaptured. We are kept aware throughout of a *conscious* re-creative effort of the will (both Sean's and Ford's), and the film's comedy and drama spring from a common source: the intrusion of reality into the dream.

Ford lures us into the dream by lavishing all his gifts of composition on the most prosaic sights of the countryside. When Sean arrives at the railway station in the opening scene, for example, there is a brief glimpse of Barry Fitzgerald's horse and cart parked outside. We see it, from Sean's viewpoint, framed through a station window, an image as delicately symmetrical as a Whistler engraving. And as Lindsay Anderson wrote in his excellent *Sight and Sound* review:

Sean's first glimpse of Mary Kate is presented with a pre-Raphaelite relish for sharp and varied colouring, as well as a kindred romanticism of view: a fairy-tale shepherd girl, auburn hair, scarlet skirted, dressed in two shades of blue, driving her sheep down the rocky dell, yellow gorse in the foreground, the countryside opening out greener in the distance . . . a landscape in which soft and rugged cordially combine, as they do in the whole personality of the picture.

But everywhere Sean goes he finds his dream confounded and contradicted. He eventually finds himself threatened with a second expulsion from Eden unless he abandons the purpose of his flight from America: he has to use his fists to win the hand of Mary Kate (Maureen O'Hara) from her tyrannical brother, Squire 'Red Will' Danaher (Victor McLaglen). Even the beauty of Innisfree has its illusory aspects. A consummate romantic, Sean plants roses in his garden (in memory of his mother), puzzling Mary Kate, who thinks turnips would be more practical; and the radiantly green field yields only rocks when he tries to cultivate it. When he proudly shows off his little thatched cottage to a neighbour, he is given a left-handed compliment: 'It looks the way all Irish cottages should, and so seldom *do*. And only an American would think of painting it emerald green!'

Mary Kate turns out to be a fiercely independent woman, so concerned with her household possessions and her dowry that she refuses to sleep with Sean after their marriage until he fights Red Will for them. Ford's description of *The Quiet Man* as his first love story is not strictly accurate, for his previous feature, *Rio Grande*, had also paired Wayne and O'Hara as a couple torn apart by cultural differences – the wife is a Southerner who leaves her husband after he burns her ancestral home, 'Bridesdale', during the Civil War. *Rio Grande* was exacted by Republic Pictures as part of Ford's deal to make *The Quiet Man*, and as Lindsay Anderson suggests, Ford may have deliberately used it as a rough draft because of 'the need to creep with some wariness up to this ticklish subject'. Sean's desire for Mary Kate, like his return to the thatched cottage, is so romanticized that it distorts his perceptions. When he spies her on the hillside, he asks Michaeleen og Flynn (Fitzgerald), 'Hey, is that real? She couldn't be.' Flynn responds, 'Nonsense, man, it's only a mirage brought on by your terrible thirst.'

Sean misinterprets Mary Kate's insistence on the dowry as simple greed, associating it with the 'dirty money' he won for killing his ring opponent, when it is actually a token of her traditional rights as a married woman. She, correspondingly, misinterprets his refusal to fight Red Will as a lack of feeling for her, and the townspeople misinterpret it as cowardice. They too have been caught up in a dream vision, seeing him as a 'Homeric' hero come home to glory. The crisis is precipitated by Sean's desire to remain lodged in his childhood reveries. He sees Innisfree as the merely quaint, other-worldly vision which the less astute critics have accused Ford of creating, and it is so charming that he refuses to become dissociated from it. Like all Ford heroes, Sean is ultimately forced to reconcile his private obsessions with the demands of society and tradition.

When the fight finally occurs, it has become the nexus of so many points of communal conflict that it ranges all over the countryside, surrounded by a horde of spectators. Ford shoots it repeatedly in long-shot to emphasize its communal, dance-like aspects, and gives us a score of vignettes within the action. The dramatic crisis is rooted in Sean's private conflicts, but it finally affects the whole community. To enter the community, he must understand and accept the rules and traditions of its basic unit, the family. It is his refusal of his public role (his standing in the community) which prompts Mary Kate to refuse her private role. The film ends in consummate harmony, with all the villagers gathering to give tribute to a visiting Anglican prelate (the parish priest hides his collar and urges the crowd to 'cheer like Protestants'), and Sean and Mary Kate running into their cottage to complete their marriage. But before we see the couple, Ford gives us a long series of 'curtain call' shots of the other characters. Individual harmony is a condition of communal harmony.

The Quiet Man begins like *The Man Who Shot Liberty Valance* (a train pulls into a station carrying a passenger back to the land of his youth), and it might well have ended the same way, with the train pulling out of the station. But when Sean and Michaeleen leave the station, they ride under a bridge in their horse and cart, and another train passes over them: it is as if they are tunnelling under the modern world's bright, cold sophistication (the train is mockingly painted emerald green) and re-entering the past. In the cart, Sean gives Michaeleen an inkling of the horrors of his immigrant's life in America – the death of his overworked, widowed mother; his years working in the Pittsburgh blast furnaces; his murderous climb to wealth – and Michaeleen adds the definitive Fordian denunciation: 'America ... Pro-hi-bition!' None of these elements is present in the short story by Maurice Walsh from which Ford and Frank Nugent adapted the film. It is a conventional fantasy of wish-fulfilment: small man whips big bully because he happens to be, secretly, a professional prizefighter. The character in the story is, like Sean in the film, a native Irishman, but his journey home is based on simple nostalgia, not on a rejection of his immigrant dream of America. Along with Sean's guilty motivation, Ford and Nugent added the dimension of sexual blackmail in his relationship with Mary Kate and added the vital communal figures of Flynn, Father Lonergan (Ward Bond), and the Protestants, the Reverend and Mrs Playfair (played by Barry Fitzgerald's brother, Arthur Shields, and Eileen

The Quiet Man: Michaeleen og Flynn (Barry Fitzgerald) as matchmaker

Crowe). Walsh's Ireland is indeed that Glockamora fantasy of which
Connery complained; Ford's, for all its romance, is situated in the realities of
rural life in the Republic of Ireland: the latent political turmoil (the priest and
two cohorts are running an IRA cell), the exploitative economic system (Red
Will is not only the town bully, he also owns most of the land), and the
omnipresence of religion, which Ford underscores with frequent background
use of churches, stained-glass windows, church graveyards and Gaelic
crosses.

As in *Wagon Master*, Ford accompanies the action with a continual choric
flow of folk songs, suggesting a pattern to which the characters must accommodate themselves. Sean's first gesture of kinship to the villagers is visiting
the pub to buy a round of drinks. Stony silence greets his offer; the pub-
crawlers don't know the stranger's motive. Then a bearded patriarch (Francis
Ford) asks his name, and the names of his father and grandfather as well.
Hearing Sean's reply, the bartender wondrously removes his hat, and the old
man proclaims, 'So it's himself you're named after! Well, that being the case,
it *is* a pleasant evening and we *will* have a drink!' He thumps his stick on the

. . . and as bookmaker

bar to start the celebration. Ken Curtis starts playing 'The Wild Colonial Boy' on his accordion, and the group joins in the song as Flynn downs drink after drink in single gulps. Ford does not give us a close-up of Sean during the song, nor individual shots of the other celebrants; instead, he climaxes the ritual with a warm fresco of the entire group gathered in a circle round the bar. A gesture made, a gesture returned, and then a communal gesture made – all at an individual's instigation, yet finally a give-and-take between him and the group.

The words of the song and the spirit manifested in the singing attest to the depth of Innisfree's involvement in tradition. The songs are a means of communicating the 'troubles' and the 'secrets', a point which Ford later made explicitly in Dan O'Flaherty's speech in *The Rising of the Moon*. The colonial boy, of course, is Sean, but it could also be his grandfather, whom, we have learned from Father Lonergan in a foreshadowing of the song, 'died in Australia ... in a penal colony', as did Jack Dugan in the song. There is a devious appropriateness, too, in the way Squire Danaher strides into the pub precisely on the words 'He robbed a wealthy squireen'. When Mary Kate, on entering her nuptial cottage, sits at a spinnet to sing 'The Lake Isle of Innisfree', it is as if she is reading Sean's emotions and giving them voice. All the villagers fit into this musical framework: Michaeleen, with his syncopated stops and explosions; the Playfairs, with their cultivated, harmonious brogues; Red Will, with his Gypo Nolan-like hesitations and the grammatical constructions which make the English language sound so atonal ('If he was the last man on earth, and my sister the last woman, I'd still say no'); and the bit players, whose florid rhetoric conforms to the theatrical tradition of 'beautiful speech'.

Detractors of Ford like to attack his use of 'type' characters, and none of his films is more susceptible to this charge than *The Quiet Man*. On the face of it, every one of the 'types' Donald S. Connery objects to can be found here, except perhaps the 'cantankerous old farmer who sleeps with his boots on' (you will find *him* in *The Rising of the Moon*). But the Irish are a people notoriously prone to play-acting, and Connery admits, 'The trouble is that every time I am solemnly told in Ireland that the stage Irishman does not exist I meet one the next day.' Take Barry Fitzgerald's Flynn, one of the most memorable characterizations in all of Ford. If his performance is 'stage Irish', it belongs to a time-honoured theatrical tradition, that of Synge, Yeats, O'Casey and Lady Gregory, of the Abbey Theatre whose players Ford uses in a number of the minor parts, notably Jack McGowran as Red Will's little sycophant Feeney (an odd touch – Feeney is the Anglicized version of Ford's real surname).

Like the other villagers, Flynn is highly conscious of his own quaintness, and since he is the official Town Character, he plays it to the hilt. When his cart passes an old castle, he solemnly informs Sean that it is 'the ancestral home of the ancient Flynns', and adds out of the corner of his mouth, 'It was taken from us by ... by ... the Druids.' His joke is not entirely an idle one; this is a community so dominated by memories of fabled traditional glories that the present is hardly as real as the past. Michaeleen wanders off to the pub, during a howling storm, with the words, 'It's a fine soft night, so I think I'll go join me comrades and talk a little treason' (a line cited by Nugent as an example of Ford's own skill as a scriptwriter). Except for Dan Tobin, Michaeleen is the only one of the villagers who knew Sean in his childhood, which Sean himself hardly remembers. He is Sean's self-appointed guide to the country's customs, sights and people, a go-between whose occupations include cabbie and hauling service, matchmaking and running the local book.

What keeps the character from being merely a brilliant theatrical turn is Ford's insistence on the tensions between sham and reality within the role: in particular, on the way Flynn's jollity and garrulity mask an essential melancholia and lack of belonging. Flynn is at the service of everyone, but until Sean's arrival, he belongs to no one in particular; and after Sean is safely married off, he is alone again, back in his eternal role of matchmaker — this time for Red Will and the Widow Tillane (Mildred Natwick), whose superannuated courtship is a comic counterpoint to that of Sean and Mary Kate. The two most revealing glimpses into his dependency are his tipsy admission to Mary Kate that if she weren't being courted by Sean, 'I could marry you meself,' and his utter despair as he sinks to the floor of the pub, head in hands, after Sean walks away from Danaher's challenge. Like the drunken doctors who abound in Ford's work, Flynn insists on taking personal responsibility for the community, a self-sacrificial role which would be tragic were it not recognized as vital by the community itself.

There is no official government in this community, no mayor, because the order springs naturally and organically from the villagers' acceptance of their traditional roles. In fact, the nominal leader of the community, Father Lonergan, is so seldom called upon to make a decision that he spends most of his time fishing for 'the king of all salmon', a wry twist on the traditional role of a priest as a 'fisher of souls' (his first name, Peter, completes the irony). In a harmonious Fordian community, institutional religion is just another traditional institution, no more and no less. The pub is more central to the life of the community than the church, and no one seems to think this unnatural, least of all Father Lonergan. Only in times of personal crisis does the church play an active role, and even then it seems rather ineffectual. Lying on his

The Quiet Man: the winning of Mary Kate

deathbed, Francis Ford (making his penultimate appearance in his brother's work) picks his teeth and shakes his head in disinterested admiration as the curate intones some purple Last Rites. When he hears the noise of the fight outside, he springs out of bed and runs into the street, stumbling into his pants. And there is so little religious divisiveness in this part of Ireland that the Reverend Playfair has only three parishioners (a good thing, too, if Arthur Shields' war-mongering Calvinist minister in *Drums Along the Mohawk* is any indication). He spends most of *his* time playing tiddlywinks and reading the sports pages. Ford treats Playfair with much affection, particularly because he is, like Sean, something of an outsider. It is fitting that he is the only villager who realizes that Sean was once 'Trooper Thorn'; a former boxer himself, he has clippings on Sean's career in his scrapbook.

The vital role of religious sentiment in a Fordian community is not the outward show of piety but the preservation of social ties, especially those of the family. All of Lonergan's activity in the film is social – his shadowy work in the IRA, his lying to Red Will about the Widow Tillane's feelings in order to convince him to let Mary Kate free to marry Sean, and his counselling of Mary Kate on her sex life (in Gaelic!). It is delightfully appropriate that

Ford's love story, 'the sexiest picture ever made', is narrated by a celibate. Religious feeling plays such a large role in *The Quiet Man* not because of Sean's guilt feelings – he can handle those himself, and when he can't he goes to the Anglican, not the Catholic, clergyman for help – but because his attempt to recapture the simplicity of his childhood is so bound up in the religious consolations he associates with his mother's memory. When he asks the Widow Tillane to sell him back the family cottage, 'White O'Morn', he explains: 'Ever since I was a boy and my mother told me about it, Innisfree has been another word for Heaven to me.' The widow, thinking of her own fruitless life, snaps, 'Innisfree is far from being Heaven,' and chides him for trying to turn the cottage into a 'national shrine'. His childhood was not as idyllic as the sentimental remembrances of his suffering, homesick mother made it seem (the family left Innisfree, after all), and his life in America was probably not as brutal as the memory of the fight made it seem. The truth lies somewhere in between, and this is what Sean must acknowledge before he can accept himself, fight Danaher and win Mary Kate.

At the beginning, he sees her in the same impossibly romantic aura of sanctity with which he remembers his mother. When he discovers that she has come to sweep up the cottage for him, he pulls her into his arms, kisses her and tells her that she has 'a face like a saint'. To which she hisses: 'Saint indeed!' Ford continually links Sean's passion for Mary Kate with religious symbolism and with the wind, a symbol of natural passion but also an archetypal symbol for the presence of God. Their first touch comes when Sean, meeting her on the doorstep of the church, abruptly scoops holy water into his hand and holds it towards her, an almost unconscious gesture; a storm is howling the night he finds her in the cottage; and their courtship is concluded in a graveyard, surrounded by Gaelic crosses, during a thunderstorm. This last scene is such an extraordinary combination of religion and eroticism that it is worth examining in detail just how Ford builds up to it, and how many nuances he can find in the most casual behaviour.

The courting ritual begins with a communal gathering outside Red Will's house. Sean is still rather bewildered at the intricacy of local customs; in America he would just 'honk my horn and the girl'd come a-running.' After an uncomfortable drive through the countryside in Flynn's ridiculous courting cart – the couple sit facing in opposite directions – they break away, steal a tandem bicycle, and pedal off for a quick ride which recalls the celebrated bicycle idyll in *Jules et Jim* but is distinguished most of all by its lack of real spontaneity. Instead of the breathtaking long-shots and sweeping whip-pans which give Truffaut's scene such a sense of liberation, Ford uses a series of repetitive pans to follow the action from a consistently formal middle distance, giving the *impression* of exhilaration but undercutting it with a feeling of mechanized rigidity; we realize that Sean and Mary Kate are merely going through the motions of a youth they never really had. Flynn, who had been prudishly insisting on the 'proprieties', starts off in pursuit but soon bows to the superior wisdom of his horse, which stops on force of habit outside Cohan's Pub. The couple's momentary freedom is suddenly weighed down by the forces of tradition: castles and ruins loom out of the landscape. Sean reluctantly observes the 'proprieties' by averting his eyes while Mary Kate strips off her shoes and stockings to wade through a stream; then he casts propriety to the winds by hurling away his derby and gloves and splashing across the stream in pursuit.

Again they are in the free, open air — but just as quickly they are in the archway of a graveyard, surrounded by reminders of eternity and the destiny which weighs down their briefest attempts to escape. It is still a dream to Sean: 'If anybody'd told me six months ago that today I'd be in a graveyard in Innisfree, with a girl like you who I'm just about to kiss ...' He breaks the proprieties by kissing Mary Kate, and immediately a *Wuthering Heights* storm erupts, thrusting a giant branch into the foreground. What follows is as close to a nude scene as Ford has ever come. Sean removes his coat, wraps it round Mary Kate, and the rain soaks him to the skin as he embraces her, the wet stockings tangled in her hand and draped over his shoulder.

We are not made to feel here that religion and the past are repressive influences; on the contrary, Sean yearns for their security. When they break their kiss, Mary Kate rests her head against Sean's chest and he stares solemnly off into the future, the camera tracking slowly towards them and finally holding on their faces for nearly a minute as the soundtrack mingles the drone of the rain with a dirge-like reprise of 'The Lake Isle of Innisfree', the ballad of mingled yearning and loss. Ford then dissolves to a half-serious, half-comic image of the couple holding a frozen pose for their wedding portrait, gravely contemplating the eternity of their relationship until the photographer's flash powder explodes and off-camera a spinnet begins playing 'The Humour is on me now'. It is typical of the humanist function of religion in the film that the curate stops playing the song when Father Lonergan enters, only to have Lonergan sit down at the keyboard and launch into a lustier rendition of the lyrics. There are proprieties, and there are proprieties.

The mock-epic fight which resolves the conflict over the dowry is treated more as a communal celebration, a comic version of Ford's traditional quest, than as a serious fight. It is sublimely unimportant who wins, and at the conclusion the hero and villain stagger arm-in-arm to Sean's cottage for supper, sloshing through a stream as they deliver a massively off-key rendition of 'The Wild Colonial Boy'. The moral issues have been decided before the fight begins; the real climax of the film comes when Sean picks up the dowry money, strides up to Danaher's blazing furnace (a subliminal reminder of his life in America?), and tosses it inside, with Mary Kate opening and slamming the door for him. The sexual undertones of the door gesture conclude a motif from Sean's earlier search of the station for Mary Kate, when he leapt off his massive black stallion to open doors all the way down the length of the train before finding her. The burning of the money, like the burning of the scalp in Hawks' *The Big Sky*, conveys the feeling of liberation from a psychic obsession. Interestingly, Ford told Peter Bogdanovich that this was the only mistake in the film ('He should have tossed it to one of the fellows and said, "Give it to charity," or something'), perhaps because it so strongly asserts instinct over tradition. But the flamboyance of the gesture, like the flamboyance of the fight itself, emphasizes its essentially comic quality. Mary Kate and Sean both win what they want: Mary Kate a public demonstration of her husband's concern for her, Sean a recognition of his moral integrity by Mary Kate and the rest of the community. Anyway, as Ford pointed out, giving the money to charity would not have made much difference, because 'Who would he give it to anyway? Not the parish priest – he has more money than the Lord Mayor of Dublin.'

The Quiet Man could have been a grim story. After all, like *Sergeant York*, it is the story of a pacifist-killer. But tragedy and comedy are a matter of the point of view, and it is important to note that Ford does not present Sean's obsession as funny: the murderous fight is depicted in a horrifying flashback, the brilliant glare from the ring lights flooding Sean's anguished face as he stares down at his opponent's corpse and the flashbulb-popping photographers hovering round it. The crowd-pleasing slapstick and romance of *The Quiet Man* are never more than a beat away from pain and humiliation, and the film's biggest laugh comes at Sean's lowest moment – when he goes off in pursuit of Mary Kate after their calamitous wedding night and Flynn, entering the nuptial chamber with a crib, spies their collapsed bed and exclaims, 'Impetuous! Homeric!' Like a bawdy song at a wake, *The Quiet Man* is a way of facing the pain, ignominy and chaos of life. It is Ford's most convincing and beautiful affirmation.

The Rising of the Moon

The Rising of the Moon is perhaps the least known of Ford's great works. The effortless nonchalance of its style, its tone of 'blarney', no doubt accounts for the almost complete lack of critical attention paid to it. John Baxter considers it 'an irritating, though occasionally charming work', and Bogdanovich and

The Rising of the Moon: Old Dan harangues the magistrate (Noel Purcell, Cyril Cusack)

Haudiquet give it scant notice in their excellent books on Ford. Made in Ireland in 1957 with a cast of 'unknowns' (actually prominent Irish stage actors), it was one of Ford's purely personal, decidedly uncommercial projects, like *Wagon Master* and *The Sun Shines Bright*, and it has been eclipsed by its proximity to *The Last Hurrah*, based on a famous novel and made in Hollywood as a highly publicized reunion with a host of veteran character actors.

The Rising of the Moon and *The Last Hurrah* look at the same subject from different sides of the Atlantic: the dwindling away of Irish communal traditions in the face of modern social pressures. The latter film, which deals with the Irish immigrant community in Boston, has hard, bright, sculptural lighting, as if it were all taking place in a mausoleum, and is climaxed with the most grandly protracted deathbed scene since Dickens (a full eighteen minutes of screen time). *The Rising of the Moon* is jovially melancholic, for the Ould Sod is within touching range. On the face of it, the three stories which make up the film seem arbitrarily selected to illustrate different 'humours' in the Irish character (the working title, thankfully only that, was *The Three-Leaf Clover*). An old man is marched off to jail for assaulting a seller of bad whisky; the passengers of a train gleefully make nonsense of the timetable; a policemen lets a fugitive revolutionary escape during the 'troubles'. On closer inspection, however, *The Rising of the Moon* reveals a rigorous, almost schematic orderliness. It deals with what could be called the national consciousness of the Irish people (more precisely, the people of the Irish Republic), evolving a concept of folk heroism by means of a subterranean chain of logic running through the three stories. Ford's better-known Irish films, *The Informer* and *The Quiet Man*, both present the land through a single character's perspective; here, Ireland itself is the hero, a mass hero gradually revealed through successive incarnation in a series of individuals. It is the dream-world of *The Quiet Man* brought into the waking air, an *insider's* view of the national mystique. The soft pastels of the earlier film give way to the sharp, argumentative clarity of black-and-white.

All three of the apparently dissimilar stories centre on the Irish people's anarchic tendency to resist any kind of externally applied order. In the first story, ironically entitled *The Majesty of the Law*, a policeman reluctantly makes an arrest, and the arrested man wins a moral victory by preventing his antagonist from paying the fine; in the second, *A Minute's Wait*, absolute anarchy rules in the railway station; and in the third, *1921* (based on Lady Gregory's one-act play *The Rising of the Moon*), the film comes full circle as a policeman refuses to make an arrest, and Ireland wins a moral victory over the British. The old man's insistence, in the first episode, on the importance of folk 'secrets' (such as the art of making good liquor) is gradually revealed, in the 'tragic moment' of the last episode, as not a whimsical conceit but a matter of national life and death. The intermingling of the primitive and the modern in the first two episodes – it is noteworthy, for instance, that the seller of bad liquor has a car, and his old antagonist walks – establishes the Fordian context in which we view the national crisis of the climactic story. Fittingly, the full meaning of the folk secrets is revealed through a narrative movement *backward* in time. The final effect of the film could be summed up in a passage from Sean O'Casey:

I'm afraid we're withering. Even the shadow of what we once were is fading ... Someone or something is ruining us ... What do we send out to the world now but woeful things – young lads and lassies, porther, greyhounds, sweep tickets, and the shamrock green. We've scatthered ourselves about too much. We've spread ourselves over the wide world, and left our own sweet land thin.

Or as Ford put it in a BBC interview: 'I think our ancestors would be – can you say "b-l-o-o-d-y"? – I think they'd be bloody well ashamed of us if they saw us now.'

126

The Rising of the Moon

Tyrone Power, the host-narrator of *The Rising of the Moon*, introduces *The Majesty of the Law* from a doorstep on a busy, noisy street in modern Dublin by giving his credentials (his family was from County Waterford) and affecting a brogue to say, 'As we are a quiet, peace-loving people, nothing much ever seems to happen in Ireland ...' More seriously, he adds, 'This story is about nothing, yet perhaps it's about everything.' Ford's use of an *émigré* host reinforces our awareness of the dissolution of the traditional community, and Power's commentary also emphasizes the bardic, ballad-like nature of the film. Much of the meaning of the drama is illustrated by the songs on the soundtrack. When the reluctant magistrate (Cyril Cusack) journeys by foot and boat to the homestead of Old Dan O'Flaherty (Noel Purcell), a tenor voice is singing:

> Oh, the Garden of Eden has vanished, they say,
> But I know the lie of it still . . .

Old Dan, massive but arthritic, irascible but touchingly gentle, is the repository of centuries of tradition. He lives in a national monument, his family castle, and in a moving tableau he gets down on one knee with the

The Rising of the Moon: anarchy at the station

castle looming behind him and laboriously digs up a stone to carry with him
to prison as a memento of home. The camera first frames the castle, tilts down
to the ground with Dan, then tilts up to show him kissing the stone, as three
groups of his kinsmen and neighbours watch in the background. As he walks
away, an old woman in a shawl bows her head to him.

Dan's self-defence at the impromptu 'trial' before the magistrate – conducted over cups in his own home – is a long, eloquent harangue, similar
in spirit to O'Casey's words, about the ancient and honourable art of
liquor-making, which is 'not what it used to be'. Old Dan is speaking for
Ford:

Liquor-making takes time. There was never a good job done in a hurry, for there are
secrets in it. Every art has its secrets, and the secrets of distilling are being *lost*. Hear,
when I was a boy, there wasn't a man in the Ballanee but had a hundred songs in his
heart. But with the people going here, there, and everywhere, and off to Canada,
Australia, America, So' Boston ... with the coming of the automobiles and ... and
... and the films, and the raddio and that other new thing along with it – all the songs
are lost, and all the *secrets* are lost.

A key to the film's attitude to tradition is the tone in which the old revolutionary ballad of the title is sung behind the credits – dulcet, nostalgic, melancholy, a receding echo of the martial spirit in which it was conceived, back in the eighteenth century. The poignancy of the song, and the point of Dan's lament, is that posterity, for whose sake a revolution is fought, eventually forgets the meaning of the struggle. Dan's slow, measured movements (such as the way his gnarled hands, in close shot, pull back a floor stone to uncover the money he could use to pay the fine, if he had a mind to) have the stateliness of ritual, a beauty mysterious to the innocent eye. That the magistrate, a child of the new order, partially understands this beauty is made clear in the wary reverence with which he approaches Dan's castle, in his decision to go *to* Dan rather than ordering Dan to come to him, and in the regret with which he finally brings himself to state the charges. In the last shot, Dan puts his arm round the magistrate as they walk towards the jail. What gives the episode its deep emotional power is the dignity Ford invests in both men and the serio-comic way he discreetly brushes round the edges of the larger issues implicit in their meeting.

The second episode is an *entr'acte* as joyous and uninhibited as a country dance – and at the wildest moment of anarchy, the train passengers assembled in the station's bar erupt into a revolutionary ballad as the homely barmaid dances a jig. The image of the train, symbol of modern industrialized Ireland, stopped in the rustic station for a 'minute's wait' of two hours is a succinct visual metaphor for the triumph of primitivism over regimentation. (If anyone doubts the relevance of train travel to themes of national order, remember that it was Mussolini who was elected on the slogan, 'He Made The Trains Run On Time'.) Ford's narrative gifts are exercised with dazzling virtuosity in this episode, with more than a dozen characters vividly rendered and an ingenious series of complications (including two marriage contracts) engineered in little more than a reel of film. The elderly station porter to the barmaid, whom he has been courting for eleven years:

Paddy: Do you mind if I call you Peggy?
Peggy: No – Paddy.
Paddy: Well, I . . . I don't know how to put it . . .
Peggy: Go on. Go on.
Paddy: (*triumphantly*) How would you like to be buried with my people?
Peggy: It would be lovely!

Ford's handling of the crowd scenes is full of rhythmic and spatial gags, such as the low-angled shot of the passengers frantically dashing into the coaches in the background while the driver and fireman saunter along in the

The Rising of the Moon: the nuns in prison

foreground. It is this great visual control, paradoxically, which allows the episode to assume its air of utter spontaneity; any lapse in story-telling rhythm, and the artifice would seem laboured. *A Minute's Wait* ends with a glorious shot of the train, bathed in steam and sunlight and vibrant with the resounding voices of the local hurling team, as it pulls away from the station, leaving behind the priggish English couple who have persistently failed to appreciate the joke. (When an injured hurler is borne past the train on a stretcher, the woman asks, 'Charles, is it another of their rebellions?') The train now seems to stand for rural Eire itself, riding through the present brash with the spirit of ancient allegiances, on a journey to nowhere, and in no hurry to get there. As one of the passengers puts it, 'Do you know what I like about all this? It's the gettin' on and the gettin' off.'

In *1921*, a young rebel named Sean Curran (Donal Donnelly), whose imminent execution is being protested by crowds marching and praying outside a British Army jail, escapes with the help of the Abbey Players and disguises himself as a ballad-singer. The actors hover round Curran as he makes himself up in the wings, just feet away from the tragedy being enacted on-stage (we see a funeral procession – what could happen to Ireland if the revolution

The Rising of the Moon: the policeman, his wife and 'blood money'

should fail), and as they pass back and forth from the stage to the real-life drama in the wings, the scene becomes a commentary on the nature of tradition. Seeing Curran, the 'corpse' says 'I die happy', and lies down on his stretcher.

What makes Old Dan seem an anachronism is that he is like an actor who has lost his audience; what makes the routines absurd in the *entr'acte* is the idea of life becoming theatre; and in the last episode, it is a consciously assumed absurdity, the lie of theatre, which enables an actor (the rebel) and his audience (his people) to create a shared truth in which reality and drama, modernity and tradition, pragmatism and idealism, pool their creative forces. This is a moral as well as an aesthetic equation, for as Kierkegaard had it, the poet is the hero's better nature, and, conversely, the hero is the poet's better nature. Ford intermingles hero and poet in the image of the rebel turned ballad-singer, the man who carries both the songs and the secrets within him. Ford and Frank Nugent have made some revealing additions to the Lady Gregory play. Besides updating it to the Black and Tan War – the play was first performed by the Abbey Players in 1907 – they added the entire first section dealing with the actresses from the Abbey Company, disguised as nuns, who spirit Curran from the jail. With this in mind, the film's hero-poet metaphor becomes even more striking: by incorporating the play's original performers into its plot, Ford and Nugent are stressing the importance of theatre in the life of the Irish (in fact, the play provoked a great deal of controversy because of its 'treasonous' nature) and suggesting that it is only through a continual retelling of the 'secrets' on stage (and in song) that the nation can survive.

The casting of the simple, slow-witted Irish policeman who meets the ballad-singer is one of those fascinating correspondences which lend such resonance to Ford's work: he is played by Dennis O'Dea, the street singer who insolently sang 'The Minstrel Boy' as British soldiers frisked him in *The Informer*. Sean Curran tries to reawaken the 'secrets' in the policeman by offering his wife copies of 'The Peeler and the Goat' (a joke he does not appreciate) and of the IRA ballad, 'The Rising of the Moon'. The policeman's wife (played by Eileen Crowe, the Protestant minister's wife in *The Quiet Man*) goads him by recalling how he used to sing 'The Rising of the Moon' while they were courting. But the song which echoes most in our ears is the one which begins:

> The minstrel boy to the war has gone,
> In the ranks of death you'll find him ...

At the beginning of the episode, Ford has sketched in the policeman's resentment of the British soldiers, their condescension towards him, and his anguish and confusion over having to enforce their policies. Ford's anti-British bias is extreme, of course – the first time we see Curran he is praying in his cell, with harp music on the soundtrack, and even the policeman joins in the recital of the rosary outside the prison – but it is to his credit that the British major in charge of the execution (Frank Lawton) is, like the policeman, portrayed as a man divided against himself.

Puffy and slightly dissolute in appearance, the major steadies himself with a drink and nervously paces his headquarters while Curran awaits him with a martyr's calm. Several close-ups reveal the major's distaste for duty even as he mouths the conventional sympathies to the nuns, shamed by his own hypocrisy. When one of the nuns becomes lachrymose about how the 'tender hearted' Curran once 'cried for a dead bird', a soldier sneers and lights a cigarette, but the major barks at him to put it out. Our compassion for the major is increased when we realize that the nuns have been exploiting his sympathy (one of them turns out to be wearing high heels, like the nun in *The Lady Vanishes*), and his bitter outcry against his role has acquired an added dimension since the film was made: 'Four years of war and I end up a hangman. How much longer are they going to keep us here?'

The *1921* episode is virtually a remake of *The Informer*, but here the crisis is seen not from the point of view of a solitary outsider, but from that of a representative of society who is also, at heart, a rebel – the policeman. The visual style of the episode is just as expressionist as that of *The Informer*, a maze of vertiginously tilted camera angles, startling in contrast with the visual off-handedness of the first two episodes. However, the distortion is not a subjective effect, as was *The Informer's* nightmarish externalization of Gypo's internal conflicts, but a reflection of the violent tensions which are threatening to pull the country and its traditions apart. The overtones are positively sacrilegious in the shot of the nuns hurrying up the steps of the jail with a machine-gun barrel pointing menacingly towards the camera in the extreme foregound. By the end of the episode, the camera has gradually and unobtrusively returned to eye-level, reflecting the restoration of social equilibrium.

Like Gypo Nolan, the impecunious policeman is tempted to turn informer by the 'thirty pieces of silver' offered on a rebel's wanted poster. But unlike Gypo, he does not have to make his decision in solitude. The community makes it with him. His wife, who had been among the crowd protesting at the jail, joins him at his harbour post with a pep talk about how they could use the reward to buy a farm, making him blurt out that it is 'blood money' (the same words Dan O'Flaherty used to describe his antagonist's hand-out). Then she distracts him by talking about 'The Rising of the Moon' while Curran slips away. The boat leaves the harbour, the policeman cries 'I have a gun! I'll shoot!', but a flute softly begins playing 'The Rising of the Moon' on the soundtrack, like the voice of memory or the voice of conscience, and the camera moves in to a close-up of his face as he murmurs, '*Sean Curran*', remembers the 'secrets', and lets the ballad-singer escape. Returning to his jubilant wife, he joins her in a chorus of the song, and the last shot of the film makes the words concrete: Sean Curran is seen standing in heroic silhouette on a boat floating to freedom in the moonlight.

Putting the dissolution of traditional values at the beginning of the film, in *The Majesty of the Law*, redoubles the effect of the affirmation of tradition at the end. But it is a measure of Ford's melancholia about progress that it is the policeman of the *past* who saves his country, and the policeman of the present who takes it to jail. And the fact that in the last shot the hero is facing in a contrary direction to the movement of the boat (it is moving left, and he is looking right) seems to imply that Ireland's greatest victories are behind her.

7. Rebels: *The Sun Shines Bright* (1953), *The Searchers* (1956)

The Sun Shines Bright

Ford's personal favourite among all his movies was not one of his great popular successes. Nor was it an Oscar winner or a *succès d'estime*. He told Burt Kennedy in a 1968 interview that *The Sun Shines Bright* was 'the only one I like to see over and over again'. Strange, at first glance, that this moody period piece should have taken precedence over his fabled Westerns, his sea stories or his Irish tales. The milieu is more Faulkner than Ford – a Kentucky border town in 1905 – and there is little of Ford's typical feel for landscape and action.

The title is paradoxical, for most of the film takes place at night, in deserted streets, smoke-wreathed halls, plush sitting-rooms and shadowy verandahs. The narrative line is so whimsically followed (or avoided) that the story often seems obscure or fantastic. Ford said it was a picture done 'for my own amusement', intended only to recoup its costs. Republic Pictures kept it on the shelf for more than a year, finally releasing it 'cut to shreds', and the financial débâcle which ensued finished off Argosy Pictures, Ford's production subsidiary.

One might gather from all this that Ford's love for the film was another case of an artist favouring his 'sick child' above the others. But the three Irvin

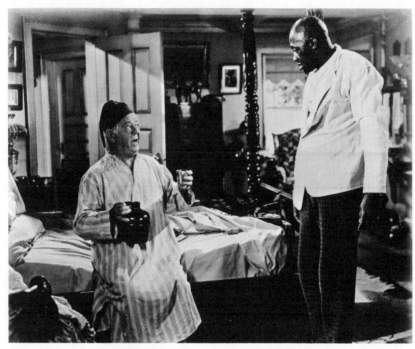

The Sun Shines Bright: Charles Winninger as the Judge, with Stepin Fetchit

S. Cobb stories on which Laurence Stallings' superb script is based – 'The Sun Shines Bright', 'The Mob from Massac' and 'The Lord Provides' – touch on every Ford base: the film is simultaneously a work of nostalgic Americana, a raucous comedy, a caustic social protest and a Christian parable. And Charles Winninger's Judge William Pittman Priest is probably Ford's idealized self-image – humble, sagacious, comic, melancholic. Billy Priest, the old clown who sneaks drinks at a temperance rally and has to take a dose of 'medicine' to 'get my heart started' in moments of crisis; Billy Priest, who leads the funeral procession of a prostitute on election day; Billy Priest, who leaves his Confederate encampment to escort a 'captured' Yankee flag back to the GAR Hall; Billy Priest, the indomitable rebel who defies a town gone mad from lynch fever; this *is* John Ford.

The Sun Shines Bright is a reworking of one of Ford's finest 1930s films, *Judge Priest*, which had Will Rogers in the title role. Like the later film, *Judge Priest* centres on a series of incidents in which the Judge shames the community into an awareness of its intolerance – he defies class barriers by helping his nephew woo a girl from a disgraced family, pointedly involves his black factotum in his legal activities, and exonerates the girl's father from a trumped-up assault charge by revealing his Civil War heroism. According to Stepin Fetchit, who plays the Judge's companion Jeff Poindexter in both films, Ford remade *Judge Priest* because 20th Century-Fox cut a scene in which the Judge rescues Jeff from a lynching: 'They cut it out because we were ahead of the time . . . This time the Negro that gets saved was played by a young boy – I was older then. But they kept it in.' Even accounting for *Judge Priest's* missing sequence, the blacks play a much larger role in *The Sun Shines Bright*, which uses them like a chorus. This can be attributed to several factors: the later setting (1905 rather than 1890), and the film's heightened concern with the decadence of the Old South; Ford's growing interest in the breakdown of social order; and the more enlightened temper of the times when Ford returned to the subject.

It is possible to see Ford's blacks merely as stereotypes, and leave it at that – from the moonstruck Jeff to Ernest Whitman's patriarchal Uncle Pleasant to the grinning banjo band at the Great Lemonade and Strawberry Festival. But they are stereotypes in the same way that the Irish in *The Quiet Man* are stereotypes. Although many whites today are embarrassed by this kind of traditional humour (which most non-bourgeois blacks enjoy), the use of a Stepin Fetchit no more makes Ford anti-black than his use of the oafish Victor McLaglen or the impish Barry Fitzgerald makes him anti-Irish. (Ford drew this connection himself: 'The Irish and the Negroes are the most natural actors in the world.') When he uses Stepin Fetchit, he is employing a sharply defined ethnic image as familiar in American culture as Mark Twain's Jim. And as *Film Quarterly* put it, 'Cooler second sight must admit that Stepin Fetchit was an artist, and that his art consisted precisely in mocking and caricaturing the white man's vision of the black: his sly contortions, his surly and exaggerated subservience, can now be seen as a secret weapon in the long racial struggle.' Like Mark Twain, Ford is sufficiently sure of his touch to be able to ridicule the sources of racial discrimination even while brushing round the edges of stereotypes. He could never *ignore* a man's origins or the colour of his skin because, as a social commentator, he must acknowledge that these are among the basic data of American culture. Ethnic humour is never divisive in Ford, but always a sign of sanity and fellow-feeling, a refusal to evade distinguishing characteristics in the name of a spurious and enfeebling homogeneity. A devastating bit of irony in *The Sun Shines Bright* says more about the absurdity of prejudice than a score of 'committed' films: when the Judge on his bench says, 'Come here, boy' to the young black, the boy and his elderly uncle enter the frame from right and left at exactly the same moment.

Two versions of a Southern judge: Will Rogers in *Judge Priest* (1934) . . .

What we remember most clearly from *Judge Priest* is the warmth and spontaneity of Will Rogers' improvisatory performance. Despite Ford's tendency to over-indulge Rogers' fondness for hammy stammering and folksy nose-scratching (Rogers was an early practitioner of the 'method'), it is a more rounded and intimate characterization than Charles Winninger's broadly sketched performance. But what makes *The Sun Shines Bright* more powerful as a film is the complex portrayal of the community of Fairfield, built up from many small moments of poetry and drama: the festival with its promenading cadets and girls who seem removed in time even as they go through their clock-like movements; the image of Judge Priest, faintly absurd in his white Southern gentleman's outfit, as he stands outside the jail with Uncle Pleasant to await the mob; the old Confederates' palsied rush into the courtroom when they hear the strains of 'Dixie'; the majestic funeral procession, with the astonished populace falling in one by one behind the Judge and the carriage bearing the town whores; Jeff's reflective harmonica commentary as the Judge and his cronies sit on the verandah lamenting the disruption of communal order.

The Sun Shines Bright is like a *précis* of the Judge's life, a testing and a

... Charles Winninger in *The Sun Shines Bright* (1953)

summary of his ideas in a series of events which dovetail into each other with
the uncanny symmetry of a dream. But the film finally seems less concerned
with the Judge himself than with the community's reaction to him. Rogers is
the catalyst for most of what happens in *Judge Priest*; Winninger, on the
other hand, is largely acted upon. It is a film about the last stand of honour
and decency, and Ford's casting of a roly-poly old vaudevillian in the role of
the town's noblest citizen is a beautiful touch, suggesting the frailty and
perhaps even the anachronism of the principles he represents. The law, to
Ford, is not an impersonal system but a human instrument requiring delicate
handling, and Judge Priest, to use Chesterton's description of a judge in one
of his Father Brown stories, is 'one of those who are jeered at as humorous
judges, but who are generally much more serious than the serious judges, for
their levity comes from a living impatience of professional solemnity; while
the serious judge is really filled with frivolity, because he is filled with vanity'.

The twentieth century hangs over *The Sun Shines Bright* like a shroud.
When we first see the Judge, he and Jeff are walking away from the camera; a
steamboat whistle blows, like the voice of memory, and they halt and turn
awkwardly in their paths, looking towards the camera. This is to be Billy

Priest's Last Hurrah. *Judge Priest* was set in a time when the Civil War was still a living memory for most of the town's populace. But in *The Sun Shines Bright*, the Judge's political opponent (played by Milburn Stone, *Young Mr Lincoln's* villainous Stephen Douglas), whose slogan is 'Go Forward With Horace K. Maydew', scoffs at the idea of letting the old-timers use 'an empty sleeve or a gimpy knee' from the Civil War as 'a blanket to smother the progress of the twentieth century'. (The particular note of venom here can be traced to Stallings, a Georgian who lost a leg at Belleau Wood and went on to write *What Price Glory?*, which Ford filmed the year before *The Sun Shines Bright*.) The old men are the strength of the community, but their memories are richer and more satisfying than either the chaotic present or the appalling prospects of the future. And their number is so small that when a knock is heard on the door of the half-empty Confederate meeting hall, Judge Priest muses, 'All that's left of us is here. Maybe it's a ha'nt . . . a ghost!'

The personification of the town's past is old General Fairfield (James Kirkwood, who was in Griffith's *Home, Sweet Home*), its namesake, who sits magisterially aloof from the events around him but continues to exert his shadowy influence as *paterfamilias*. Never stepping outside his mansion, subject to an occasional pilgrimage by the Judge and hushed veneration from the other veterans of the Fairfield Brigade, he seems like a living ghost. And an oddly comic one at that: he sits in a dressing-gown under his Confederate flag, refusing out of pride and shame (because of the scandal involving his daughter, the prostitute) to show his face in public. The general cuts a splendid figure, but Ford kids him a bit by having him solemnly tell the Judge, 'You loom large in my memoirs.' The Judge is touched by this declaration, as we are, but he also realizes that General Fairfield's sterile fixation on the past is as dangerous and crippling to the town as Maydew's callous cult of the future. When the general enters the church – preceded by a long shadow – the Judge is in the midst of his daughter's eulogy, the New Testament story of Christ's refusal to condemn the woman 'taken in sin'. He pauses, then looks the general in the eye and continues, 'He that is without sin among you, let him first cast the stone at her.' The general's entrance, and his taking a seat in the front row with the prostitutes, has a mythical effect: the very spirit of the town has been moved.

The Sun Shines Bright is closest in spirit among Ford's works to *Wagon Master*, because like Elder Wiggs, the Judge proselytizes Christian values through *secular* communal activity, as the name 'Judge Priest' indicates. The fact that there does not appear to be a priest or a minister in Fairfield underscores the importance Ford places on personalized religion. In fact, religion *per se* does not enter the schema of the film until after the prostitute's

The Sun Shines Bright: old memories of two Southern gentlemen (Charles Winninger, Russell Simpson)

death, when the madam visits the Judge and asks him to arrange the funeral. He consults a Bible, and, after an obvious inner turmoil over the decision's effect on the election, closes it and tells her, 'Worry no more, Mrs Cramp. The Lord will provide.' The moral vision Ford gives us in *The Sun Shines Bright* is that of a child, a magical, exaggerated, innocent vision in which a lynch mob, after being rebuffed like a gang of unruly schoolboys, undergoes such a complete transformation that it reappears at the end of the film marching behind a banner reading 'He Saved Us From Ourselves'.

There are few actual children in the film, however, and the only major characters not approaching senility are the general's disgraced granddaughter, Lucy Lee (Arleen Whelan), and her suitor Ashby Corwin (John Russell), the 'profligate seed of a noble line', in the Judge's colourful phrase. But Ford repeatedly stresses the need to become 'as little children' in order to purge hypocrisy and self-righteousness – most clearly in the funeral sequence, when the Judge asks Ashby to say a prayer and he responds with the child's night-time prayer 'Gentle Jesus'. Like *How Green Was My Valley*, *The Sun Shines Bright* is a larger-than-life, wide-eyed fantasy of past innocence, seen from the viewpoint of an old man looking back on a vanished society: there Huw Morgan looking back on his own childhood, here Ford looking back with the same ingenuous perspective which the Judge has in the 'second childhood' of old age.

In the opening sequence, the camera, mounted on a steamboat, sweeps along the harbour line (horse carts, cotton bales, a banjo-strumming black) in a lazy lateral movement which beautifully captures the feeling of time standing still. Later, when Lucy Lee goes to the school, the bell rings and a group of black children run out to group round her. And the theme song 'My Old Kentucky Home' has undergone a small but significant alteration since Ford used it in *Judge Priest*: the line 'In summer, the darkies are gay' has become 'In summer, the *children* are gay'. What gives this vision of harmony its moral force is our awareness of its precariousness and impermanence. For all its sense of communal life, the film contains none of the traditional family unity which gave *How Green Was My Valley* its sense of order. The Judge is a widower (this is not made clear in the film, though it may have been in a cut scene, but the most poignant moment in *Judge Priest* was the character's address to his dead wife's portrait); the general's family is chaotically scattered; and the prostitutes are a constant Fordian testament to maternal longing. The absence of nuclear family life is actually the impetus for the film's religious spirit, its gathering of all the characters, however old, eccentric, wretched or abandoned, under the mantle of 'children of God'. The prostitutes, the old soldiers and, especially, the blacks, form communal 'families' based on a childlike sense of protectiveness, and the Judge (who is still 'Little Billy' to the old general) reconstitutes the benevolent paternalism of the fabled Old South by bringing them all together. Pointedly, it is the superannuated and socially disreputable communities within the disorganized community of Fairfield which are its real source of unity and strength.

Both the lynching attempt and the funeral procession are depicted as communal actions, even though in the one the streets are empty (but for the mob) and in the other the streets are lined with spectators. Before we see the mob, Ford shows us the horrified reactions of a few black families; then the sheriff, society's surrogate, throwing away his badge and turning tail; and only then the face of the boy shivering in the jail. The community as a whole participates in the lynching by its absence, and we find later that the leader of the mob is the man who actually committed the rape of which the boy is accused. The funeral procession is one of the most sustained visual cadenzas in Ford's work, an almost silent passage of several minutes in which all the plot and thematic threads are drawn together with dazzling economy and precision. As the 'progress' candidate harangues a crowd in the street, he is

The Sun Shines Bright: the personality of the law (Grant Withers, Charles Winninger)

interrupted in mid-sentence by a silent, dignified procession. The horse-drawn, crepe-hung hearse marches sombrely up the street, followed by the Judge, a solitary figure in white. Behind him is the carriage of prostitutes. All the various white factions of Fairfield gather on the streets to watch this odd procession. A gaggle of women breaks into hooting and catcalls, Ford cuts to the drawn faces of the more civilized ladies in the carriage, and the commander of the Yankee veterans pushes rudely through the hecklers to join the Judge in the procession: a brief moment, but a telling one – an unchivalrous gesture justified by a director whose watchword is chivalry at a moment when chivalry is at issue. Seeing Yankee and Confederate marching together again, people from the crowd begin to join them. Ford keeps cutting from the methodical, relentless movement of the procession to the edgy, tentative movements among the crowd.

Two old biddies (Mae Marsh and Jane Darwell) are sitting in a carriage, like the whores. '*Well!* No decent woman will ever be seen with Billy Priest from now on!' says Mae Marsh, breaking the silence. 'No, I don't suppose they will,' Jane Darwell replies, and adds her imposing presence to the ranks.

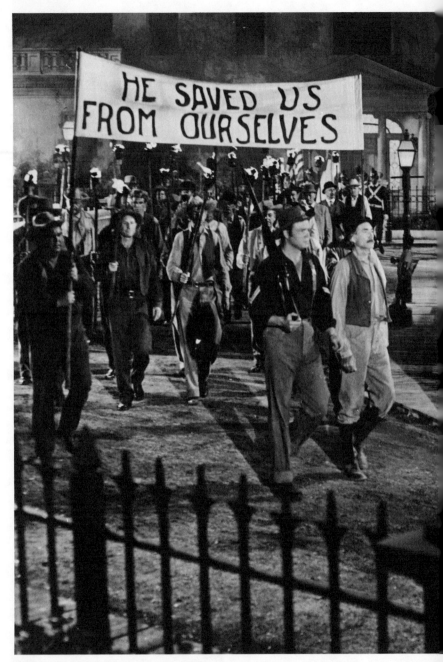

The Sun Shines Bright: Judge Priest's last hurrah

An old-timer in a coonskin cap (Francis Ford *in excelsis*) is drinking from a jug under a sign reading 'Maydew Will Drive the Moonshiners Out'. He squints to see what is happening, plugs up his jug, picks up his gun and beats a gimpy-legged track towards the street. By the time the procession reaches the general's mansion, it has swelled considerably. The general stands on his porch in his dressing-gown as the hearse moves past, seen in stately long-shot framed by the branches of a magnolia tree. As he turns ambiguously back into the house, we hear the first strains of 'Swing Low, Sweet Chariot' from the black community, assembled outside the little frame church in the shanty district. They sing softly but with gathering authority, led by Uncle Pleasant in a frock coat; this is a community of idealized outcasts, like the Mormons in *Wagon Master*. The procession halts outside the church, Judge Priest giving marching orders to the pall-bearers and Uncle Pleasant singing 'Deep River'. In an eerie ellipsis, Ford cuts to the coffin being carried over the heads of the crowd, so that it seems to move wraithlike, of its own impetus, into the church, like the chariot of the song 'coming for to carry me home'.

As the Judge implores the community to 'receive a child' in Christ's name, the camera settles on the prostitutes, stung by the beauty of the Judge's gesture and the pain of his words. During the sermon Ford's camera follows the Judge's every move back and forth, up and down, as he acts out Christ's writing in the sand. This is an extraordinary gesture on Ford's part. Fred Zinnemann has recalled that Ford once told him, 'You know, you could be a pretty good director if you'd stop fooling around with that boom and quit moving the camera so much. To me, the camera is an information booth. I like to keep it still and have the characters come to it and tell their story. I don't move the camera unless there is a very, very good reason for it.' Although Ford does not actually *move* the camera here, this is one of the rare times he used the camera to *follow* a character's actions for a protracted period of time within a limited space; usually his fixed framing keeps the characters subservient to the camera's viewpoint, but here the camera's imitation of the Judge's movements completely immerses us in *his* viewpoint and that of the parable. After Ashby's prayer, there is a silent pause as he bows his head, and then Ford dissolves to the profane bleating of a tuba playing 'Hail, Hail, the Gang's All Here' in the election parade.

The film ends with a joyous $8\frac{1}{2}$-like coda: the entire town, group by group, marching in tribute past the Judge's home. The sublime image of a horse dancing to 'Dixie' in faraway long-shot is our first sight of the parade. As in the opening of *The Prisoner of Shark Island* and the ending of *Rio Grande*, the playing of the defeated faction's anthem becomes an emblem of rebirth, a celebration of traditional harmony. The little Judge stands on his porch, profoundly moved, as the Confederates, the Yankees, the lynch mob and even the temperance ladies march past. The parade continues to the home of General Fairfield, who is standing on his porch in full uniformed regalia, as elegant and stiff as a waxwork. Before the Judge enters his house – with the street cleared, the tumult and the shouting over – the blacks move on, away from the parade, and sing 'My Old Kentucky Home' in his honour.

By any standard of historical accuracy, Ford's view of the Old South is rosy and unreal, and by contemporary standards, his solution to the racial problem is drastically limited by its overtone of paternalist condescension. The beauty of *The Sun Shines Bright* is in its innocence; the film is not a piece of historical documentation but one man's fervent creation of a simpler, kindlier and more gentlemanly America than ever existed. Five years later, when Ford filmed another story of an old paternalist politician, *The Last Hurrah*, he bitterly echoed the finale of *The Sun Shines Bright* by having Mayor Skeffington walk home alone on the evening of his defeat, with his opponent's victory parade marching in the opposite direction to the tune of 'Hail, Hail, the Gang's All Here'. Ford knew there is no room for a Judge Priest in modern America.

The Searchers

> I should like to do a tragedy, the most serious in the world, that turned into the ridiculous.
>
> Ford, just before shooting *The Searchers*

The Searchers has that clear yet intangible quality which characterizes an artist's masterpiece – the sense that he has gone beyond his customary limits, submitted his deepest tenets to the test, and dared to exceed even what we might have expected of him. Its hero, Ethan Edwards (John Wayne), is a volatile synthesis of all the paradoxes which Ford had been finding in his Western hero since *Stagecoach*. A nomad tortured by his desire for a home. An outlaw and a military hero. A cavalier and a cut-throat. Ethan embarks on a five-year odyssey across the frontier after his brother's family is murdered and his niece taken captive by the Comanches. Like Ulysses, he journeys through a perilous and bewitching landscape.

Even more than in Ford's earlier Westerns, the land is felt as a living, governing presence. Previously the great rocks were a backdrop, omnipresent but glimpsed from a distance. Usually it is the Indians (the test) who move among the rocks in Ford's Westerns; the pioneers, vulnerable and exposed, move through the plains below. Here, much of the important action takes place up among the rocks, crevices and cliffs. The epic detachment conveyed by the vast aerial views (there are many more high-angled shots than is usual in Ford) lends an almost supernatural aura to Ethan's quest which is denied to the more prosaic characters of the other Westerns. The demons which drive him onward, almost against his will, seem to emanate from the 'devilish and grinning' land around him. The killing of the family, an action horrifyingly abrupt and brutal, is only the first in a long chain of bizarre events which bedevil Ethan and, finally, drive him mad. Within the classical symmetry of the story – the film begins with a door opening on Ethan riding in from the desert and ends with the door closing on him as he returns to the desert – Ford follows a subjective thread.

Apparently the only serious contemporary critique of *The Searchers* was a review in *Sight and Sound* by Lindsay Anderson, who was amazed to find that Ethan was 'an unmistakable neurotic', and asked, 'Now what is Ford, of all directors, to do with a hero like this?' Anderson's disillusionment with Ford after *The Searchers* was prophetic of the line which the English-speaking critical establishment has only recently begun to reconsider. Odd as his incomprehension may seem today, we must remember that we are looking at the film with full knowledge of the sombre cast Ford's vision took in such late works as *Two Rode Together*, *Liberty Valance* and *Seven Women*. *The Searchers* did violence to that 'simple, sure, affirmative' heroic vision which seemed (and indeed still seems to many critics) to be Ford's *raison d'être*.

The film is not in fact an aberration, but a crystallization of all the fears, obsessions and contradictions which had been boiling up under the surface of Ford's work since his return from World War II. Jean-Luc Godard hints at this in his delightful comment: 'Mystery and fascination of this American cinema ... How can I hate John Wayne upholding Goldwater and yet love him tenderly when abruptly he takes Natalie Wood into his arms in the last reel of *The Searchers*?' Ethan is both hero and anti-hero, a man riven in two by his passions, radically estranged from his society and yet driven to act in its name. His strengths and failings, like the promise and danger of the land around him, are inextricable. *The Searchers* is, on the surface, a highly romantic subject – a knightly quest – but the knight's motives are impure, and as the search progresses, Ford begins to undercut his morality. There is no Penelope to mark the end of his quest because the woman he loves is his brother's wife and she has been killed at the onset, an event which makes his peregrinations absurd. Ethan starts out seeking the return of his nieces, Debbie and Lucy, but after he finds Lucy's mutilated corpse and realizes that Debbie is being made into an Indian squaw, he becomes nihilistic, seeking only revenge. When he finally catches up with Debbie, he tries to kill her. And the search itself would have been a failure had not Old Mose Harper (a

Return of a nomad: John Wayne and Dorothy Jordan in the opening sequence of *The Searchers*

Shakespearean fool played by Hank Worden) accidentally found Debbie after Ethan had spent years losing her trail. Ethan loses her again, and Mose finds her again. It is this grotesquerie, and the anarchic humour which accompanies it, which Anderson found incomprehensible.

The first images of *The Searchers* are an invocation of myth. A door opens inside the darkness of a pioneer cabin, a woman appears, and the camera glides behind her through the door and outside to reveal Ethan, a tiny moving form, gradually materializing on horseback out of the morning mist surrounding one of the great rocks of Monument Valley. Ethan rides slowly, silently, inexorably towards the little homestead, Ford cutting again and again from him to the waiting family; the intercutting gives a feeling of magnetic attraction. When Ethan dismounts and shakes hands, wordlessly, with his brother, his face is mysteriously shadowed by the turned-down brim of his battered hat. The ostentatious way he wears his sword and his fading Confederate cloak alerts us to his futile absorption in the events of the past. As Ethan goes to kiss his brother's wife, Ford gives us, for the first time, a full shot of the home, harmonious with the landscape. The home is a shrine of civilization in the midst of the wilderness, a shrine almost as ridiculous as it is sacred, for we see only one other pioneer home in the entire film. The communal impulse around which the generative principles of Ford's universe are organized is centred precariously round these tiny dwellings. The two pioneer families are infinitely precious and infinitely vulnerable.

Ethan is a descendant of Fenimore Cooper's Leatherstocking, whose character, as Henry Nash Smith put it in *Virgin Land*, is based on a 'theoretical hostility to civilization'. Ford's Western heroes, whether they are outlaws (Harry Carey in the early silents, the bandits in *Three Bad Men* and *Three Godfathers*, Ringo in *Stagecoach*) or lawmen (Wyatt Earp, the soldiers in the Cavalry films), all have a primitive awe for the family. Some of them seek revenge for the murder of members of their own families; others sacrifice themselves for orphans; the cavalrymen act to keep the plains secure for the pioneer homesteads. All, to some degree, are also loners and outcasts from civilization. Their role as the defender of primitive society forces them to live in the wilderness with the enemies of that society, the Indians. But of all Ford's Western heroes, only Ethan turns his violence *against* his family – against Debbie, who could just as well be his own daughter – and that is what makes him such a profound and disturbing figure. Although Thursday might be seen as a less complex 'rough draft' for Ethan (who is more like Thursday and York combined), the only really comparable example in Ford's career is the mother in *Pilgrimage* (1933), who sends her son to his death in World War I rather than lose him to the girl he loves. Here, as in *Pilgrimage*,

The Searchers: 'an isolate, almost selfless, stoic, enduring man' (John Wayne as Ethan Edwards)

Ford has faced up to a contradiction which, as Jim Kitses points out, is also at the basis of Anthony Mann's Westerns: 'Mann's vision of the family as microcosm of humanity is profoundly ambiguous: the highest good, the source of all evil.'

As Ethan's search progresses, it becomes increasingly difficult to appreciate the difference between his heroism and the villainy of Scar, his Indian nemesis. Certainly Scar and Ethan are the only characters who fully understand each other, because their motives are so similar. We learn eventually that the massacre, which seemed at first a totally wilful action, was performed in revenge for the death of Scar's own children. 'Two sons killed by white men,' he tells Ethan. 'For each son, I take many scalps.' The pattern of primitive revenge is endless; Ethan will eventually take Scar's scalp. (And as an added fillip, Scar does not know the word for scalp, and has to be supplied with it – scalping was the white man's invention.) There is a very strange scene early in the pursuit when Ethan shoots out the eyes of an Indian corpse so that, according to Comanche belief, the dead man will never enter the spirit-land and will have to 'wander for ever between the winds'. Seemingly a blind act of vindictiveness – or a gesture of contempt towards an alien culture – the act in fact has undertones of kinship. Ethan himself is doomed to wander for ever between the winds. He takes on the nature of a primitive in desperate recognition of his own failure to find a place in civilized society. Ethan hates Indians – is he envious of their license?

Since the end of the Civil War (three years before the film begins), Ethan has been fighting in Mexico and, evidently, robbing banks; he has developed a seemingly limitless knowledge of Indian tricks, customs and language. He is, as D. H. Lawrence wrote of Leatherstocking, 'a man who turns his back on white society. A man who keeps his moral integrity hard and intact. An isolate, almost selfless, stoic, enduring man, who lives by death, by killing, but who is pure white. This is the very intrinsic-most American. He is at the core of all the other flux and fluff. And when *this* man breaks from his static isolation, and makes a new move, then look out, something will be happening.' What lures Ethan out of the wilderness is a home impulse – his love for Martha – but it is also an anarchic impulse, for his presence threatens to destroy the stability of the family. Ethan's attachment to his sister-in-law is futile, and any overt action would be unthinkable, the shattering of a taboo.

Martha shares his feelings – it is she who opens the door on the wilderness – and she inadvertently speaks them to the Reverend Samuel Johnson Clayton (Ward Bond) on the morning of the massacre. When the communal breakfast is finished, Clayton, alone now, stands up to drink a last cup of coffee. His eyes wander, and he sees Martha through the doorway of her bedroom, caressing Ethan's cloak. He slowly turns back, staring straight ahead and sloshing the coffee reflectively in his cup, as Ethan enters behind him to accept the cloak and kiss Martha goodbye. As Andrew Sarris puts it, 'Nothing on earth would ever force this man to reveal what he had seen.' When the massacre occurs (the very day after Ethan's arrival), it has the disturbing feeling of an acting-out of his suppressed desires – destruction of the family and sexual violation of Martha. With the links between Scar and Ethan in mind, it becomes easy to see why Ford, much to the consternation of certain critics and against his custom, cast a white man (Henry Brandon) in the Indian role. Scar is not so much a character as a crazy mirror of Ethan's desires.

The Searchers stands midway between the 'classical' or psychologically primitive Western and what could be called the 'neo-classical' Western (more commonly, if rather crudely, known as the 'psychological' Western). It was not, of course, the first Western to criticize the basic assumption of the genre – that the solitude of the hero, because it is an instinctive revulsion against the hypocrisy of civilized society, is *a priori* a good thing. In the decade before

The Searchers appeared, a whole rash of Westerns were made in which the hero's solitude was presented as socially unjust (*High Noon*), wasteful (*The Gunfighter*), callous (*The Naked Spur*), insane (*Red River*) or impossibly pure (*Shane*). Little as Ford was usually influenced by film trends, he could hardly have escaped coming to terms with the radical questions posed by this departure. In the same interview in which he said he wanted to make 'a tragedy, the most serious in the world, that turned into the ridiculous', Ford said that *The Searchers* would be 'a kind of psychological epic'. The terms are contradictory, certainly, but contradictions are what the film is about.

Its debt to *Shane*, the apotheosis of Western epic romanticism, is clear (particularly in Shane's wordless flirtation with Mrs Starrett), but the influence of Howard Hawks' *Red River* is far more important. Tom Dunson in that film was the first anti-hero John Wayne had ever played. In the films he made with Ford before *Red River*, the director had stressed his gentleness, his simplicity, the quiet authority beneath his rough exterior. After *Red River*, however, Ford began to use Wayne in parts which were more psychologically complex: the ageing Cavalry captain in *She Wore a Yellow Ribbon*, the neurotic lieutenant-colonel in *Rio Grande*, the pacifist boxer in *The Quiet Man*. This change in Ford's view of Wayne was evidently no coincidence. Discussing Ford recently, Wayne said, 'I don't think he ever really had any kind of respect for me as an actor until I made *Red River* ... Even then, I was never quite sure.' And Hawks has revealed that Ford, after seeing *Red River*, told him, 'I never knew that big sonofabitch could act'.

Dunson, like Ethan, is a good and noble man soured by a tragic mistake. It is a strong performance, but what makes Wayne's Ethan so marvellous is the way that Ford, instead of keeping the character's innate gentleness buried, lets it break through the sullen façade in sudden flashes of sentiment and humour. Besides the character influence, the two films are remarkably similar in plot: both begin with a woman being killed by Indians because the man she loves has deserted her; both have the man rescue a boy – in *The Searchers* the half-breed Martin Pawley (Jeffrey Hunter), his brother's ward – and embark with him on an obsessive epic task; both transfer our allegiance to the boy when the man becomes deranged; and both end with a showdown in which the man is unable to kill his kin – in Dunson's case his ward Matthew, and in Ethan's, Debbie. And there are more localized connections as well: Dunson's bracelet which the Indian takes from Fen becomes Ethan's medal which Scar takes from Debbie; Dunson's cold-blooded murder of the 'quitters' is echoed in Ethan's ambush of Futterman and his men, an action unprecedented for a Ford hero; and Hank Worden's performance as a barmy trailhand foreshadows the Mose Harper character (with perhaps a borrowing from

Worden's crazy Indian in Hawks' *The Big Sky* thrown in for good measure – one of the most astonishing visual *tours de force* in *The Searchers*, the procession of the horsemen between the parallel lines of Indians, is embryonically present in the scene in *The Big Sky* in which the Indians follow the keelboat along the river bank).

What this elaborate pattern of borrowings indicates is not so much that Ford was constructing an answer to Hawks' film (some of these elements are also present in the crude novel by Alan LeMay from which Ford and Frank Nugent adapted the script for *The Searchers*), but that the 'anti-Westerns', particularly *Red River*, jarred Ford into a new area of thinking by suggesting an alternative course for the working-out of the hero's impulses. Ford was always interested in outlaws not so much for their rebellion *per se* but for the subtle ways they are linked to the society that scorns them. In *Stagecoach* and *Clementine*, he seemed to be endorsing an uneasy equation between force and morality by portraying revenge as socially beneficial and morally pure. The revenge transformed the community by cleansing it of its internal pressures – which were also the hero's internal pressures – and it won the hero the community's respect because he had done a necessary deed of which they, because of their civilized stultification, were incapable.

Now what is Ford, of all directors, to do with a hero like Ethan? *Red River* may have a parallel plot, but it is really about something altogether different, the maturing of the relationship between Dunson and Matthew. *The Searchers* is about Ethan's relationship to society, and his desire for revenge, unlike Ringo's or Earp's, serves only to estrange him further from his society, which is also geographically isolated from him. The film's abruptly shifting moods and moral emphases – which Anderson laid to 'the director's unease with his subject' – are determined by the imbalances in the relationship between Ethan and the other pioneers. For instance, since Ethan finds it impossible to enter society through marriage, all the marriages the film portrays are grotesquely unbalanced. Either the female dominates the male (the Edwardses, the Jorgensons), or the female is held in literal bondage to the male (Scar and his wives), or the partners are wildly incongruous (Laurie Jorgenson and the goonish cowboy she turns to in Martin's absence; Martin and Look, the chubby Indian wife he inadvertently buys at a trading post).

Fundamentally alone though Ethan is, all his dilemmas are shared by the community around him. When Brad Jorgenson learns, as Ethan did, that his lover (Lucy Edwards) has been raped and killed, he rushes madly off to be slain by the Indians, who are lurking in the darkness like the unseen, ungovernable forces of the libido. Martin, who is more restrained and civilized than Ethan, nevertheless resembles Ethan enough to suggest that his

The Searchers: the 'pinched awkwardness' of the Edwards' home

continual fleeing into the wilderness, away from Laurie's advances, holds a clue to what drove Ethan and Martha apart in the first place: his fundamental reluctance to become domesticated. Just as Laurie turns to the dull but dependable cowboy in despair of taming Martin, so it must have been that Martha turned to Ethan's dull brother for stability. The wedding of Laurie and the cowboy, which Ethan and Martin fortuitously but appropriately disrupt, is a grotesque parody of Martha's loveless union. It is thus fitting that the wilderness is presented with such extreme visual romanticism and spaciousness, while the scenes in the Edwards' home are marked by what Sarris described as a feeling of 'pinched awkwardness and cramped closeness', caused by Ford's unusual concentration on low-angle shots, making the heavy ceiling beams seem to press down, claustrophobically, on the characters.

Philippe Haudiquet points out another important structural dichotomy:

Conjuring up the recent American past in his Westerns is Ford's way of abolishing time. Very often the action of his films unfolds outside real time, according to the secret and mysterious rules of an ideal time ... In *Stagecoach*, the attack on the

The Searchers: desert confrontation (John Wayne, Jeffrey Hunter)

coach by the Apaches seems to last an eternity, when in fact it takes no more than five minutes. Inversely, in *The Searchers*, the lengthy, circuitous trek of Ethan Edwards and Martin Pawley does not appear to last more than a few weeks, when in actuality it takes several years. The significance of this is that time has a different meaning for Ethan and Martin, who live a nomadic existence, and for the Jorgensons (particularly Laurie), who live a fixed life on the land.

In Fordian terms, Ethan's quest, apparently so solitary and nihilistic, is perceived as exerting a dominant influence on the way the other characters live. Even after Martin becomes, in effect, the hero by attempting to restrain Ethan's nihilism, he is merely following the principles with which Ethan began. And despite Martin's actions, it is finally Ethan who makes the decision about whether to kill Debbie or take her home. Gestures against Ethan tend to remain only gestures; minor characters are continually frustrated in their attempts to change his course, and Ford makes the frustration tactile by repeatedly showing them pushing at Ethan's gun or angrily throwing things to the ground. Towards the end, Martin draws a knife on Ethan, but throws it down when Ethan remains immobile. Martin cries, 'I hope you die!', and Ethan responds with his characteristic assertion of invulnerability: 'That'll be the day.'

The one white character who is able to give Ethan pause is Clayton, who keeps his schizoid roles of minister and Texas Ranger in a subtle, if disturbing, balance: shouting 'Hallelujah!' when he gets off a good pistol shot and snapping 'Bible!' as if calling for a gun. The difference between Clayton and Ethan is succinctly expressed in their first meeting since the end of the war, when Clayton asks Ethan why he didn't show up for the surrender. 'Don't *believe* in surrenders,' says Ethan, adding sarcastically, 'No – I still got *my* sabre, Reverend. Didn't turn it into no ploughshare, neither.' Ethan, the eternal rebel, carries his rebellion to the point of madness. Clayton compromises, and this is what makes him a leader. The two men are several times seen tossing things back and forth – a canteen, a coin, a gun – in wary gestures of mutual forbearance. Although they never come to blows, they are close to it several times. What holds Ethan back is the same fundamental indecision which holds him back from Scar. To make a decisive move against either one would imply a commitment to either civilization or primitivism, and that is Ethan's dilemma: he can't make the choice. When he finally meets up with Scar, it is the ultimate expression of John Wayne *macho* – he stands literally inches from Scar's face and growls insults at both his body (*'Scar*, eh? Plain to see how ya got your name') and his soul ('You speak pretty good American – for a Comanch' – someone teach ya?'). Scar is equal to the *macho* ('You speak good Comanch' – someone teach you?'), but he is similarly unable to make the decisive physical move.

When Scar dies, it is not the White Knight but Martin, the half-breed, who kills him. In transferring the actual heroic deeds, the killing of Scar and the finding of Debbie, to Martin and to Mose, the fool, Ford is destroying the myth of the heroic loner. If Ethan's search is motivated by a desire to preserve the community, then the community, even against its will, must participate in the action. It would never have taken place if the outsider had not initiated it, but it is fundamentally a communal action. If the pragmatists (Clayton, the Jorgensons, Martha) are needed to stabilize society, the visionaries (Ethan, Martin, Mose) are needed to motivate it and define its goals. All, whether they realize it or not, are part of society, a fact which Ford underscores visually with his repeated shots through the doorways of homes. But the film is, as Ford said, the 'tragedy of a loner': Ethan must reject a society he can neither accept nor understand, and the society must reject him, since he belongs to neither the white nor the Indian world.

Martin belongs to both worlds, which is why he is able to accept both

The Searchers: the stability of home (Vera Miles, Olive Carey, John Qualen)

Debbie's miscegenation with Scar and Laurie's desire for a home. As Peter Wollen wrote in his section on Ford in *Signs and Meaning in the Cinema*, for Martin 'the period of nomadism is only an episode, which has meaning as the restitution of the family, a necessary link between his old home and his new home'. Until the search is consummated, Martin is unable to accept Laurie and civilization, for her perspective is just as distorted as Ethan's. Resplendent in the virginal white of her wedding dress, she urges that Ethan be allowed to kill Debbie because 'Martha would want him to'. Martin has told Laurie that Ethan is 'a man that can go crazy-wild, and I intend to be there to stop him in case he does', but it is chillingly clear that Ethan's craziness is only quantitatively different from that of civilization in general. The United States Cavalry, reflecting Ethan's and Laurie's malaise, has bypassed its role as truce-keeper and become a tool of white supremacy. (It was around this time that Ford first commissioned a screenplay for *Cheyenne Autumn*.) Immediately after Ethan begins slaughtering buffalo so that the Indians will starve, a Cavalry bugle merges with his gunshots. Ford gives the Cavalry his traditional romantic trappings – jaunty marching lines, 'Garry

Owen' on the soundtrack – but he undercuts their romanticism as he does Ethan's.

The Cavalry has frozen into an inflexible role. They make their entrance against a background of snow; they gallop through a river whose natural current has turned to ice; and – pre-dating *Little Big Man* by fourteen years – we are taken into an Indian village whose inhabitants they have massacred. Like Scar and Ethan, the Cavalrymen have been trapped in a social tragedy whose terms have been established long before their arrival. The innocent Indians they slaughter, like the family slaughtered by Scar, have become pathetic pawns in a cycle of retribution which will end only when one race exterminates the other. In this context, it is surely no accident that Mose Harper is both the craziest of all the characters and the one who has the most obsessive need for civilization: all he talks about is being able to sit in a rocking-chair. That is what he does when he arrives with Ethan at the burned-out home and what he is doing at the end, when Debbie comes home. An even more ambiguous figure than Ethan, Mose wears a feather in his hat, does war dances, and speaks in a curious Indianized lingo, which is maybe why he finds Debbie so easily.

Miscegenation, next to war itself, is probably the most dramatic form of collision between two cultures, and by exploring a community's reaction to it Ford is testing its degree of internal tension. The dark man, red or black, occupies a peculiar position in American mythology: he is both a cultural bogey and a secretly worshipped talisman of the libidinous desires which the white man's culture takes pains to sublimate. The Western genre in both literature and film, which usually replaces the black man with the red man, is particularly expressive of the American psychical dilemma; Leslie Fiedler's celebrated thesis about American culture, which was received with scandalized disbelief at the time of its propagation, is rooted about equally in the writings of Fenimore Cooper and the New England Puritans, for, as Borges remarks, 'New England invented the West'. (Ethan's name, which in the book was Amos Edwards, suggests a fusion between Ethan Allen and Jonathan Edwards – between the adventurer and Puritan impulses in the American personality.) When Ford, starting with *The Sun Shines Bright*, began to probe deeper and deeper into the causes of social dissolution, racial conflict came to assume almost obsessive proportions in his stories, providing the dramatic centre of *The Searchers*, *Sergeant Rutledge*, *Two Rode Together*, *Cheyenne Autumn*, *Seven Women*, and even the comic *Donovan's Reef*. LeMay's novel lingers over the grisly details of the murders and rapes committed by the Indians on the frontier women. Ford's treatment of the massacre, by contrast, is marked by a devastating

The Searchers: arrivals and departures

elision. The Gothic shot of Scar's shadow falling on Debbie in the graveyard and the fade-out on his blowing the horn are far more suggestive than an actual depiction of the massacre would have been. Our minds work much as Ethan's works when, in the next scene, he stares at the burning home with a fixated expression of horror. He is contemplating the unthinkable.

The emotion Ford emphasizes in the moments before the massacre is the women's fear – conveyed through Martha's anxiety for Debbie, the scene in the graveyard, and the camera's compulsive pull into a large close-up of Lucy screaming (a very uncharacteristic shot for Ford and, as such, a doubly brutal shock). When Ethan, towards the middle of the film, finds a group of white women driven mad by their years among the Indians (one of them croons distractedly to a doll), he reacts with revulsion, and the camera pulls in to a large close-up of *his* face. He has become possessed by the same fear which possessed the women in the home. Eldridge Cleaver, once a rapist himself, has given a cogent analysis of why this act above all, above even the murder of a white man, is so inflammatory: 'In a society where there exists a racial caste system . . . the gulf between the Mind and the Body will seem to coincide

The Searchers: a dual heritage (Natalie Wood, Jeffrey Hunter)

with the gulf between the two races. At that point, the fear of biological miscegenation is transformed into social imagery ... The social distinction is made sacred.' Therefore, as Cleaver puts it, 'rape is an insurrectionary act'. It is revealing that the arch-racist Ethan finds Martin's 'marriage' to Look, the Indian woman, amusing rather than frightening. It has nothing to do with white culture. If a white man impregnates a dark woman, he is planting his seed in an alien culture; but if a dark man impregnates a white woman he is, in the eyes of the primitive white, violating her. The scene in which Ethan finds the mad white women is so disturbing that the spectator may momentarily wonder whether Ford is not succumbing to the same fear of miscegenation and trying to convey it to us with the subjective camera movement towards Ethan. But our first glimpse of Debbie as a woman makes it clear that the fear has a purely neurotic base. Like Martin, she has accepted her dual heritage; resigned to her role as Scar's wife ('These are my people'), she nevertheless remembers her childhood ('I remember ... from always') and is fluent in both English and Comanche. Miscegenation has not destroyed her identity, but deepened it.

Ethan's climactic encounter with Debbie occurs in a rock cleft similar to the one in which, years before, he had found Lucy's body. He takes her roughly by the shoulders – the first physical contact they have made in five years – and, in the same movement, suddenly swings her body into his arms. He says softly, 'Let's go home, Debbie.' It is not *just* the physical contact that prevents Ethan from killing the last of his family; there is also a sense of the profound memories which are flooding back into his consciousness as he touches her. The lifting gesture, which seems almost involuntary, recalls the moment inside the home long ago when he lifted the child Debbie into his arms. Gone now is the hatred caused by his knowledge that she has slept with the man who violated his lover; gone are the years when she no longer existed for him as his own flesh and blood, but only as Scar's squaw. The proximity of his scalping of Scar is vital. When Ethan rises after the scalping, we do not see the corpse. We see only his face, and it is a face almost identical to the one which looked upon the burning home, a face purged of all passion. When Ethan chases Debbie, it is more out of reflex (this is the moment he has been steeling himself to for years) than from any real hatred or desire to kill her. He has been freed from his memories of Martha by a deeper, tribal memory.

At the end, the symbolic sublimation of red into white takes place as Martin accepts Laurie and the family embraces Debbie, still wearing her Indian clothes, on the doorstep of their home. And it is then that Ethan, who seemed on the verge of entering the Jorgensons' doorway (the future), steps aside to let the young couple pass him by and turns away to 'wander for ever between the winds' like his Indian nemesis. Scar and Ethan, blood-brothers in their commitment to primitive justice, have sacrificed themselves to make civilization possible. This is the meaning of the door opening and closing on the wilderness. It is the story of America.

8. What Really Happened: *Sergeant Rutledge* (1960), *The Man Who Shot Liberty Valance* (1962), *The Civil War* (1962)

Sergeant Rutledge

According to Colonel James Warner Bellah, author of the stories on which Ford based his Cavalry Trilogy, scriptwriter Willis Goldbeck came to him with a Frederic Remington painting of black Cavalrymen and suggested that they write a script 'to present the story of the coloured soldier and his contribution to the Western march of American empire'. In a series of story conferences which Bellah described as 'hard labour', Ford took this reactionary idea and transformed it into a brutally frank examination of American social injustice, all the more provocative since it centred on an enduring *modern* fear – of blacks, not of Indians – at a time when civil rights was the most urgent national issue. The black soldier of the title (Woody Strode), a liberated slave who invariably identifies himself as '1st Sgt Braxton Rutledge, C Troop, Ninth United States Cavalry', stands on trial before an all-white court-martial, prosecuted and defended by white officers, for the rape and murder of a white girl.

Sergeant Rutledge dares to confront the radical issue between whites and blacks: sex. Eldridge Cleaver said that when he committed his 'insurrectionary' rape, 'it delighted me that I was defying and trampling upon the white man's law, upon his system of values, and that I was defiling his women . . . I

Sergeant Rutledge: the trial

wanted to send waves of consternation throughout the white race.' The crime of which Rutledge is accused is both symbolically and literally insurrectionary, for he is also accused of killing the girl's father, his commanding officer. As an added outrage, a gold cross was torn from the girl's neck, 'a symbol of the purity he has destroyed', in the words of the post's German doctor. Ever since the riots surrounding the release of *The Birth of a Nation*, Hollywood had avoided this issue like the plague. As Seymour Stern wrote in his study of Griffith's film, 'White liberals may miss the point, but white radicals rarely miss it ... those in the middle do not appear to know what the objective is. They seem to think it concerns the right of a Negro to ride in the same bus or streetcar with white girls, while remaining forever forcibly excluded from the white girls' beds.'

Ford had used the trial-as-theatre many times before, most brilliantly in *Young Mr Lincoln*, as a dramatic metaphor for a society's coming to terms with communal guilt by acquitting an ostracized defendant. The spirit of Lincoln hovers over this later trial as well, even to the curiously apposite touch of giving the black sergeant the same name as Lincoln's lost love. In

Sergeant Rutledge: black demigod, white fear (Woody Strode, Jeffrey Hunter)

Rutledge, however, Ford has largely eliminated the constant reference point of his earlier trials, the courtroom audience. The spectators are repeatedly admonished that the facts are too sensational or obscene to be spoken in polite company (polite company indeed: one of the spectators is brandishing a lynching rope), and the court is cleared at the most delicate moments of testimony. This is society's belief that when a charge springs from irrational, ungovernable impulses, it is unwise to play on emotions; simple facility in stirring an audience's feelings is not enough. Yet in the irrational presentation of the case for Rutledge's defence, which centres entirely on his service record and does not attempt to refute the seemingly overwhelming circumstantial evidence against him, and in the final outcome of the trial (as in *Lincoln*, the real villain emerges from the courtroom audience during the defence's summing up), Ford makes it clear that he regards a court's human fallibility, its responsiveness to the emotional appeal, as its greatest asset.

Unlike Kurosawa's *Rashomon*, which also deals with the flashback reconstruction of rape and murder, *Rutledge* does not present the testimony as a clash of irreconcilable viewpoints. Ford does not show a lie. Instead, each flashback is not only presented as the absolute truth but the testimony of the various witnesses even manages to follow a strict chronological order. From a purely legal standpoint, the trial is a mockery. The judge (Ford's house windbag, Willis Bouchey) and his tribunal continually interrupt the proceedings with wisecracks and opinions; the judge's wife (Billie Burke) and her gaggle of old hens (including Mae Marsh, the black rapist's prey in *The Birth of a Nation*) pester and bully him throughout; the tribunal breaks into a fast game of poker during the only recess; events are depicted in the flashbacks which the witnesses could not have seen or understood; the prosecutor (Carleton Young) constantly makes thinly veiled racist slurs; both lawyers accuse each other of 'cheap legal tricks' and flourish pieces of evidence which severely tax credulity; and at the climax of the trial, defence attorney Cantrell (Jeffrey Hunter) actually slaps and pummels the murderer in the witness chair, shoving him on to his knees as he screams out his confession.

Of the actual circumstances of the crime, Cantrell knows nothing. Rutledge, because he knows that even the suspicion of involvement in 'white woman business' is enough to hang him, refuses to deny the charges. It is Cantrell's, and Ford's, position that the essence of the man, revealed in crisis, contradicts what is said against him. And that the white community, finally, must look to itself for the source of the problem. The rapist-killer turns out to be the white sutler, whose confession is a harrowing statement of guilty desires and sexual repression: 'I had to! I had to! Don't you *understand*? She ... the way she walked ... the way her body moved ... she drove me

Sergeant Rutledge: the night of the crime (Constance Towers, Woody Strode)

crazy ... I had to have her!' As in *The Sun Shines Bright*, a black has been made the scapegoat for the sickness of white society.

Kurosawa, the more modern moralist, presents the universe as absurd and truth as incomprehensible; there are as many truths as there are men who seek it. Ford, the traditionalist, presents the universe as comprehensible, if illogical; the truth will out, and the truth is the standard against which men must judge themselves. Constant reference is made in *Rutledge*, both verbally and implicitly, to 'the book': the book of procedures which ostensibly governs the court-martial, the book of military duty, and, most important, the book of history which the black troopers see as their ultimate vindication. Rutledge allows himself to be implicated in a lie because he is sacrificing himself to a greater truth: 'The Ninth's record's gonna speak for us all some day, and it's gonna speak *clean* ... You're not gonna risk any part of this regiment's record for one man's good.' Yet what Rutledge, in his desire for martyrdom, does not realize is that not only he but the entire black community of the fort (and, by extension, the country) is on trial, because he is their acknowledged representative, their 'top soldier', idolized by the rookies and respected by the tribal elder, the sagacious and fatalistic old Sergeant Matthew Luke Skidmore (Juano Hernandez). Ford characteristically accompanies his destruction of a false legend (black rapacity) with the creation of a new one, that of the idealized black man which Rutledge's comrades celebrate in a song, 'Captain Buffalo' ('John Henry was a weakling next to Captain Buffalo'), as he stands outlined against the campfire smoke and the sky, slowly turning his head in a statuesque pose.

Woody Strode's Rutledge is both more and less than a man. A former athletic hero with a monumental physique, shaved head, erect bearing and huge moonlike eyes, Strode looks like an African ebony carving (besides bearing an uncanny resemblance to Stepin Fetchit!). He is the personification of the black image that white society instinctively fears and tries to render impotent – the 'Supermasculine Menial' of which Cleaver speaks – and the kind of male demigod which black society erects to insist on its sexual identity. Strode said recently, 'I've never gotten over *Sergeant Rutledge* ... It had dignity. John Ford put classic words in my mouth ... You never seen a Negro come off a mountain like John Wayne before. I had the greatest Glory Hallelujah ride across the Pecos River that any black man ever had on the screen. And I did it myself. I carried the whole black race across that river.'

There are several contradictory ironies operating in Ford's argument. First of all, Cantrell's conviction of Rutledge's innocence ultimately rests on his knowledge that Rutledge has no desire for white women. The first item Cantrell offers in his defence is the sergeant's impeccably gallant behaviour towards Mary Beecher (Constance Towers, the Southern blonde heroine of Ford's previous feature, *The Horse Soldiers*) in an isolated train station on the very night the crimes were committed. The second part of the defence is even more ironic: Rutledge's loyalty to the troop when, in that Glory Hallelujah ride, he returns from escaping to warn them of an Indian attack. The complexity of the issues involved in the courtroom drama arises in large part from Ford's delineation of the fort's social structure. There are four separate communities portrayed in the film – the white superior officers, the white civilians attached to the fort, the black troopers and the Indians outside the walls. A counter-society, like that of the blacks, exists only as a shadow of the more powerful society which subsumes it, and the Indians, lowest on the American totem pole, serve only as the test through which the blacks are able to prove themselves to the whites.

The film takes place so late in the frontier period – 1881, after the effective end of the Indian Wars – that its social stratification is virtually that of modern America. The only course open to the blacks, next to suicide, is to find a place in white America in which their manhood is respected. And America has traditionally valued its minorities' manhood only in the sexless situation of warfare. Significantly, the film's Indians are not involved in any real warfare against the whites but only a symbolic, suicidal warfare – a 'sport uprising' for young reservation escapees who have never before tasted battle. (That is how Cantrell describes it, but it is a melancholy fact that the only Indians we see at close quarters are the same weather-beaten old-timers who had worked with Ford since *Stagecoach*.) When the Indians 'attack' the Cavalry, they ride laterally past the troopers, madly discharging their rifles and getting picked off like ducks in a shooting gallery. It is this kind of futile *macho* Rutledge rejects when he returns to the troop: 'It's because the Ninth Cavalry was my home. My real freedom. And my self-respeck. And the way I was desertin' it, I wasn't nothing but a swamp-runnin' nigger. And I ain't that! Do you hear me? I'm a *man*.' Strode recalled that Ford was nervous about using the word 'nigger' in this scene: 'I said, why not? It would be the first time a black man ever called *himself* a nigger on the screen. And I wanted to hit home.'

There is no single image in the film more eloquent than the shot of Rutledge as he listens to Cantrell read his freedman's papers after the arrest: seen from a low angle, Rutledge raises his shackled hands to his chest in a mute gesture of accusation. He and the other black soldiers are individuals in battle, because they freely chose to be there, but only pawns of white justice and sympathy in the courtroom. Ford underlines this point with a violent visual schematization. The courtroom sequences, tense, monotonous and

Sergeant Rutledge: individuals in battle

constricting, clash with the sweeping action and vivid coloration of the Monument Valley flashback sequences, contrasting talk with action, principles with deeds, rhetoric with reality. The lyricizing device of background music occurs only in the battle sequences, leaving the words of the courtroom suspended in a hollow, abstracted silence. Ford uses an unnatural lighting effect borrowed from the trial in *Mary of Scotland* – the courtroom dimming into darkness while a witness remains in spotlight or in silhouette – to cue in several flashbacks, as if to point up the metaphysical distinction between society's distorted view of an action and what the action really meant to the person involved.

The end of the film, superficially, is a triumph, but it is really only a triumph for white society, which has been redeemed from an act of barbarism. Under other circumstances, Rutledge would probably have been found guilty and condemned to hang, or would perhaps have been lynched without a trial. The film closes with a heroic image out of Remington – a line of black troopers marching exuberantly along the horizon with 'Captain Buffalo' echoing on the soundtrack. But though the specific and symbolic injustice has been righted, the historical injustice remains. Long after the film has ended,

Sergeant Rutledge: desertion

the viewer is haunted by a scene which calls into question everything Rutledge, Ford and America itself stand for. Trooper Moffat dies on the battlefield in Rutledge's arms, a man without a country damning the United States in his last breath. Profoundly stirred, Rutledge climbs on his horse (as we hear a distant echo of 'The Battle Hymn of the Republic') and then rides off into the recesses of Monument Valley as the soundtrack resounds with 'The Battle Cry of Freedom'. But his desertion, we know, will be only temporary, and the dying man's last words hang in the air as Rutledge rides away:

Moffat: My three little girls . . . what's gonna happen to them, Brax?

Rutledge: Some day, Moffat, they gonna be awful proud of you.

Moffat: (*laughs*) Some day. You always talkin' about some day, like it gonna be Promised Land here on earth. *Brax*! We're fools to fight the white . . . white man's war . . .

Rutledge: It ain't the white man's war. We're fighting to make us *proud*. Some day your little girls . . . Moffat, do you hear me? (*He dies*) Moffat!

The scene immediately following Moffat's death is, if anything, even more challenging, because it brings Rutledge and his friend Cantrell into public

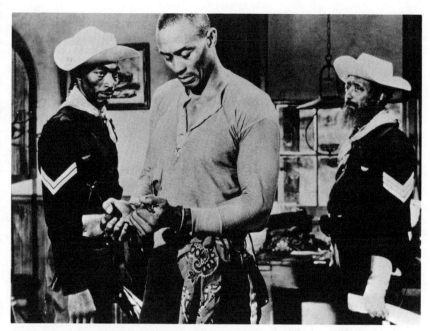

Sergeant Rutledge: Rutledge under arrest (Woody Strode)

conflict for the one and only time in the film and rawly exposes the contradictions of Cantrell's role. Even the stirring tune of liberation underlying
Rutledge's escape has a double meaning; its alternate title is 'Rally Round the
Flag, Boys'. When Moffat dies, Rutledge makes an Indian-like signal to the
waiting troop, slowly waving his arms up and down like a bird – a gesture
symbolizing both the flight of Moffat's soul and his own impending flight to
freedom. Then Ford shows Rutledge, in medium shot, staring intently towards Cantrell while tying a bandanna round his neck. As Rutledge rides away,
Cantrell fires a warning shot with his pistol and Rutledge's comrades shout
'*Sir!*' Then, in an act for which Mary will later damn him as a 'cheap,
contemptible, tin-plated book soldier', he takes aim with his rifle; Mary
pushes it away. All this time Rutledge has been riding off, his back to
Cantrell, calmly heading towards his destiny. If one can gauge Ford's attitude
towards civilization by that of his leading lady, then Mary's contempt for the
Army and the West is indicative of his mounting scepticism since *The
Searchers*. After Rutledge has returned to the troop, Mary rejects Cantrell's
advances by telling him, 'No, Tom. I hate this land. It killed my mother, and
now it killed my father. I wish I'd never come back to it.' Cantrell's reply

is curiously lacking in real conviction, and he seems to realize it: 'But, Mary, it's a *good* land. It really is. Maybe not now ... but like Rutledge says, some day.'

Whether Ford and his surrogate Cantrell would have been so quick to defend Rutledge if the sergeant were an 'uppity' black chafing at white discipline and miscegenatory barriers is doubtful, and this raises anew the question of Ford's own attitude towards racism. It is one thing for Ford in *The Searchers* to present Scar, who *is* guilty of murder and miscegenatory rape, as a victim of social circumstances. It would be another thing altogether for him to do the same with Rutledge, because Scar is a past threat to the stability of American culture, and a Scar-like Rutledge would be a present threat. No one, of course, would expect Ford to defend Rutledge if he actually were a rapist and a killer. But it is a legitimate question to ask why Rutledge could not have been both innocent of the crime *and* rebellious, and what this indicates about the limitations of Ford's perspective.

The film's view of America, as expressed through Rutledge, is perhaps an unduly optimistic one, given the facts. But it could be argued that Ford, like any good defence attorney, makes Rutledge such an innocent and noble figure because he is attempting to present the best possible case for his client – i.e. black America. (Similarly, the absence of miscegenatory overtones in *Cheyenne Autumn* – when the situation of the white missionary woman accompanying the tribe would seem to make it dramatically inevitable – also registers as a deliberate omission for the sake of a 'best possible case'.) As a cultural commentator, Ford realizes the hold miscegenatory fear still exercises on white America, and in order to argue for the black's integration into white society, he presents the black in terms acceptable to whites. Perhaps this is the necessary first step towards integration, both of society externally and of the neurotic American psyche.

Sergeant Rutledge often calls to mind the work of Samuel Fuller, the great nihilist of the American cinema: first in its use of the glacial Constance Towers as the virginal heroine (she plays a stripper and a prostitute in two post-*Rutledge* Fuller films, *Shock Corridor* and *The Naked Kiss*), but mostly in its frank arousal of the audience's cultural hysteria. Like Fuller, Ford dredges up a truckload of psychic garbage from beneath the level of good taste, shocking us into considering questions we usually suppress. For instance, when the prosecutor begins making innuendoes about the night at the railway station, Ford makes them concrete in a shot of Mary running into the extreme foreground as Rutledge's black hand suddenly clasps over her mouth. It is Rutledge's first appearance in the flashbacks, and Ford abruptly cuts back to the courtroom, allowing the viewer's mind to indulge in the most lurid kind of speculation about what really happened that night.

As Rutledge's innocence becomes more and more obvious, there is less and less of this Gothic imagery. The difference between Ford and Fuller is that Fuller probably would have made Rutledge guilty. His *Sergeant Rutledge* probably would have ended in a lynching (as does Ford's next film, *Two Rode Together*), and the viewer would have been left to contemplate the ashes of American civilization. Ford, more defiantly perhaps, refuses to give up on America and its traditional ideals. That he is skirting a very touchy issue by making Rutledge innocent is undeniable. But rather than presenting an absolute view of America – whether nihilistic or entirely idealistic – he is simply admitting the unpleasant facts: a Scar-like black culture would lead to a renewal of genocidal warfare. Ford presents the truth about American racism rather than a fantasy of harmony and equality.

The Man Who Shot Liberty Valance

> It is practically the only question of the age, this question of primitivism and how it can be sustained in the face of sophistication.
>
> Jean Renoir

The Man Who Shot Liberty Valance opens on a shot of an iron horse passing through a tranquil Western landscape. We have seen this image in countless Westerns; like a folk song, it releases a flood of memories and associations. Yet the way Ford lets the camera linger a moment on the heavy trail of black smoke hovering in the wake of the train seems to question the convention. Decades earlier, Ford had uncritically celebrated the building of the transcontinental railway in *The Iron Horse*, but now the train, the traditional symbol of progress and the pioneering spirit, has become a polluting and corrupting force.

The opening and closing sections of *Liberty Valance* are set in the last days of the frontier period, the beginning of modern America. From this perspective, we study in a long flashback the events surrounding one of those epochal gunfights which carry all the romance and meaning of the Western myth for us today. *Liberty Valance* is told from the viewpoint of a transplanted Easterner, Ransom Stoddard, who had once 'taken Horace Greeley's advice literally'. Stoddard (James Stewart) became a prime mover in the early history of the territory as the legendary Man Who Shot Liberty Valance, and is now its United States senator. Yet by the end, his heroism has been revealed as sham, and the train carrying him and his wife back to the East in the final shot describes an arc exactly the inverse of the opening shot. Inside the train Mrs Stoddard gazes at the valley: 'Look at it. Once it was a wilderness. Now it's a garden. Aren't you proud?'

That is the basic question of the film. Hallie Stoddard's juxtaposition of the words 'wilderness' and 'garden' invokes the familiar vision of the Western migration defined in *Virgin Land*:

They plowed the virgin land and put in crops, and the great Interior Valley was transformed into a garden: for the imagination, the Garden of the World ... When the new economic and technological forces, especially the power of steam working through river boats and locomotives, had done their work, the garden was no longer a garden. But the image of an agricultural paradise in the West, embodying group memories of an earlier, a simpler, and, it was believed, a happier state of society, long survived as a force in American thought and politics.

Stoddard has not only symbolically transformed the wilderness into a garden, through his showdown with the equally legendary Valance (Lee Marvin), but when the film opens he is on the verge of literally transforming it, as the author of an irrigation bill. He has destroyed the Old West to give birth to modern America. But the ruthless logic of the flashback will prove that he was not the prime mover, merely a catalyst for inevitable historical forces; the Old West destroyed itself to make way for him and the way of life he represents – law, book learning, progress.

Although Ford's sympathies clearly lie with the archaic simplicity of the wilderness – with John Wayne's Tom Doniphon, who shot Valance and let Stoddard take the credit – the film is not an indictment of Stoddard. Like Tom, Valance and Hallie, he is caught up in a process of destruction and change which he is all but powerless to control. In fact, Stoddard is almost a comic figure, and the casting of James Stewart (in a role Henry Fonda would have played had the film been made twenty years earlier) emphasizes the ambiguity. Stoddard's predicament as a false hero bears an uncanny likeness to the situation Edward G. Robinson faces in a 1935 Ford comedy, *The Whole Town's Talking*, when his resemblance to a famous killer brands him with the newspaper sobriquet of 'The Man Who Looks Like Mannion'. But because Stoddard *sought* his title, even if he has not really earned it, his situation is tragic.

Superficially, *Liberty Valance* is one of Ford's least typical Westerns – a film of darkness and interiors, the only landscapes the shots of the train and a handful of visits to the flat, nondescript terrain of Tom's ranch – but in terms of ideas and feelings, it is perhaps the most personal and most typical of all his films. Ignoring the evidence of *The Horse Soldiers* (1959), *Two Rode*

Together (1961), *Donovan's Reef* (1963) and *Cheyenne Autumn* (1964), all of
which contain splendid and extensive location work, the less perceptive critics
have decided that Ford's confinement to a drab and familiar set was due to the
torpor of old age. Pauline Kael, who disliked the film because Ford 'doesn't
bother going outdoors much anymore', had earlier criticized his 1940s
Westerns for indulging in 'the "affectionate", "pure", "authentic" scenery of
the West'. Damned if you do, damned if you don't. But *Liberty Valance* does
break the classic John Ford mould, which may explain why even some of his
erstwhile admirers have been equally disdainful. The pasteboard town of
Shinbone, where, in Manny Farber's words, 'the cactus was planted last
night', has the same function as the neutral backgrounds of Dreyer's *Jeanne
d'Arc* and Hawks' *Rio Bravo*: it avoids the conventional romanticizing of
period detail to force all our attention on to the faces of the characters. There
are probably more close-ups in *Liberty Valance* than in all of Ford's 1940s
Westerns combined.

Ford alters the externals of the classical Western in order to re-examine its
metaphysic. The town we see in Stoddard's tale, with its buildings too close
together, the mud too close to the stars and a painted horizon, is as much a
symbolic evocation of his past as the fog-shrouded canvas Dublin of *The
Informer* is of Gypo's tormented soul. The conflict in *Liberty Valance* is as
much between reality and symbol, truth and legend, memory and conscience,
form and substance, as among the archetypal characters who enact it. Like
the gaucho stories of Borges ('The Challenge' in particular), it draws its
peculiar claims on the imagination through its extremely self-conscious,
ritualistic perspective on an essentially irrational, 'disinterested' duel – in
Borges' words, 'a story that may belong to legend or to history or (which may
be just another way of saying it belongs to legend) to both things at once' –
which exerts a symbolic cultural influence out of all proportion to its immediate cause. *Two Rode Together*, which Ford made just before *Liberty
Valance*, is a virtual double of Borges' spooky frontier story 'The Captive'.
The meeting-ground between these two artists is their preoccupation (more
marked in their late work) with the power of legend to overshadow reality,
and the way a remembered past can crowd out the present.

In *Liberty Valance*, instead of the dovetailing series of recollections Ford
and his scenarists (again Goldbeck and Bellah) used in *Rutledge*, there is
basically only one (the exception is Doniphon's revelation of the truth about
the showdown to Stoddard himself in a brief flashback within the flashback).
Stoddard relates his story to a chorus of three newspapermen in a museum-
like carpentry shop/undertaking parlour, with Tom's pine coffin lying in the
adjoining room. There is a Hawksian bleakness in the first view of the

undertaker, about to toss a bucket of wood scrapings from the coffin into the street and stopping when he sees the senator's entourage. Tom has died in obscurity, his only other mourners the former marshal Linc Appleyard (Andy Devine) and Tom's old black retainer Pompey (Woody Strode). When Stoddard lifts up the coffin lid, he shoots an evil glance at the undertaker and commands, 'Put his boots on, Clute. And his gun belt. And his spurs.' The badgering editor is played by Carleton Young, who was the prosecutor in *Rutledge*, and Stoddard's story has the feeling of a guilty confession before the court of history. The senator's hammy, rhetorical personality partially dictates the self-consciously theatrical manner of Ford's own story-telling. Stoddard even cues in the first scene of the flashback, Valance's robbery of the stagecoach on which he came to Shinbone, with a corny reference to the old propped-up stagecoach in the corner. He opens the door, letting a cloud of dust stir inside the coach, then wipes a generation's accumulation of dirt from the 'Overland Stage' shingle and declares it to be the very coach of the tale.

Perhaps the oddest thing about the film is that most of the actors in Stoddard's re-creation are older, by decades, than the characters they are playing. Ford's detractors found this the limit of absurdity, as if the old man had slipped into dotage. But we are not seeing the characters as they were in the past. Nor are we seeing them altered by the memory of an old man (Stoddard or Ford). They are the people of the film's present projected back into the past, acting out its fateful moments but incapable of altering them. There is also a theatrical dustiness to the make-up of the people in the film's present and an exaggerated gravity in their bearing. In his excellent article 'Cactus Rosebud', Andrew Sarris suggested the logic behind this:

Throughout the entire flashback, Andy Devine fulfills his duties as town marshal by cowering behind doorways to avoid Liberty Valance. Yet Devine's mere participation in the fierce nobility of the past magnifies his character in retrospect. For Ford, there is some glory in just growing old and remembering through the thick haze of illusion.

And Robin Wood has added:

The Old West, seen in retrospect beside Tom Doniphon's coffin, is invested with an exaggerated, stylized vitality; in the film's 'present' (still, of course, *our* past, but connected to our present, as it were, by the railroad that carries Senator Stoddard and Hallie away at the end) all real vitality has drained away, leaving only the shallow energy of the news-hounds, and a weary, elegiac feeling of loss. What is lost for the characters is defined in concrete, dramatic terms.

Liberty Valance contains an exceptionally complex network of allusions to Ford's previous films, evoking audience memories, placing the story in the

The Man Who Shot Liberty Valance: the John Ford Stock Company (Andy Devine, John Wayne, Jeanette Nolan, John Qualen, Vera Miles, James Stewart)

totality of the Western tradition, and adding a further process of correspondence to that of the time structure. Typically, his Stock Company recall roles they have played before, but here with a much closer resemblance than usual – Doniphon, who is building a nuptial cottage for Hallie, recalls Ethan Edwards in *The Searchers* and Sean Thornton (with his White O'Morn) in *The Quiet Man* ; Vera Miles' Hallie and John Qualen's Ericson remind us of their Jorgenson characters in *The Searchers*; Strode's strong but subservient Pompey is a demilitarized version of Sergeant Rutledge; and Devine recalls his Buck, the driver, in *Stagecoach*, down to the point of having a 'Hoolietta', though by now his daughter, not his wife. (Andrew Sarris observed that Devine, 'Ford's broad-beamed Falstaff, must stand extra guard duty for the late Ward Bond and Victor McLaglen. Ford, the strategist of retreats and last stands, has outlived the regulars of his grand army.') Even more strikingly, other famous Ford characters are re-created, almost parodistically, by new actors: Marvin, with his whip and his cretinous henchmen, resembles Brennan in *Clementine* and Kemper in *Wagon Master*; and Doc Boone from *Stagecoach* is split in two by Edmond O'Brien's drunken editor Peabody and Ken Murray's drunken Doc Willoughby (when Valance is shot, the doctor calls for whisky and, not for the first time in a Ford Western, swigs it down before attending to the patient).

The general audience could be expected to recognize at least some of these correspondences. Others are more in the nature of a private reminiscence on Ford's part: the framing of the film between the entrance into the valley and the exit resembles the structure of *The Searchers*; when Hallie visits the ruins of Tom's house, the Ann Rutledge theme from *Young Mr Lincoln* appears on the soundtrack; her carriage ride from the railway station to the home recalls Sean's pilgrimage in *The Quiet Man*; Valance draws the 'dead man's hand' before the gunfight just as Luke Plummer did in *Stagecoach*; and Tom's burning of the house he was building for Hallie shockingly parallels Scar's burning of Martha's home in *The Searchers*.

Robin Wood has drawn attention to the close thematic links with *Clementine*, and also the marked divergence in tone. But one could go much further (Ford encourages it in the film) in analysing *Liberty Valance* as, literally, a remake of *Clementine*, the classic 'town-taming' Western, from a more complex moral and historical perspective. To do this is hardly to contend, as William S. Pechter has done, that *Liberty Valance* is more an 'essay' than a drama, meaningful only as a gloss on Ford's previous work. Ford is not merely toying with his past; like Stoddard, he is attempting to perceive in it a grand design. What Ford is doing in his 'essay' on *Clementine's* themes is actually only a more elaborate and self-conscious version of what every Western director does – he is using a set of historical and formal assumptions as a departure point for a revaluation of the Western myth. As Renoir has said, 'The marvellous thing about Westerns is that they're all the same film. This gives a director unlimited freedom.'

Like Wyatt Earp, Stoddard is a young man from East of the territory who is insulted and robbed on the outskirts of a wild cattle town; using the law as a vehicle for personal revenge, he ends by civilizing the town, taking the sweetheart of the 'good bad man', and passing into myth. The name 'Shinbone' is a parodistic echo of 'Tombstone', and the credits of both films appear on signposts. Stewart's lawyer, like the young Fonda (here more Lincoln than Earp, though, and more Jefferson Smith than either), embodies all the virtues America traditionally reveres: temperance, tolerance, a passion for justice, meekness and reverence towards women (he is beaten for demanding that Valance give back a widow's brooch), and ambition. Earp asks, 'What kind of town is this?', and Stoddard, 'What kind of a community have I come to here?' In the confrontation between the lawman (Earp, Stoddard) and the outlaw (Clanton, Valance), there is a powerful mythic symbolism: the one represents mind and morality, the other instinct and licence (down to the irony of the name 'Liberty'). In the eyes of history, therefore, the killing is a mythically perfect act, idealism and social responsibility triumphing over self-serving nihilism. But *Liberty Valance*, like *Fort Apache*, shatters the purity of a myth even as it shows history accepting it. Valance was not shot by the man of the law, but by another primitive, Doniphon. The deed was not done in public but from a dark alley, in ambush; 'cold-blooded murder', Doniphon himself calls it, adding, 'but I can live with it'. Furthermore the outlaw and his killer are not motivated by pure evil and pure good: Valance is the hired gun of the big ranch interests who are fighting statehood so that they can keep the territory an 'open range', and Doniphon saves Stoddard's life for Hallie's sake.

The flashback is organized in a rigorous but unobtrusive pattern of seven sequences, each chronicling a step in Stoddard's rise to power. We see him first in abject humiliation at the hands of Valance during the robbery; then being introduced into the Ericson 'family', which also includes the marshal, Hallie, Tom and Pompey; waiting on tables in the Ericsons' restaurant and being taunted by Valance in the long, brilliant sequence which culminates in the tense staring match between Doniphon and Valance; working with Peabody on the newspaper and with Hallie in the schoolroom; being taught to shoot by Tom; being elected territorial delegate along with Peabody over Valance's objection at the town meeting in the saloon; 'shooting' Valance; and finally winning nomination to the United States Congress at the territorial convention.

What we are really seeing is not the building of a legend but a gradual stripping away of Stoddard's illusions. We are constantly taken 'backstage', a motif introduced before the flashback even begins, when Stoddard leaves the room with the coffin to tell his story in the anteroom. Other uses of a 'backstage' area include the frenzied kitchen in which Ranse carries on his courting of Hallie out of Tom's sight; Peabody's office adjoining the school-room, in which he prints the newspaper Ranse uses in the civics lesson; the room Tom is building for Hallie at his ranch, which we see under construction during the shooting lesson, with Pompey applying the whitewash; the alleyway behind the restaurant where Pompey waits to spirit Ranse out of town; the bar in which Valance prepares for the gunfight by drinking, terrorizing a gambler and getting the dead man's hand; the alleyway in which Tom waits to ambush Valance; and finally the little back room of the convention hall in which Tom tells Stoddard what really happened during the shooting and orders him to take the nomination, again for Hallie's sake ('You taught her how to read and write, now give her something to read and write *about*'). The mythic actions occur on stage – in the dining-room, the school-room, at the ranch, in the saloon, on the streets of Shinbone, and in the convention hall – but the truth is revealed in the wings.

It may seem incongruous, given the obvious momentousness of the theme, that *Liberty Valance* is also one of the funniest of Ford's movies, funnier, in fact, than an actual comedy such as *The Quiet Man*, but we know better by now. Like *The Searchers*, *Liberty Valance* constantly undercuts the self-conscious gravity of epic gestures with sudden eruptions of farce and mayhem. The humour provided by Appleyard's spectacular incompetence is no mere distraction; it does as much to fill in the anarchic context of the Old West as Valance's psychopathic whipping and shooting. To Stoddard, as to Lincoln, the law is virtually a religion (Tom seems to recognize this in his teasing nickname for him, 'Pilgrim'), but Ford treats the law as low comedy. Shortly after Stoddard rejects Tom's suggestion that he start carrying a gun by telling him, 'I don't want to *kill* 'im – I want to put him in jail,' Appleyard chimes in with the information that 'the jail's only got one cell and the lock's broke and I sleep in it'. The alarming irony of this kind of humour is that when Stoddard appeals to the law, he is appealing, like Kafka's Joseph K., to a mythical system. To save the territory from chaos, Stoddard finally has to resort to what Valance calls 'Western law', i.e. barbarism, and when he is offered a Congressional nomination for violating his principles, he leaves the room in disgust ('I'm going home, Tom' – but where's home?) until Tom makes him face the facts.

Several critics have pointed out the profound contradictions of a film with, in V. F. Perkins' words, 'a story which celebrates the submission of the Old West to the rule of law and order, and a style which evokes nostalgia for the primitive nobility of its untamed frontiers.' They might have also mentioned another paradox: a film which exposes the falsity of legend, play-acting, and appearance is itself extravagantly expressionist in its lighting, acting and business. The long restaurant sequence, for example, develops the town's moral dilemma with great clarity and simplicity, but it is the use of digressions and asides, unerringly calculated and presented, which enables Ford to create an entire milieu in about a reel of screen time. Outside there is the palpably threatening darkness of the streets, the townspeople moving quickly and cautiously past the restaurant, constantly on guard against Valance; inside there is the warmth and camaraderie of the spacious, brightly lit and homely dining-room; further inside is the hub of the little community, the bustling, cheerful kitchen with its gargantuan steaks and its clouds of aromatic steam.

When Valance and his henchmen enter, the harmonious, egalitarian atmosphere is immediately disrupted. The tension is graphically conveyed in the

The Man Who Shot Liberty Valance: 'Everybody in this country *kill*-crazy?' (Lee Marvin, James Stewart, John Wayne)

person of the stuttering cowboy whose seat, and steak, Valance appropriates, and in the maniacal giggles of the crazier of his two henchmen (Strother Martin – the silent, hawk-faced one is Lee Van Cleef). The confrontation begins with a close-up of Valance's hand thumping the whip on the table, the camera pulling rapidly away from it as if from the vortex of a storm. Valance laughs giddily at Stoddard's appearance in an apron, and trips him to the floor. Doniphon suddenly appears on the right of the screen: 'That's my steak, Valance.' Valance jumps up and announces, 'Three against one, Doniphon.' 'My boy, Pompey, in the kitchen door,' Doniphon replies, and Pompey is shown cocking his shotgun. Strother Martin moves in from background left to pick up the steak and Doniphon brutally kicks him *in the face* – a movement so off-hand it is comic. Here Ford shows the influence of the black humour which had been creeping into the genre, and in particular the scene in Hawks' *Rio Bravo* in which Wayne slams a man across the face with his rifle and says, 'I'm not gonna hurt him.' But it is also a symptom of the mounting sense of the grotesque which characterizes Ford's 1960s work as civilized values seem more and more attenuated, and society more decadent.

Doniphon, his eyes riveted on Valance, moves towards him and the two men freeze into a tableau, staring at each other with *macho* grins (like Ethan and Scar, but this time not broken down into an exchange of over-the-shoulder shots) as Ford holds and holds and holds the shot – irresistible force meeting immovable object. Stoddard, who cannot abide a transgression against his moral system, breaks the impasse by 'rising up out of the gravy and the mashed potatoes' (as Peabody puts it), slamming the steak on the plate, and screeching, 'What's the matter? Everybody in this country *kill*-crazy?' The intervention of the third man – the civilized modern man – is the difference between *Liberty Valance* and *The Searchers*. In the earlier film the clash was between two absolutist moral codes, but here, since Ford is analysing the meaning of modern rather than primitive America, the clash is made relative by Stoddard's presence.

This scene also contains the moment which, in retrospect, looms as the climax of the entire pattern of personal and historical tragedy. Before the confrontation over the steak, Tom, in his best Sunday clothes, comes through the kitchen door with a cactus rose for Hallie. Like everything else in the film, the rose is a simply perceived image which carries a multiplicity of meanings. A rose in the desert is a living anachronism – the unnatural, touching spectacle of a plant blooming in the dust – and the cactus is also a carrier of water and life. Hallie's girlish greeting, 'Why, Tom, *look* at you! You're all dressed *up*!' assumes an almost unbearable poignancy on repeated viewings of the film. She pulls back from him shyly and hesitates, half in clumsiness and half in shame, as Tom holds out the rose. It is at this moment that Doniphon first realizes that, in his absence, the tinhorn lawyer has been charming Hallie with his books and his dreams of the future. In conversation with Ranse after Pompey has planted the rose outside the door, Hallie says, 'Maybe some day, if they ever dam the river, we'll have lots of water, and all kinds of flowers.' This is the root of Stoddard's famous and symbolic irrigation bill. It was Tom who inspired it, with his romantic but destructive uprooting of the rose, and Hallie who set the idea in motion.

After the face-off with Valance, Tom walks out into the alley, and Hallie, in a flash of prescience, rushes to the door to watch him leave. Ford lap-dissolves the shot of Hallie in the doorway over the beginning of the school-room sequence, which is the town's first step towards civilization. The cactus rose comes to stand for Hallie's roots in the wilderness ('Any more color' n' you'd be prettier than that cactus rose,' Tom tells her), and also her tragic desire to see the wilderness transformed into a garden. When the Stoddards return to Shinbone for Tom's funeral, she takes a cactus rose from the earth round the burned-out addition to the ranch and places it on his coffin. It is as if she were planting it again, as if its roots, and hers, come from his very clay.

Just before Stoddard starts his tale, Ford shows Hallie opening the hat box containing the rose, but he does not show the rose actually placed on the coffin until the tale is completed. As Sarris wrote, 'From the cut from the hat box to that climactic moment nearly two hours later when we see a cactus rose on the coffin, the cinema of John Ford intersects the cinema of Orson Welles. As Hitchcock and Hawks are directors of space, Ford and Welles are directors of time.' When Stoddard notices the rose, and realizes that Hallie is still in love with Tom, the composition is as intricate as the ambiguities of his position in history: the rose is in the foreground as he moves forward in middle frame to shut the door of the coffin room, stopping when he sees the rose, with the door half-closed and Hallie's solitary figure visible in profile in the far background. Sarris again: 'Everything that Ford has ever thought or felt is compressed into one shot . . . photographed, needless to say, from the only possible angle.' As the senator closes the door on the past, the camera moves in to a close-up of the cactus rose. It is the last thing we see in Shinbone before Ford dissolves to the train leaving for the future.

The most remarkable discovery the viewer makes after close study of the film is that it is Hallie, not Tom or Ranse, who makes every important decision, even down to the nod of her head when Ranse wordlessly asks her if he should reveal the truth to the press. Although Ann Rutledge offers a close parallel in her inspiration of Lincoln's career (the reason Ford uses her theme in the scene at the burned-out ranch), it was really not until *The Quiet Man* that women's feelings and influences began to assume equal prominence in Ford's work. In the 1960s women move to centre stage (the culmination of this trend is, of course, *Seven Women*), because they stand for the urge towards civilization, and Ford's late work is concerned with the question of whether civilized values can survive in the modern world. When Valance enters the restaurant, the camera makes a sudden rush up to Hallie's face as she stops cold (recalling the shot of Lucy Edwards just before the massacre in *The Searchers*), but it is important to note that we never feel her instinctive fear of Valance as specifically a *sexual* fear. Valance is hardly capable of rape, because rape, whatever else it may be, is at least a social act. His defilement of women – such as his theft of the widow's brooch – is *symbolic* defilement, an outrage to the principles of family and community. It is a bitter irony that to save the man she wants to marry and, by extension, to preserve civilization, Hallie has to arrange for a cold-blooded murder; it recalls the dénouement of *Wagon Master*.

Like Hallie and like his predecessors in Ford's Westerns, Tom also

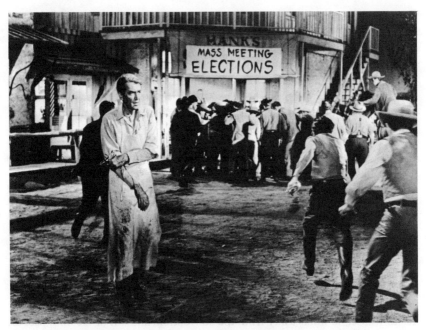

The Man Who Shot Liberty Valance: (*opposite and above*) the making of a legend

becomes a social agent through desire for a family. Ranse has ideals, but Tom's desires are more concrete. Ranse wants 'democracy', 'law' and 'statehood'. Tom simply wants Hallie. It is because his desire is so pragmatic that he is able to eliminate the physical threat of lawlessness while Ranse, the idealist, sets himself up for slaughter. But in doing away with 'Western law', Tom also destroys the only way of life he can accept, and later that night he literally tries to destroy himself in the flames of his home. As he lies on his back in the buckboard, watching the house burn, he is in the same position Valance's corpse occupied when it was driven out of town, and the position Ranse occupied when Tom brought him into Shinbone – abject, rootless and fundamentally alone. Pompey, whose presence in the film (like Stepin Fetchit's in *The Sun Shines Bright*) has more to do with its poetics than with its plot, has rescued Tom so that they can continue their primitive, sexless vagabond friendship. (When James Stewart criticized Woody Strode's costume as being 'a little Uncle Remusy', Ford snapped, 'I put that costume together – that's just what I *intended*!') American civilization has passed over the Tom Doniphons just as it passed over the blacks and the Indians.

When the Stoddards return to Shinbone for the funeral, Appleyard tells

187

them that Tom had not carried a gun for years, and he tells Hallie, in a splendid bit of historical irony, 'I guess the only one of us from the old days still workin' steady is the senator.' Tom, like Valance, was an anarchist – he told Ranse on their first meeting, 'Liberty Valance is the toughest man south of the Picketwire ... next to *me*' – but unlike Valance, who scorned women and lived 'where I hang my hat', he was an anarchist at war with himself. Manny Farber observed that Ford's casting and direction completely isolate Doniphon from the other characters:

Wayne's acting is infected by a kind of hoboish spirit, sitting back on its haunches doing a bitter-amused counterpoint to the pale, neutral film life around him ... Wayne is the termite actor focusing only on a tiny present area, nibbling at it with engaging professionalism and a hipster sense of how to sit in a chair leaned against the wall ... a craggy face filled with bitterness, jealousy, a big body that idles luxuriantly, having long grown tired with roughhouse games played by old wrangler types like John Ford.

But Ford is tired of games too. Tom's politics, such as they are, are dictated by his feelings towards Hallie: while he is courting her, he acts as chairman of the meeting to elect a delegate to the statehood convention, but after ceding her to Ranse, he walks away from the convention, and out of the film, past an anti-statehood poster. Like Ethan, he is condemned to aimless wandering. His last words to Hallie, when he sees her cradling Ranse on her breast after the shooting, are, 'I'll be around.' Our minds may flash back to another Fordian farewell – when the outlaw Tom Joad told his mother, 'I'll be all around in the dark. I'll be everywhere – wherever you look.' Doniphon will haunt Ranse and Hallie.

One of the things which makes the film so much more suggestive than its source, a Dorothy M. Johnson short story, is that Stoddard's memory of the shooting is put in a much broader context. In the story, Stoddard mulls over the events as he returns to town for the funeral, but he does not reveal the truth to anyone. Ford changed things so that Stoddard would confess the truth to society's watchdogs, the newspapermen. But the editor tears up his notes and throws them into a stove, telling Stoddard, 'This is the West, sir. When the legend becomes fact, print the legend.' His action was foreshadowed by York's lie at the end of *Fort Apache* and by a 1955 television show Ford directed, *Rookie of the Year*, in which John Wayne, playing a sportswriter, refuses to print the truth about a legendary baseball hero who has become an alcoholic. The Johnson story exposes legend as an ignoble hoax; for Stoddard to tell the truth would be a disgrace, and it would probably end his career. But in Ford's telling, the confession ennobles

Stoddard's character (the influence of Ford's Catholicism?) and allows us to see the historical process not as an absurdist comedy of errors but as a tragedy which subsumes both heroes and villains into a vast, inexorable scheme.

Ford is not suggesting that the lie has become truth – after all, as Peter Bogdanovich notes, 'Ford prints the fact' – but instead that the lie was part of history, and the *symbol* of Stoddard the hero has become a fact. Law triumphed over anarchy; the wilderness did become a garden. To expose the symbol as a lie would be to deny the meaning of history. And the public, as the ending of *Fort Apache* makes abundantly clear, would not believe it anyway. Once the historical process has been given a catalyst, it can't be stopped: that is the tragedy. And the reason Ford 'prints the fact' is to ask the public, '*Are* you proud?' On the train back East, Ranse and Hallie decide to return to the wilderness once the irrigation bill gets through Congress; in context, an impossibly naïve idea. Ranse, contented, starts to light his pipe. But he is interrupted by the pompous and effusive conductor, who presents him with a spittoon and, when thanked, replies, 'Don't you worry about that, Senator. Nothing's too good for the man who shot Liberty Valance.' The camera moves in on Ranse and Hallie. Their faces are drawn, silent and almost opaque. Stoddard blows out the flame in his hand. And then the train vanishes into history.

The Civil War

The Civil War, the middle segment of the five-part Cinerama spectacle *How the West Was Won*, is a brief sketch about a farm boy's coming of age at the battle of Shiloh. 'Ballad' is a word that often comes to mind when discussing Ford's narrative style, and it is nowhere more appropriate than here. Scarcely more than a reel in length, the episode encompasses several of his central themes – the disintegration of family, the sacrifices of war, the ambivalence of legend – with the haunting simplicity of a folk song. Like the Union marching tune 'When Johnny Comes Marching Home', heard twice on the soundtrack, *The Civil War* says little and suggests a great deal. Its lack of a reputation undoubtedly stems from the banality of the film surrounding it, an inflated, simplistic attempt at a national epic told through the experiences of a single pioneer family. The historical ambiguities latent in the screenplay by James R. Webb, who later wrote *Cheyenne Autumn*, are all but swamped by the sheer size of the production. Buffalo stampedes, Indian attacks and train wrecks careen across the three-panelled screen (it was the first story film made in Cinerama) as every Western sub-genre is hastily recapitulated.

Spencer Tracy's narration, bitter and pointed for Ford, seems otiose when spoken over the vast *National Geographic* panoramas of federal parks and game preserves which dominate the Henry Hathaway and George Marshall sections. In a movie whose *raison d'être* is extravagance, Ford keeps his scenes muted and intimate, composing mostly in counterpoint to the snake-like shape of the screen. He hated Cinerama, complaining particularly about the way the edges of the screen 'curl' in moving shots 'and the audience moves instead of the camera'. He mitigates the distortion by composing in depth, disguising his cuts, and consistently arranging things in triangular patterns: at one point he puckishly sets up his camera so that the twin pillars of a porch exactly block out the dividing lines between the panels. Ford also avoids the dislocating effect of elaborate cross-cutting in his action sequences. The Battle of Shiloh itself is evoked in a few shots of infantry charges and Cavalrymen sweeping through a river, and in the eerie image of a receding line of successively discharging cannons which opens and closes the conflict. What Ford said of his *April Morning* project, another tale of a boy's first taste of combat, could also be applied to *The Civil War*: 'It's not really a battle story, it's a character sketch.'

Describing Ford as a Civil War 'buff' is a considerable understatement; indeed, he once told Gavin Lambert, presumably with tongue in cheek, that it was the principal interest in his life, with movies secondary. Dan Ford recalled that on an evening drive outside Washington, D.C., his grandfather had been sitting quietly for nearly an hour when he suddenly remarked, 'Lee must have had a hell of a time getting his troops through these swamps.' And William Clothier said, 'I have never, in all my life, met any man who knew as much about the history of the Civil War as John Ford. He can tell you the name of every general who was in the Union Army and the Southern Army. He is absolutely familiar with every piece of wardrobe that was worn by troops in the Civil War. When we would go on location – for instance, on *The Horse Soldiers*, which was a Civil War film – Mr Ford would have a box of books which was larger than his wardrobe.' In light of this, it is odd that Ford never made a full-scale film about a major incident of the war. *The Horse Soldiers* is about a secret Cavalry mission far behind Confederate lines; *The Prisoner of Shark Island* is about Dr Samuel Mudd, the man who set John Wilkes Booth's leg; *Judge Priest* contains a magnificent Griffith-like flash-back to Gettysburg. For the most part, though, the Yankees and Confederates who wander throughout Ford's films are living the war only in their memories.

Pressed on this point in our interview, Ford testily came up with the rather evasive answer that it was difficult to find a story to hinge his ideas on. Perhaps what he really meant was that the Civil War was such utter chaos –

The Civil War: the assassination attempt (Russ Tamblyn, George Peppard)

brother against brother, the nation ripping itself apart – that he was unable to sort out his feelings and ideas about it into a coherent pattern, as he had done with the Indian Wars and World War II. Ford's Shiloh battlefield is a landscape out of a horror film. The events of 6 April 1862, 'the bloodiest day of the war on the Western front', are depicted as the grotesque fragments of a national nightmare. A ghastly cloud of quicklime rises into the night sky as a huge grave is dug for a mound of corpses; Private Zeb Rawlings (George Peppard) stares into a river running pink with blood, unaware that moments earlier his own father had been pronounced dead on an improvised operating table as red and slimy as a butcher's block; Zeb saves General Ulysses S. Grant (Harry Morgan) from a freakish assassination attempt by killing a new-found friend, an impulsive Confederate deserter (Russ Tamblyn).

It is probably not coincidental that Shiloh was the battle Ford's Uncle Mike was mustered into when he climbed off the boat from Ireland and was tricked into the Union Army; at Shiloh Uncle Mike deserted (as the Confederate tempts Zeb to do) and joined up with the South. Tracy narrates over the digging of the mass grave: 'In the morning, it had looked like a Confederate victory. But by nightfall, no man cared to use the words "win" or "lose".' As in *They Were Expendable* and *Fort Apache*, Ford takes the nation's worst catastrophe as his metaphor for the general conflict. Philippe Haudiquet has commented:

War, with its sound and fury, may provide Ford with spectacle – deployment of troops, alignment of artillery pieces, Cavalry charges – but he regards it as nothing less than the most frightful butchery. He is not content with showing troops being decimated, ripped up with machine-gun fire, he takes us into the worst part of the battlefield, the field hospital. He shows operations taking place under bombardment (*They Were Expendable*), amputations being made without anesthesia (*The Horse Soldiers*), young soldiers dying . . . In *The Civil War* . . . such scenes, brief, dense, and presented in their logical order, give us the most exact image of war.

Ford characteristically interweaves great and small actions, private conflict and national destiny, in developing his microcosm of the war. Zeb's confusion ('It ain't quite what I *expected* – there ain't much glory in lookin' at a man with his guts hangin' out') is mirrored by Grant's torment over the charges of incompetence laid on him in the aftermath of Shiloh. The South caught him by surprise, and only Sherman's intervention and Confederate disorganization prevented a total rout. Grant temporarily lost his command when the news of his casualties and his alleged drunkenness during the battle reached Washington, and the spectre of Shiloh was to plague him to the end of his days. In his *Memoirs* Grant recalled, 'Up to the Battle of Shiloh, I, as well as thousands of others, believed that the rebellion against the government would collapse swiftly and soon, if a decisive victory could be gained over any of its armies.' Shiloh destroyed that certainty just as surely as it destroys the young soldier's delusion that the war will be a brief, glorious adventure. With his predilection for showing 'what really happened', Ford re-creates a celebrated passage from the *Memoirs* in a few biting images:

Some time after midnight, growing restive under the storm and the continuous pain, I moved back to the log-house under the bank. This had been taken as a hospital, and all night wounded men were being brought in, their wounds dressed, a leg or an arm amputated as the case might require, and everything being done to save life or alleviate suffering. The sight was more unendurable than encountering the enemy's fire, and I returned to my tree in the rain.

Ford's only licence is to replace the rain with a hideous, ink-black darkness, lit only by torches bobbing in the extreme background or flashing past the camera in the extreme foreground.

The Civil War is prefaced with premonitions – a shadowy tableau of Lincoln (Raymond Massey) staring out of the window of his Illinois law office, contemplating the future; and a brief glimpse of a secessionist riot in a border town. From this noisy, lurid encounter, Ford dissolves to an almost unnaturally placid long shot of a majestic colonnade of trees, an endless corridor of tranquillity, as Corporal Peterson (Andy Devine) slowly approaches the camera in a carriage. Mindlessly humming 'The Battle Hymn of the Republic', he is as ignorant of the future as the boy he is coming to tempt away from home. There is a vague foreboding, too, in the surreal calm of the Rawlings farm: in the vast field, the distant view of a broad river, the warm browns and whites of the family's clothing which clash so disturbingly with the gaudy colours of the corporal's uniform. Peterson's message to Zeb – 'There ain't much glory in trompin' behind a plow' – is later given a grisly echo in Zeb's words on the battlefield.

Inevitably for Ford, it is the mother (Carroll Baker) who realizes what the future holds. Her grief over Zeb's departure finds expression in a few simple gestures. Holding a long black cloth, she tenderly adjusts the lapels of his ludicrously undersized dress suit. Grasping his shoulder, she averts her eyes. When he leaves, she wanders over to the fence enclosing her parents' graves, tries to pray, and slumps to the ground, her head sinking below the railing and only her arm, with the black cloth, trailing behind. Zeb himself is tragically unaware of the meaning of his actions. Ford frames him in silhouette from inside the home, like Ethan in *The Searchers*; like Ethan he is governed by forces he cannot comprehend. Seen through the doorway, he bounds off the porch, shouting 'Yahoo!' and kicking his legs like a schoolboy. But then, just as suddenly, he spins round and stares after his mother, who is disappearing into the darkness of the home. This dim intimation of the future soon fades from his mind, however, and we see him walking down the colonnade of trees, telling his dog to go back home. His jaunty step is belied by the ghostly chorus of 'When Johnny Comes Marching Home' echoing like a dirge on the soundtrack.

When he returns home from war we hear the same tune, now loud and buoyant, but belied again, this time by the solitude which greets him ('We'll all be there when Johnny comes marching home'): the gravestones of his mother and father have joined those of his grandparents. The first glimpse of his younger brother, Jeremiah, carries a subtle remembrance of Shiloh. As Zeb stands at the graves in the extreme background, Jeremiah tosses a pail full of water from the porch, and the long graceful arc it makes in the sunlight recalls the macabre image of the bucket routinely sloshing down the bloody operating table in the field hospital after their father's death. Zeb is the prototypical American, for despite his experience at war and the war's decimation of his family (or *because* of it), he must still keep pushing towards the territory ... as a Cavalryman fighting the Indian Wars.

The Civil War: General Sherman and General Grant (John Wayne, Harry Morgan)

His motive for re-enlistment is no more than rootlessness. Imitating his father's voice, Zeb tells Jeremiah their father's story about how he killed a bear because 'I wanted to go somewhere, and the bear got there first', and adds, 'I just wanta go somewhere too.' This is a tragic submission to the ethos of 'manifest destiny', which is about to rekindle another civil war, this time between whites and Indians. When Zeb rises from the porch at the end, resplendent in his military cape, he momentarily strikes a classic heroic pose, head back, leg cocked at an imperious angle. After Zeb disappears (and the dog, symbol of his childhood, slinks away), Ford holds on the agrarian life he and the nation have left behind: a tableau of the porch, with a tree limb bobbing gently in the brilliant sunlight at the far corner of the frame, as his brother, chagrined and wasted, bows his head in mourning.

The bizarre chain of accidents which has allowed Private Rawlings to save Grant – and, by extension, the Army and the country itself – has the same fateful grandeur which elevates the gunfight in *Liberty Valance* into the realm of national myth. Ford was fascinated by the ambiguities of Grant's position in history and tried without success to raise interest in a film biography. There are tantalizing fragments of the unmade film, however, in *The Colter Craven Story*, an episode he directed for Ward Bond's television series *Wagon Train* in 1960.

Bond tells Grant's story (seen in flashback) to another drunkard, a doctor who lost his nerve at Gettysburg, in order to steel him for an operation. Most of the scenes with Grant centre on the way he doggedly regains his self-respect after leaving the Army and returning to his Illinois home; particularly memorable is a haunting long shot of his wife and two sons waiting on a shadowy street corner as he alights from a steamboat. Incredibly, the flashback ends with Grant's worst disgrace – Shiloh. In Ford's view, the fact that a disgraced drunkard has risen to become a disgraced general carries a logic above and beyond the individual's feelings; in a peculiar way, the higher disgrace has a nobility all its own. Grant's image, like Senator Stoddard's in *Liberty Valance*, has the ability to survive any tarnishing or exposure, because it means more than the man behind it. In *The Colter Craven Story*, the disillusioned Grant is given a new sense of mission when Bond meets him by chance at Shiloh and discovers that his old friend 'Sam' Grant and General Ulysses S. Grant are one and the same man. In *The Civil War*, Grant looks strangely composed and very small beside the wildly dishevelled Sherman (played, as in *The Colter Craven Story*, by John Wayne), who talks him out of resigning.

Grant wants to quit not so much because of the battle itself, which both men agree was not entirely his fault, but because of the effect it will have on his image – because of 'the general lack of confidence in me' created by newspaper correspondents who are always writing that he has been drunk even when he has not, just to build up the legend. Sherman ridicules Grant's notion in a speech which surely reflects Ford's own attitude: 'A month ago they were saying I was crazy, insane. Now they're calling me a hero. Hero or crazy, I'm the same man. Doesn't matter what the people think. It's what *you* think, Grant.' Yet in a sense it *does* matter what the people think, although it matters less to the generals than to the people themselves.

As the generals talk, Zeb and the rebel deserter eavesdrop behind them; what happens in the foreground of history cannot ultimately be separated from what happens in the background. When Sherman speaks Grant's name, the rebel (who moments before had passed up a chance to kill Zeb, arguing that 'Westerners' should stay out of an 'Eastern' war) raises his pistol. It is as if the revelation of Grant's identity, and the myth which surrounds it, has suddenly galvanized the rebel into a recognition of his own role in history. His movements are zombie-like; he is no longer an individual. And when Zeb strikes down his friend's hand and bayonets him, he too is acceding to his role. It is at this moment that the horror of war takes hold of Zeb. Dropping the bayonet, he grasps his friend's inert body and shakes it madly, demanding, 'Why did you make me *do* that?' Moments before, he had been ready to join the rebel (and Grant) in desertion. But desertion would have implied nothing less than that he quit the stage of history. The role has consumed the man.

9. The Last Place on Earth: *Seven Women* (1966)

Until quite late in his career, Ford's view of women was relatively uncomplicated. They were the source of stability, the passers-on of tradition, civilization and growth. In *How Green Was My Valley*, Huw says of his family, 'If my father was the head of our house, my mother was its heart.' The women were the ideal, simple, pure and all but untouchable; they stayed close to their dominion, the home, and mostly let the men take care of the complex and disturbing outside world. The 'fallen' women in Ford's films, the saloon girls and prostitutes, are, if anything, even more saintly than the home women, because their longing for a home is so acute. This limited compass did not prevent Ford from creating a vivid gallery of female performances. Margaret Mann in *Four Sons*, Claire Trevor in *Stagecoach*, Edna May Oliver in *Drums Along the Mohawk*, Sara Allgood in *How Green Was My Valley*, Donna Reed in *They Were Expendable*, Anna Lee in *Fort Apache*, Mildred Natwick in *Three Godfathers* and Joanne Dru in *Wagon Master* are as memorable as any of his male characters from the period.

There *was* a sub-species of Fordian woman which never received much attention because it seldom reached centre stage. This is the puritanical old biddy type, most strikingly represented by the hawk-faced Ladies' Law and Order League which ran Dallas out of town in *Stagecoach*; the attentive

197

A streak of misogyny: feminine discomfort in a scene cut from *Cheyenne Autumn*

viewer may also recall seeing gaggles of cackling women hanging outside the saloons in other Ford Westerns to jeer when a drunk came flying through the door. Between this extreme of malevolence and the heroines' extreme state of piety there was almost nothing until, in the 1950s, Ford began to acknowledge and systematically explore some of the unattractive aspects of his heroines' superhuman tenacity and determination – aspects he had touched on in the amazingly anomalous *Pilgrimage*, with its remarkable performance by Henrietta Crosman as the possessive mother. (If *Pilgrimage* is the exception which proves the rule in Ford's earlier period, it also exemplifies the rule by having the mother take on a surrogate son in atonement for causing her own son's death.) The reassessment began with his ambivalent treatment of Mary Kate's fanatical insistence on a dowry in *The Quiet Man*, and escalated with his revelation of Laurie's racism in *The Searchers*.

What makes Ford's work in the 1960s so moving is his courage in trying to come to terms with problems he had tended to simplify or evade in the past; a desire to cut through long-accepted dogmas and traditions to find out 'what really happened'. One need only compare Hallie in *Liberty Valance* with her earlier counterpart, Ann Rutledge in *Young Mr Lincoln*, to see how disillusioned Ford was becoming with the woman's traditional role as catalyst for the man's ambitions. All of which should make it clear that *Seven Women*, although unquestionably a departure for Ford, is not the complete aberration many critics have claimed. It is instructive to compare two statements Ford made about the film. To Peter Bogdanovich he said, 'It was a good switch for me, to turn around and make a picture all about women.' In the interview for this book, he said, 'I've directed women before.' As usual with Ford, the truth lies somewhere in between.

If there is one characteristic common to all Ford's heroines, it is this: they suffer. Their children leave home, their husbands are killed, their homes are burned. If they are single, they struggle to keep their men from leaving or neglecting them; if they are prostitutes, they are humiliated; if they are queens, they are beheaded. One could almost describe Ford's obsession with feminine suffering as a streak of misogyny. 'I always want to make the leading lady fall down on her derrière,' he said once. But every idealist is prone to dwell on the subversion of his ideal, and Ford more so than most. One of his leading ladies recently described him as the most perverse man she had ever met. What rescues Ford's view of women from being merely sentimental is his willingness, even eagerness, to acknowledge the contradictions implicit in his, and their idealism, by bringing it face-to-face with the most unpleasant reality.

Schematization is an occupational weakness of critics, but it is hard not to see *Seven Women* (a film without a hero) as the logical end-point of Ford's attitudes towards civilization, just as *Liberty Valance* was of his attitudes towards history. The entire film takes place in and around the tiny mission (one is tempted to write 'fort') which the women have erected in the most alien landscape the American mind could conceive, China in 1935, during a period of civil war. As one of the women puts it, they are in 'the last place on earth'.

Robin Wood was not the first critic to find *Seven Women* 'eccentric', but he was the first to attempt to situate his objections in the context of Ford's *oeuvre*:

The essence of the film is a thinly concealed nihilism. The lack of real religious feeling in Ford prevents him from finding any transcendent spiritual values in the missionaries and their work; any positive belief in the mission as a community, or as an epitome of civilization, is made nonsense of by its futility, by its inner tensions and outer ineffectuality.

Wood is correct when he observes that the mission is 'nonsense' as a community. It is in fact the *reductio ad absurdum* of the communal ethic, for everything which could threaten its stability – irreligion, sexuality, violence,

Seven Women: the mission set

dissent, any kind of instinctual behaviour – has been walled out. This is the exact inverse, for Ford, of a true religious community, the kind he portrayed in *Wagon Master*. What enables the Mormons to survive is their social adaptability, their openness to the outside world, concretely expressed in the metaphor of their desert journey. To emphasize the unnaturalness of the group's isolation in *Seven Women*, Ford shoots the film in a hermetically sealed studio set with only a few glimpses of the world outside that the women are trying to ignore. The perverse thing about these missionaries is that, in their lust for purity, they have constructed a sanctuary which all but invites attack. Just as Ethan's odyssey in *The Searchers* becomes a parody of a heroic quest, the mission in *Seven Women* becomes a parody of civilization: the ideals which gave it birth have turned into a stale, joyless repetition of form which collapses in its first confrontation with the world it is supposed to contain.

By the time of *Seven Women*, Wood alleges, Ford had acknowledged 'the disintegration of everything he had believed in', using the missionaries as symbols of the decay of traditional values in the face of modern reality. This is a subtle distortion which falsifies the film. Ford *had* lost his faith in the permanence of social structures, but that faith was always tenuous at best. He had not lost his faith in human nature. The character of Dr D. R. Cartwright (Anne Bancroft) embodies everything Ford believed in: candour, compassion, moral commitment, defiance of hypocrisy, sacrifice. She is also completely alone, utterly rootless, far more radically estranged from society than Ethan or Tom Doniphon. The fact that she is a woman makes her solitude, for Ford, all the more terrible and all the more heroic. *Seven Women* superficially seems to turn its back on the ideals of community and tradition which had always animated his work, but it is precisely our sense of the *loss* of these values which makes the doctor's sacrifice so important; this sense of loss coupled with her rekindling and passing on of communal values in the last part of the film.

What *Seven Women* ultimately affirms is the necessity of individual integrity in the face of nihilism. It is difficult to speak of such values today without sounding platitudinous; Robin Wood, like many other critics, does a much better job of defining what Ford is against than of defining what he is for. Ford reacted with characteristic bluntness when Bogdanovich asked him why the doctor sacrifices herself for the others: 'She was a doctor – her object in life was to save people. She was a woman who had no religion, but she got in with this bunch of kooks and started acting like a human being.' E. M. Forster, who, like Ford, found the complexities of the twentieth century alarming and insoluble, could have been describing Dr Cartwright when he wrote of Margaret Schlegel, the heroine of *Howards End*:

She was not a Christian in the accepted sense; she did not believe that God had ever worked among us as a young artisan ... But in public who shall express the unseen adequately? It is private life that holds out the mirror to infinity; personal intercourse, and that alone, that ever hints at a personality beyond our daily vision.

This is the kind of humanistic 'religion' Ford postulates in *Seven Women*.

Probably more damaging to the film's reception than the objection articulated by Wood was the uneasiness most critics felt about the reason for the Chinese setting. The bandits who erupt into the mission have been seen as the worst Caucasian fantasies about Oriental life running wild. To see the film as an anti-Communist or anti-Oriental tract, however, is to seriously misread its emphasis. Politics is at most a peripheral issue in the film, even though it takes place during a civil war, for it is not stated what faction the bandits belong to, or even if they belong to one at all. They are just bandits. The one specific political reference in the film is the brief scene in which the mission leader pleads with the retreating Republican Army command not to leave the district in the control of the bandits; here Ford is clearly holding to the conservative line that once established authority breaks down, chaos is sure to follow. The overriding political meaning to the film, however, is simply a revulsion against the lawlessness engendered by war, a lawlessness whose evil transcends questions of faction or ideology: the first action the bandits take on entering the mission is to slay another Chinese, and later that night they herd together a bunch of Chinese refugees and shoot them all – men, women and children. The prologue to the film puts it clearly: this is 'a time of lawlessness and violence'.

This is the context; now to the drama. The real conflict of the film is not between the women and the bandits but among the women themselves, just as the real drama of Ford's cavalry films is not between the cavalry and the Indians but within the cavalry. The mission's founder and director, Agatha Andrews (Margaret Leighton), underscores the Fordian parallel between religion and militarism when Dr Cartwright challenges her authority: 'Everyone who joined this mission enlisted in a war. They are soldiers, Dr Cartwright, soldiers in the Army of the Lord.' Militant religious leaders are, of course, commonplace in Ford, ranging in degree of fanaticism from John Carradine's saintly Preacher in *The Grapes of Wrath* to Arthur Shields' minister in *Drums Along the Mohawk*, who offers a prayer to the 'God of battles' and later collapses in horror when he is forced actually to kill a man. Miss Andrews' closest counterparts, however, are the members of the Ladies' Law and Order League in *Stagecoach*.

Following the ominous shots of the bandit cavalry gathering and charging behind the credits, Ford delineates the political hierarchy within the mission in a cleverly executed theatrical tableau. The camera pauses on the quietly ironic inscription over the gate ('Unified Christian Missions Educational Society' – 'Unified' rather than 'United') and then follows Miss Andrews' car into the courtyard as she returns from a medical mission. A Chinese servant boy bows to her, and she haughtily accepts the tribute. The only male on the mission staff, Pether (Eddie Albert), and his pregnant wife Florrie (Betty Field), watch anxiously from a porch on the left; to the right, with a group of boys, is Miss Argent (Mildred Dunnock), Miss Andrews' obsequious second-in-command; and in the centre, beneath a tree, is her favourite, the young and pretty Emma Clark (Sue Lyon), with a group of girls. Miss Andrews ignores the others and sweeps over to Emma, dispensing a bagful of tangerines to her girls. The Pethers worriedly ask when Florrie's doctor will arrive, and Miss Andrews fobs them off. Miss Argent follows worshipfully behind her as she goes in to read a letter from 'headquarters'.

In this brief sequence, Ford has sketched in the dramatic situation with the fluency and precision of a symphonist stating his principal themes. And we

Seven Women: Anne Bancroft as Dr Cartwright

Seven Women: a leader apart (Margaret Leighton, Mildred Dunnock, Eddie Albert, Betty Field, Sue Lyon)

have perceived the levels of conflict through the eyes of Miss Andrews, who, it is gradually revealed, is the source of that conflict. These seemingly random encounters are elaborated throughout the film. Miss Andrews, who fears and despises men, proves to have barely repressed lesbian tendencies towards Emma. The menopausal pregnancy becomes increasingly threatening. The subtle barriers of condescension separating the missionaries from the Chinese become more pronounced. And even the tangerines, Miss Andrews' perishable token of affection, turn up in the hands of the lecherous bandit leader, Tunga Khan (Mike Mazurki), as he waits in Miss Andrews' office for the subjugation of Dr Cartwright.

The mission is a cul de sac, yet at first, since Miss Andrews is our only point of reference, we tend to accept her viewpoint. She is certainly the only one of the group who can function in the outside world; it is significant that she is also a doctor of sorts, and that she *enters* the mission in the opening scene. Only gradually do we sense that the mission is a narcissistic reflection of its leader. Pether is seen lecturing a class of Chinese children. Filmed from the back, waving his arms, he is completely oblivious to his audience, almost ecstatic: 'God spake, my child. God spake to *thee*! I will thy God and Father be.' Ford intercuts this impassioned sermon with a huge close-up of a bewildered, cross-eyed Chinese boy struggling vainly to understand the words. It is a marvellous moment, a bitter, desperate joke as black as something out of Beckett. Miss Andrews, who has been watching through the window, enters to reprove Pether for his foolishness. His reply is tragic: 'I want so much to *reach* them.' We have regarded Pether as foolish only because we have accepted the Andrews frame of reference. His passion at least indicates a commitment, however absurd. To Miss Andrews, the children probably *are* hopeless, ugly and unreachable. Given time, Pether might achieve something.

But his passion, like all true passion, disturbs the mission leader. The atmosphere of self-denial and repression she has fostered in her image is conveyed in the musty settings Ford provides for the early scenes: the squared-off, dusty courtyard and its painted sky; the huge fan monotonously operated by a Chinese servant as Miss Andrews pompously dismisses the threat of violence ('This bandit, this . . . Tunga Khan as you call him, wouldn't dare to molest us – we are American citizens'); the washed-out browns and oranges of the walls and the costumes; the muted glow of the lanterns filtering through the latticed bamboo curtains as the women sit for supper (the table scenes invariably begin with a full shot from the same angle – looking towards Miss Andrews at the head of the table in the background – to express what in another Ford film we would call their traditional nature); and the mosquito netting which veils Emma's bed, Sternberg-like, as Miss Andrews enters her room and, in close-up, surreptitiously inspects the girl's half-naked body.

This shot of Miss Andrews in Emma's doorway – accompanied by a delicate, tristful theme from Elmer Bernstein's superb score – is as startling a revelation as the minister's glimpse of Martha fondling the cape in *The Searchers*. In a flash, Ford unveils the mission's façade of order. This cultivated, chaste woman, who holds the mission together purely by the force of her will, cannot control or even admit to her own suppressed instincts. Margaret Leighton's performance, one of the finest in all of Ford's work, perfectly captures the tragic contradictions implicit in religious fanaticism. Her gaunt, attenuated body, rigidly cloaked in severe brown and grey gowns, moves with a sensual restlessness. She is continually touching herself, and her large animal eyes alternately fix on the person she is addressing or on a vague point somewhere out of frame, while at the same time her head makes little jerking movements in the opposite direction. When she enters Emma's room, her hands compulsively wander over the girl's hair, twisting it in little spasmodic motions. It is as if she is possessed by her corporeality.

The Rabelaisian Dr Cartwright, on the other hand, takes perverse, i.e. Fordian, delight in outraging the prim missionaries with her blasphemy and

Seven Women: Dr Cartwright shocks the missionaries

(worse) her drinking and smoking and (worst) her tales of sexual adventure. She is the last in the long and honourable line of drunken Ford doctors; hers is a 'religion' in which instinct is not suppressed but used as a tool for understanding. It is worth noting that in *Donovan's Reef*, Ford's vision of earthly paradise (and in many ways an inverse of the Orient portrayed in *Seven Women*), the missionary has a ramshackle church and a congregation which seems to assemble only at Christmas, while the doctor is the most respected man in the community, a selfless, indefatigable worker whose retinue includes a congregation of nuns. Dr Cartwright makes her first appearance in long-shot, riding a horse through the mission gate. Off-camera, Emma is leading her girls in a song. The doctor dismounts, still in long-shot, and Ford cuts to a close-up of the back of her head as she stands surveying the mission. She turns round with a wry smile, shocking the missionaries, who were expecting a man. Pether has to reassure his wife with, 'She's as good as any man, Florrie'; the doctor snaps back, 'Better!'

Like Miss Andrews, Dr Cartwright has left America because of men; because of her failure to succeed in a man's profession and because she was jilted by a married man. That she is so obviously a man's woman, at home with her sexuality, gives her voluntary chastity and her eventual subjugation by Khan, the ultimate male chauvinist, an added sting. But there is also a certain pose of masculine swagger to her character. In her cowboy hat, boots, chaps and leather coat, she is a sort of female Ethan Edwards, fleeing civilization and the opposite sex. The film's most complex and unsettling dramatic interchange has Dr Cartwright and Miss Andrews sitting under a tree on the night Emma's life has been saved from the plague. The doctor speaks to the missionary about motherhood (the voice of purest Ford), but she is speaking to herself as well: 'You know, Andrews, you should have married. Had sons. Shared their problems. That's real living.' In the film's largest close-up – indeed, one of the most intimate shots in Ford's work – Miss Andrews stares into the darkness and, for once, candidly shares her torment with another person: 'I've always searched for something that . . . isn't there. And God isn't enough. [*Whispers*] God help me. He – isn't enough.'

The two women could hardly be less alike in attitude and demeanour, yet they eventually prove to be flip sides of the same coin. Both professionals, highly competent within their own spheres; both charismatic and strong-willed; both exiles from male society, they bring out the truth in each other because they both follow their independence to the extreme. Both are attracted to Emma, the most innocent and vulnerable of the group, because she represents the future. Miss Andrews wants to possess her and reshape her in her own image; Dr Cartwright wants to free her from illusion and constraint ('There's a real world outside . . . go and find it') by passing on the lessons she has learned from experience. The authority crisis is actually precipitated before the bandits' arrival, when Miss Andrews begins to feel her hold loosening on Emma (although one can trace its germination even further, to the beginning of Florrie's pregnancy). Richard Thompson described the terms of the conflict thus:

The final forceful intrusion of life is effected as all the women, cramped into a 12 × 12 room, are forced to watch a baby born . . . If Dr Cartwright seems more sympathetic, it is because the Fordian vision is partial to emotions and actions drawn from real life rather than to intellectual responses founded on theory . . . Bancroft has the necessary equipment for sacrifice: a grasp of the situation, humanity, heroic quality. On the other hand, the missionary ladies have no past, no future, no men or children or home – in Ford's terms, nothing to sacrifice. Bancroft is alive, whereas the missionary ladies have forfeited the changes and rewards of life for the monotonous security of the mission. The ladies know only the abstract, but Bancroft's experience with people is universal and adaptable.

The inexperienced Emma becomes the barometer with which the two leaders measure the effect of their conflict. Ford's choice of the nymphet from *Lolita* to play Emma is a revealing one, for though Sue Lyon sometimes

Seven Women: Dr Cartwright and Emma

embarrassingly overdoes the character's callowness (Ford's direction of youngsters is often heavy-handed), her pubescent shapeliness makes her missionary role seem doubly perverse. Miss Andrews, quickly sensing the girl's admiration for the doctor (a compliment on her bobbed hair), warns Emma that the doctor is 'evil'. Yet as Emma watches her coolly taking charge during the series of crises, she loses all respect for Miss Andrews. It is Emma, significantly, who witnesses the massacre of the Chinese and runs screaming out of the hut towards the bandits. When the doctor brings her back inside, Emma says, 'Dr Cartwright, now I know what evil *really* is' – and we hear a woman's scream and a rifle shot off-camera. Driven mad by the loss of her illusions, of her authority, and of Emma, Miss Andrews paces the hut like a caged animal as Dr Cartwright prepares to trade herself to Khan for the others' safety. When the missionary watches the doctor quietly assuming the martyrdom she might have wished for herself, we see her face in a sudden close-up, irretrievably deranged, bathed in raw orange light as if in a parody of religious ecstasy and illumination.

Throughout the first half of the film, Ford had kept his frames drained of bright colour. Then, when the violence from the outside world begins to make itself felt, harsh tones, mostly emanating from Ford's familiar metaphor for anarchy – fire – begin to intrude. When the refugees arrive, bringing in the cholera, two torches flash past, seen through the bamboo curtains in Miss Andrews' office. She rolls up the curtain to see what is happening. Then it is the purifying fire into which Pether and the servants cast the clothing infected by the plague. The flames give off a strange exhausted glow, like leaves in autumn, as Pether slumps to his knees, hands clasped in supplication. Later he and Dr Cartwright are startled by a distant conflagration lighting up the night sky; it is the nearby town, set to torch by the bandits. Ford does not show the burning town. Instead, he shows only the hideous sheet of orange flame rising over the mission wall; then he keeps the camera on the two faces as the light plays over them. Dr Cartwright wears a smile of fatalistic exhilaration, and Pether – who had earlier answered the doctor's warnings by intoning, 'Though He slay me, yet will I trust Him' – now realizes the full depth of their predicament: 'What kind of a man was I to get my wife pregnant at a time like this?' Like the foolish husband in *Three Godfathers*, he will die off-screen, leaving his wife and new-born child at the mercy of the unknown.

The bandits execute the Chinese by torchlight and amuse themselves by staging a brutal wrestling match within a ring of torches, a grotesque twist on Ford's traditional masculine slugging rituals. It is all being done to impress Dr Cartwright; and as Richard Thompson observes, the bandits' battle over their prize is presented in political terms, as a struggle for power within their group. Flaunting his virility, the subaltern (Woody Strode, Ford's triple-threat primitive man, adding a Chinese to his earlier portrayals of black and Indian) is challenged by the ageing but still powerful leader. As Khan rises, he strips the silk shirt from his flabby, simian torso and tosses it lewdly into the lap of the doctor, who flings it contemptuously off in the same motion. After an exchange of horrifying close-ups of the stranglehold, Khan literally breaks the neck of his opponent, and the flunkies carry the corpse off on their shoulders like a slab of meat. Anticipating Robin Wood's observation that the bandits are not three-dimensional characters, Andrew Sarris wrote: 'They are the worst kind of males the female psyche can envisage. These rampaging males wander around the countryside raping, killing, plundering, and worst of all, smashing all the windows, furniture, and bric-à-brac. They affront every canon of order imposed upon the male by the female since the beginning of time.'

Ford characteristically adds a humorous overtone, however slight, to the bandits' stunted behaviour. Tunga Khan pauses from his looting when he finds a rocking-chair on the mission porch, wondrously rocking it back and forth with his foot in a dim remembrance of infancy (cf. Mose Harper in *The Searchers*); and discovering that Mrs Pether is pregnant, the bandits group round her in childlike awe until Tunga Khan prompts them into disturbing hoots of adolescent ridicule. The bandits represent the ultimate decadence of Ford's traditional chivalric ethic, just as the missionaries represent the decadence of the home ethic: the only alternative is to be found in the person who stands aloof from both, performing a 'man's job' but retaining her sense of compassion. In fact, the ideal Ford protagonist.

The flames of the earlier scenes are finally contained in the lamp with which Dr Cartwright resolutely moves through the corridor of the darkened mission to her final tryst with Khan. Totally isolated, darkness masking the wide screen all round her in a spectacular vignette effect, she is wearing a dazzling kimono, a mockery of her former freedom but also a mockery of Khan. Ford has spent the entire film preparing us for this moment of poetry: as he said in an interview, 'I tried to keep the film down to a monotone, to start, and later on, when the girl put on the kimono, I went into rather vivid colour for a sudden change.' To the crazed Andrews, the deal with Khan is an unspeakable humiliation: 'He only wants her because she's white and he's yellow.' But the doctor is strangely liberated by her dual role as concubine and conqueror; in it, she carries the consequences of her individualism to their logical end. When Khan proposed his deal, her reaction was a moment of dead silence, an astonished beginning of a smile and an almost imperceptible tilt of the head, as if to say, 'What the hell.' She goes to get her medical bag, sees herself reflected in a mirror, shakes her head and laughs.

Waiting for release, the other women (but for Miss Andrews, who is still pacing the floor) gather round the baby and sing a Nativity hymn. Miss Argent, in revery, chants of a world of vanished order: 'I was dreaming. I dreamt it was Thanksgiving Day and I was a child, helping my Aunt Mildred cut faces in the pumpkins.' The others reminisce with her. The viewer may recall the scene in Bergman's *The Shame*, during another war, in which the antique collector fondles a musical ornament. Like the women's song and memories, it is (to quote Robin Wood) 'useless, artificial, unjustifiable in a world where people starve to death, are tortured, persecuted, massacred; yet by virtue of its very uselessness embodying the concept of civilization in its purest form'.

Religious dogma has never been less comforting in Ford than at the end of *Seven Women*, but a note of childlike faith is sustained through Miss Binns (Flora Robson), who is unlike Miss Andrews' group in several other ways: she is of another denomination (occasioning condescension from Miss Andrews), she is British, and she defends Dr Cartwright for sleeping with Khan. She speaks for Ford when she tells the others that 'Dr Cartwright has taken an oath to preserve human life', and the director places great stress on her reaction to Florrie's despairing cry, 'Who will provide for us now?': in close-up, with perfect composure, she replies, 'God will provide for us all.'

Her tangential relationship to the mission community allows her to detach herself and transcend the others' pettiness and hysteria. And she provides an intriguing balance in the struggle between Dr Cartwright and Miss Andrews over Emma, because she, like Emma, was born in China to missionary parents, and *her* mission is presented not as unnatural but as humane, realistic and serene. Yet like all Fordian women, she has a deep longing for a home: when the others talk about Christmas, she muses, 'But I've never seen it. I've never been home to England – never been out of China.' And then the recurring refrain in Ford's last films, 'Some day, I –' She never finishes the sentence.

The transference of authority which has occurred between Miss Andrews and Dr Cartwright closely resembles that between Thursday and York in *Fort Apache*, but with an important difference. The martinet commander of the fort/mission, failing to acknowledge the potency of the enemy (the Indians, the bandits), loses command to the rebellious realist. Only this time, there is no covering up the commander's mistake for the sake of posterity, because posterity seems a doubtful proposition at best as the women and the child ('a boy, if you're interested,' as the doctor says) ride their cart into the fire-lit night. And this time, the commander cannot summon up the grace and historical vision to salvage order by apologizing to the group. Miss Andrews, in the cart, is jabbering about the doctor being the Mother of Harlots; her dissolution is complete when the meek Miss Argent tells her what she can do with herself.

Paradoxically, it is the agnostic Dr Cartwright who is able to offer a spiritual consolation to Miss Argent, when she realizes that the doctor is going to take poison to preserve her independence. 'Don't,' Miss Argent begs. 'Please don't, it's a sin, it's a sin against God, it's a sin.' The doctor replies simply, 'Then pray for me.' Miss Argent leaves and then, with a sudden influx of sympathy, returns to hold her in a long embrace, Ford keeping the scene in an unbroken two-shot to express their natural, if irrational, communion. The doctor's hand remains outstretched for a long moment as Miss Argent moves out of the room. It is one of the most poignant of all Fordian farewells, and it is quickly followed by his bleakest vision of destruction. Inside Miss Andrews' office, the doctor gives Tunga Khan a cup of poisoned tea, saying, 'So long, you bastard.' She waits for him to fall, takes a drink herself and hurls down the cup. The camera pulls rapidly away, the lights round her dimming to the keening of a saxophone. She has surrendered herself to a destiny neither she nor the audience can foresee. We do not even know if the people she has freed will be able to reach safety. She herself, by their standards, is damned. She has neither the consolations of history nor the consolations of eternity, only her presence in the memory of those who knew her.

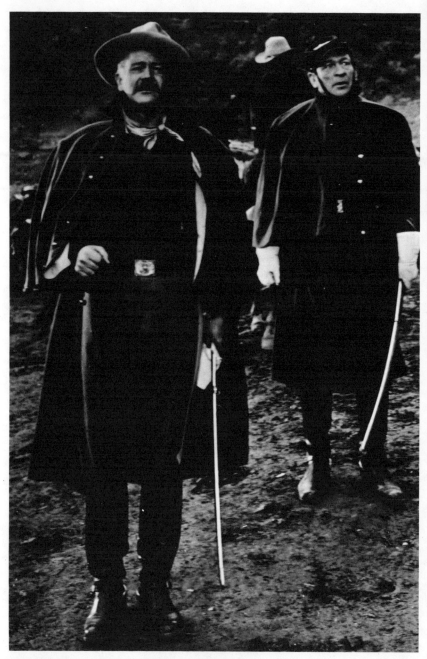

She Wore a Yellow Ribbon (John Wayne, Victor McLaglen)

Filmography

John Ford
Born: 1 February 1894, Cape Elizabeth, Maine
Died: 31 August 1973, Palm Desert, California

Following the listing of Ford's films below are full credits for each of the films discussed in this book. These are taken from several sources: William Patrick Wooten's 'An Index to the Films of John Ford', *Sight and Sound* Index series No. 13, February 1948; George J. Mitchell's 'The Films of John Ford', *Films in Review*, March 1963; a filmography by Pierre Guinle, Vincent Porter and Patrick Brion in *Présence du Cinéma*, March 1965; Patrick Brion's filmography in *Cahiers du Cinéma*, October 1966; *John Ford* by Peter Bogdanovich, 1967; *John Ford, En Dokumentation*, edited by Per Calum, 1968; and *The American Movies Reference Book: The Sound Era*, edited by Paul Michael, 1968. Some newly collected information has been added.

1917 *The Tornado, The Scrapper, The Soul Herder, Cheyenne's Pal, Straight Shooting, The Secret Man, A Marked Man, Bucking Broadway*
1918 *The Phantom Riders, Wild Women, Thieves' Gold, The Scarlet Drop, Hell Bent, A Woman's Fool, Three Mounted Men*
1919 *Roped, The Fighting Brothers, A Fight for Love, By Indian Post, The Rustlers, Bare Fists, Gun Law, The Gun Packer, Riders of Vengeance, The Last*

Outlaw, The Outcasts of Poker Flat, The Ace of the Saddle, The Rider of the Law, A Gun Fightin' Gentleman, Marked Men

1920   *The Prince of Avenue A, The Girl in Number 29, Hitchin' Posts, Just Pals*
1921   *The Big Punch, The Freeze Out, The Wallop, Desperate Trails, Action, Sure Fire, Jackie*
1922   *Little Miss Smiles, The Village Blacksmith*
1923   *The Face on the Barroom Floor, Three Jumps Ahead, Cameo Kirby, North of Hudson Bay, Hoodman Blind*
1924   *The Iron Horse, Hearts of Oak*
1925   *Lightnin', Kentucky Pride, The Fighting Heart, Thank You*
1926   *The Shamrock Handicap, Three Bad Men, The Blue Eagle*
1927   *Upstream*
1928   *Mother Machree, Four Sons, Hangman's House, Napoleon's Barber, Riley the Cop*
1929   *Strong Boy, The Black Watch* (with Lumsden Hare), *Salute*
1930   *Men Without Women, Born Reckless* (with Andrew Bennison), *Up the River*
1931   *Seas Beneath, The Brat, Arrowsmith*
1932   *Air Mail, Flesh*
1933   *Pilgrimage, Doctor Bull*
1934   *The Lost Patrol, The World Moves On, Judge Priest*
1935   *The Whole Town's Talking, The Informer, Steamboat Round the Bend*
1936   *The Prisoner of Shark Island, Mary of Scotland, The Plough and the Stars*
1937   *Wee Willie Winkie, The Hurricane*
1938   *Four Men and a Prayer, Submarine Patrol*
1939   *Stagecoach, Young Mr Lincoln, Drums Along the Mohawk*
1940   *The Grapes of Wrath, The Long Voyage Home*
1941   *Tobacco Road, Sex Hygiene* (short), *How Green Was My Valley*
1942   *The Battle of Midway* (short), *Torpedo Squadron* (short)
1943   *December 7th* (short, with Gregg Toland)
1945   *They Were Expendable*
1946   *My Darling Clementine*
1947   *The Fugitive*
1948   *Fort Apache, Three Godfathers*
1949   *She Wore a Yellow Ribbon*
1950   *When Willie Comes Marching Home, Wagon Master, Rio Grande*
1951   *This Is Korea!* (short)
1952   *What Price Glory?, The Quiet Man*
1953   *The Sun Shines Bright, Mogambo*
1955   *The Long Gray Line, The Red, White and Blue Line* (short), *Mr Roberts* (with Mervyn LeRoy), *The Bamboo Cross* (TV), *Rookie of the Year* (TV)
1956   *The Searchers*
1957   *The Wings of Eagles, The Rising of the Moon*
1958   *The Last Hurrah*
1959   *Gideon of Scotland Yard, Korea* (short), *The Horse Soldiers*

1960   *The Colter Craven Story* (TV), *Sergeant Rutledge*
1961   *Two Rode Together*
1962   *The Man Who Shot Liberty Valance*, *Flashing Spikes* (TV), *The Civil War* (an episode in *How the West Was Won*)
1963   *Donovan's Reef*
1964   *Cheyenne Autumn*
1965   *Young Cassidy* (with Jack Cardiff)
1966   *Seven Women*
1970   *Chesty* (for TV, as yet unshown)

Ford also directed sequences in *Silver Wings* (Edwin Carewe, 1922), *The Adventures of Marco Polo* (Archie Mayo, 1938), *Hondo* (John Farrow, 1953) and *The Alamo* (John Wayne, 1960). He shot several weeks on *Pinky* (1949), but was replaced by Elia Kazan, who jettisoned what Ford had shot; and he worked with his Field Photographic Unit in preparing a compilation of documentary footage, later abandoned, for the Nuremberg Trials. During World War II, Ford and his unit shot a great deal of official footage which was never publicly seen. He produced *Mighty Joe Young* (Ernest B. Schoedsack, 1949) with Merian C. Cooper, and helped Budd Boetticher edit *The Bullfighter and the Lady* (1951). He was executive producer of *Vietnam! Vietnam!*, a United States Information Agency documentary directed by Sherman Beck. His unfilmed projects included the life of Ulysses S. Grant; a remake of his 1919 film *The Last Outlaw*, to have starred Harry Carey (1943–5); Nina Federova's novel *The Family* (1947), with John Wayne and Ethel Barrymore; Reginald Arkell's novel *The Miracle of Merriford* (1965–6), with Dan Dailey; *O.S.S.*, the life of Gen. William 'Wild Bill' Donovan, Ford's commanding officer during World War II, with John Wayne; Arthur Conan Doyle's novel *The White Company*, with Wayne, Laurence Olivier and Alec Guinness; Howard Fast's novel *April Morning*, with Wayne; Maxwell Anderson's play *Valley Forge*, which he announced in 1971 as a film he would co-direct with Frank Capra; and *The Josh Clayton Story*, a Western about black Cavalrymen with Fred Williamson and Woody Strode.

Ford was a stuntman and an actor in a number of silent films directed by his brother Francis from 1914 to 1917, and a Klansman in *The Birth of a Nation* (D. W. Griffith, 1915). He also played the lead in the first two films he directed, *The Tornado* and *The Scrapper*, and appeared in a number of military training films during World War II. Ford was the subject of three films, *John Ford: Memorial Day 1970* (Mark Haggard, 1970), *Directed by John Ford* (Peter Bogdanovich, 1971), and *The American West of John Ford* (Denis Sanders, 1971), and he appeared in all three.

Straight Shooting (1917)
Production Company   Butterfly/Universal
Executive Producer   Carl Laemmle

John Ford

Director	Jack Ford
Script	George Hively
Photographer	George Scott

Harry Carey (*Cheyenne Harry*), Molly Malone (*Joan Sims*), George Berrell (*Sweetwater Sims*), Ted Brooks (*Ted Sims*), Hoot Gibson (*Danny Morgan*), Duke Lee ('*Thunder' Flint*), Vester Pegg ('*Placer' Fremont*), Milt Brown (*Black-Eyed Pete*). Running time: 5 reels. Released, 27 August 1917

Stagecoach (1939)

Production Company	Wanger/United Artists
Executive Producer	Walter Wanger
Producer	John Ford
Director	John Ford
Second Unit Director	Yakima Canutt
Assistant Director	Wingate Smith
Script	Dudley Nichols, from the story *Stage to Lordsburg* by Ernest Haycox
Director of Photography	Bert Glennon
Editors	Otho Lovering, Dorothy Spencer, Walter Reynolds
Art Director	Alexander Toluboff
Set Director	Wiard B. Ihnen
Costumes	Walter Plunkett
Music	Richard Hageman, W. Franke Harling, John Leipold, Leo Shuken, Louis Gruenberg
Special Effects	Ray Binger

John Wayne (*The Ringo Kid*), Claire Trevor (*Dallas*), Thomas Mitchell (*Dr Josiah Boone*), Andy Devine (*Buck, the stagecoach driver*), John Carradine (*Hatfield*), Donald Meek (*Samuel Peacock*), Louise Platt (*Lucy Mallory*), George Bancroft (*Sheriff Curly Wilcox*), Berton Churchill (*Banker Henry Gatewood*), Tim Holt (*Lt Blanchard*), Tom Tyler (*Hank Plummer*), Joseph Rickson (*Luke Plummer*), Vester Pegg (*Ike Plummer*), Chris Pin Martin (*Chris*), Elvira Rios (*Yakima, his wife*), Francis Ford (*Billy Pickett*), Kent Odell (*Billy Pickett Jr*), Marga Daighton (*Mrs Pickett*), Yakima Canutt (*Stuntman*), Chief John Big Tree (*Scout*), Harry Tenbrook (*Telegraph operator*), Jack Pennick (*Jerry, the bartender*), Paul McVey (*Express agent*), Cornelius Keefe (*Capt. Whitney*), Florence Lake (*Mrs Nancy Whitney*), Louis Mason (*Sheriff*), Brenda Fowler (*Mrs Gatewood*), Walter McGrail (*Capt. Sickel*), William Hoffer (*Sergeant*), Bryant Washburn (*Capt. Simmons*), Nora Cecil (*Dr Boone's housekeeper*), Helen Gibson, Dorothy Annleby (*Dancing girls*), Buddy Roosevelt, Bill Cody (*Ranchers*), Chief White Horse (*Indian chief*), Duke Lee (*Sheriff of Lordsburg*), Mary Kathleen Walker (*Mallory baby*), Ed Brady, Steve

They Were Expendable

Clemente, Theodore Larch, Fritzi Brunette, Leonard Trainor, Chris Phillips, Tex Driscoll, Teddy Billings, John Eckert, Al Lee, Jack Mohr, Patsy Doyle, Wiggie Blowne, Margaret Smith.
Running time: 97 minutes. Released, 2 March 1939

They Were Expendable (1945)

Production Company	M-G-M
Producer	John Ford
Associate Producer	Cliff Reid
Director	John Ford
Second Unit Director	James C. Havens
Assistant Director	Edward O'Fearna
Rear-Projection Plates	Robert Montgomery
Script	Lt-Cmdr. Frank W. Wead, from the book by William L. White
Director of Photography	Joseph H. August
Editors	Frank E. Hull, Douglas Biggs
Art Directors	Cedric Gibbons, Malcolm F. Browne
Set Decorators	Edwin B. Willis, Ralph S. Hurst

Special Effects	A. Arnold Gillespie
Music	Herbert Stothart
Recording Director	Douglas Shearer

Robert Montgomery (*Lt John Brickley*), John Wayne (*Lt jg. Rusty Ryan*), Donna Reed (*Lt Sandy Davyss*), Jack Holt (*General Martin*), Ward Bond (*Boats Mulcahey*), Louis Jean Heydt (*Ohio*), Marshall Thompson (*Ens. Snake Gardner*), Cameron Mitchell (*Ens. George Cross*), Russell Simpson (*Dad Knowland*), Leon Ames (*Maj. James Morton*), Paul Langton (*Ens. Andy Andrews*), Jeff York (*Ens. Tony Aiken*), Murray Alper (*Slug Mahan*), Arthur Walsh (*Seaman Jones*), Donald Curtis (*Lt jg. Shorty Long*), Harry Tenbrook (*Squarehead Larsen*), Jack Pennick (*Doc Charlie*), Charles Trowbridge (*Admiral Blackwell*), Robert Barrat (*Gen. Douglas MacArthur*), Bruce Kellog (*Elder Tomkins*), Tim Murdock (*Ens. Brown*), Vernon Steele (*Doctor at Corregidor*), Eve March (*Nurse*), Alex Havier (*Benny Lecoco*), Pedro de Cordoba (*Priest*), Trina Lowe (*Gardner's girl-friend*), Pacita Tod-Tod (*Nightclub singer*), William B. Davidson (*Hotel manager*), Robert Emmett O'Connor (*Bartender at the Silver Dollar*), Max Ong (*Mayor of Cebu*), Bill Wilkerson (*Sgt Smith*), John Carlyle (*Lt James*), Phillip Ahn (*Army orderly*), Betty Blythe (*Officer's wife*), Kermit Maynard (*Officer at airport*), Stubby Kruger, Sammy Stein, Michael Kirby, Blake Edwards (*Boat crew*).
Running time: 136 minutes. Released, 20 December 1945

My Darling Clementine (1946)

Production Company	20th-Century Fox
Executive Producer	Darryl F. Zanuck
Producer	Samuel G. Engel
Director	John Ford
Assistant Director	William Eckhardt
Script	Samuel G. Engel, Winston Miller, from a story by Sam Hellman, based on the book *Wyatt Earp, Frontier Marshal* by Stuart N. Lake
Director of Photography	Joseph P. MacDonald
Editor	Dorothy Spencer
Art Directors	James Basevi, Lyle H. Wheeler
Set Decorators	Thomas Little, Fred J. Rode
Costumes	Rene Hubert
Music	Cyril Mockridge
Technical Advisor	Wyatt Earp

Henry Fonda (*Wyatt Earp*), Cathy Downs (*Clementine Carter*), Victor Mature (*Doctor John Holliday*), Linda Darnell (*Chihuahua*), Walter Brennan (*Pa Clanton*), Ward Bond (*Morgan Earp*), Tim Holt (*Virgil Earp*), Don Garner (*James Earp*), Alan Mowbray (*Granville Thorndyke*), John Ireland (*Billy Clanton*), Grant Withers (*Ike

Clanton), Mickey Simpson (*Sam Clanton*), Fred Libby (*Phin Clanton*), Roy Roberts (*Mayor*), Jane Darwell (*Kate Nelson*), Russell Simpson (*John Simpson*), Francis Ford (*Dad, old soldier*), J. Farrell MacDonald (*Mac, the bartender*), Ben Hall (*Barber*), Arthur Walsh (*Hotel clerk*), Louis Mercier (*François*), Harry Woods (*Luke*), Charles Stevens (*Indian Joe*), William B. Davidson (*Owner of Oriental saloon*), Earle Foxe (*Gambler*), Aleth 'Speed' Hansen (*Guitar player*), Danny Borzage (*Accordion player*), Frank Conlan (*Piano player*), Don Barclay (*Opera house owner*), Jack Pennick, Robert Adler (*Stagecoach drivers*), Mae Marsh.
Running time: 97 minutes. Released, November 1946

Fort Apache (1948)

Production Company	Argosy Pictures/RKO
Producers	John Ford, Merian C. Cooper
Production Manager	Bernard McEveety
Director	John Ford
Second Unit Director	Cliff Lyons
Assistant Directors	Jack Pennick, Lowell Farrell
Script	Frank Nugent, from the story *Massacre* by James Warner Bellah
Director of Photography	Archie J. Stout
Second Unit Photography	William Clothier
Editor	Jack Murray
Art Director	James Basevi
Set Decorator	Joe Kish
Costumes	Michael Meyers, Ann Peck
Music	Richard Hageman

Henry Fonda (*Lt-Col. Owen Thursday*), John Wayne (*Capt. Kirby York*), Shirley Temple (*Philadelphia Thursday*), John Agar (*Lt Michael O'Rourke*), Ward Bond (*Sgt-Maj. Michael O'Rourke*), Irene Rich (*Mrs O'Rourke*), George O'Brien (*Capt. Sam Collingwood*), Anna Lee (*Emily Collingwood*), Victor McLaglen (*Sgt Festus Mulcahy*), Pedro Armendariz (*Sgt Beaufort*), Guy Kibbee (*Dr Wilkens*), Grant Withers (*Silas Meacham*), Miguel Inclan (*Cochise*), Jack Pennick (*Sgt Shattuck*), Ray Hyke (*Gates*), Mae Marsh (*Mrs Gates*), Dick Foran (*Sgt Quincannon*), Frank Ferguson (*Newspaperman*), Francis Ford (*Stagecoach driver*), Movita Castenada (*Guadalupe*), Hank Worden (*Southern recruit*), Mary Gordon (*Woman in stagecoach station*), Harry Tenbrook (*Courier*).
Running time: 127 minutes. Released, 9 March 1948

Wagon Master (1950)

Production Company	Argosy Pictures/Republic
Producers	John Ford, Merian C. Cooper

Associate Producer	Lowell Farrell
Director	John Ford
Second Unit Director	Cliff Lyons
Assistant Director	Wingate Smith
Script	Frank S. Nugent, Patrick Ford, from an original story by John Ford
Director of Photography	Bert Glennon
Second Unit Photography	Archie J. Stout
Editor	Jack Murray
Assistant Editor	Barbara Ford
Art Director	James Basevi
Set Decorator	Joe Kish
Costumes	Wes Jeffries, Adele Parmenter
Music	Richard Hageman

Ward Bond (*Elder Wiggs*), Ben Johnson (*Travis Blue*), Harry Carey Jr (*Sandy Owens*), Joanne Dru (*Denver*), Charles Kemper (*Uncle Shiloh Clegg*), Jane Darwell (*Sister Ledeyard*), Alan Mowbray (*Dr A. Locksley Hall*), Ruth Clifford (*Fleuretty Phyffe*), Russell Simpson (*Adam Perkins*), Kathleen O'Malley (*Prudence Perkins*), James Arness (*Floyd Clegg*), Fred Libby (*Reese Clegg*), Hank Worden (*Luke Clegg*), Mickey Simpson (*Jesse Clegg*), Francis Ford (*Mr Peachtree*), Cliff Lyons (*Sheriff of Crystal City*), Don Summers (*Sam Jenkins*), Movita Castenada (*Navajo woman*), Jim Thorpe (*Navajo*), Chuck Hayward (*Jackson*).
Running time: 86 minutes. Released, 19 April 1950

The Quiet Man (1952)

Production Company	Argosy Pictures/Republic
Producers	John Ford, Merian C. Cooper
Director	John Ford
Second Unit Directors	John Wayne, Patrick Ford
Assistant Director	Andrew V. McLaglen
Script	Frank S. Nugent, from the story by Maurice Walsh
Director of Photography	Winton C. Hoch
Colour Process	Technicolor
Second Unit Photography	Archie J. Stout
Colour Consultant	Francis Cugat
Editor	Jack Murray
Assistant Editor	Barbara Ford
Art Director	Frank Hotaling
Set Decorators	John McCarthy Jr, Charles Thompson
Costumes	Adele Palmer
Music	Victor Young
Narrator	Ward Bond

John Wayne (*Sean Thornton*), Maureen O'Hara (*Mary Kate Danaher Thornton*), Victor McLaglen (*Red Will Danaher*), Barry Fitzgerald (*Michaeleen og Flynn*), Ward Bond (*Father Peter Lonergan*), Mildred Natwick (*Sarah Tillane*), Francis Ford (*Dan Tobin*), Arthur Shields (*Rev. Cyril 'Snuffy' Playfair*), Eileen Crowe (*Elizabeth Playfair*), May Craig (*Woman at station*), Charles FitzSimmons (*Forbes*), Sean McClory (*Owen Glynn*), James Lilburn (*Father Paul*), Mae Marsh (*Father Paul's mother*), Jack McGowran (*Feeney*), Ken Curtis (*Dermot Fahy*), Harry Tenbrook (*Sgt Hanan*), Maj. Sam Harris (*General*), Joseph O'Dea (*Guard*), Eric Gorman (*Costello, the Castletown engineer*), Kevin Lawless (*Fireman*), Paddy O'Donnell (*Porter*), Webb Overlander (*Bailey, the station-master*), Harry Tyler (*Pat Cohan*), Don Hatswell (*Guppy*), David H. Hughes (*Constable*), Hank Worden (*Trainer*), Douglas Evans (*Ring physician*), Jack Roper (*Boxer*), Al Murphy (*Referee*), Patrick Wayne, Melinda Wayne, Michael Wayne, Antonia Wayne (*Children at race*), Pat O'Malley, Bob Perry.
Running time: 129 minutes. Released, 14 September 1952

The Sun Shines Bright (1953)

Production Company	Republic
Producers	John Ford, Merian C. Cooper
Director	John Ford
Assistant Director	Wingate Smith
Script	Laurence Stallings, from the stories *The Sun Shines Bright, The Mob from Massac* and *The Lord Provides*, by Irvin S. Cobb
Director of Photography	Archie J. Stout
Editor	Jack Murray
Assistant Editor	Barbara Ford
Art Director	Frank Hotaling
Set Decorators	John McCarthy Jr, George Milo
Costumes	Adele Palmer
Music	Victor Young

Charles Winninger (*Judge William Pittman Priest*), Stepin Fetchit (*Jeff Poindexter*), Arleen Whelan (*Lucy Lee*), John Russell (*Ashby Corwin*), Russell Simpson (*Dr Lewt Lake*), Ludwig Stossel (*Herman Felsburg*), Francis Ford (*Feeney*), Paul Hurst (*Sgt Jimmy Bagby*), Mitchell Lewis (*Sheriff Andy Redcliffe*), Eve March (*Mallie Cramp*), Grant Withers (*Buck Ramsey*), Milburn Stone (*Horace K. Maydew*), Dorothy Jordan (*Lucy's mother*), Elzie Emanuel (*U.S. Grant Woodford*), Henry O'Neill (*Jody Habersham*), Slim Pickens (*Mink*), James Kirkwood (*General Fairfield*), Mae Marsh (*Old lady at ball*), Jane Darwell (*Amora Ratchitt*), Ernest Whitman (*Uncle Pleasant Woodford*), Trevor Bardette (*Rufe*), Hal Baylor (*His son*), Clarence Muse (*Uncle Zack*), Jack Pennick (*Beaker*), Patrick Wayne, Ken Williams.
Running time: 90 minutes. Released in 1954

The Searchers (John Wayne, Jeffrey Hunter)

The Searchers (1956)

Production Company	C. V. Whitney Pictures/Warner Brothers
Producers	C. V. Whitney, Merian C. Cooper
Associate Producer	Patrick Ford
Production Supervisor	Lowell Farrell
Director	John Ford
Assistant Director	Wingate Smith
Script	Frank S. Nugent, from the novel by Alan LeMay
Director of Photography	Winton C. Hoch (VistaVision)
Colour Process	Technicolor
Second Unit Photography	Alfred Gilks
Colour Consultant	James Gooch
Editor	Jack Murray
Art Directors	Frank Hotaling, James Basevi
Set Decorator	Victor Gangelin
Costumes	Frank Beetson, Ann Peck
Music	Max Steiner
Orchestration	Murray Cutter

John Wayne (*Ethan Edwards*), Jeffrey Hunter (*Martin Pawley*), Vera Miles (*Laurie Jorgenson*), Ward Bond (*Capt. Rev. Samuel Johnson Clayton*), Henry Brandon (*Chief Scar*), Natalie Wood (*Debbie Edwards*), Lana Wood (*Debbie as a child*), Hank Worden (*Mose Harper*), John Qualen (*Lars Jorgenson*), Olive Carey (*Mrs Jorgenson*), Harry Carey Jr (*Brad Jorgenson*), Dorothy Jordan (*Martha Edwards*), Walter Coy (*Aaron Edwards*), Pippa Scott (*Lucy Edwards*), Ken Curtis (*Charlie McCorry*), Antonio Moreno (*Emilio Figueroa*), Beulah Archuletta (*Wild Goose Flying in the Night Sky, called Look*), Patrick Wayne (*Lt Greenhill*), Cliff Lyons (*Col. Greenhill*), Jack Pennick (*Private*), Peter Mamakos (*Futterman*), Chuck Roberson (*Man at wedding*), Bill Steele (*Nesby*), Mae Marsh (*Woman at fort*), Danny Borzage (*Accordion player at funeral*), Billy Cartledge, Chuck Hayward, Slim Hightower, Fred Kennedy, Frank McGrath, Dale van Sickle, Henry Wills, Terry Wilson, Away Luna, Billy Yellow, Bob Many Mules, Exactly Sonnie Betsuie, Feather Hat Jr, Harry Black Horse, Jack Tin Horn, Many Mules Son, Percy Shooting Star, Peter Grey Eyes, Pipe Line Begishe, Smile White Sheep.
Running time: 119 minutes. Released, 26 May 1956

The Rising of the Moon (1957)

Production Company	Four Province Productions/Warner Brothers
Producer	Michael Killanin
Director	John Ford
Script	Frank S. Nugent, from the story *The Majesty of the Law* by Frank O'Connor, and the plays

John Ford

	A Minute's Wait by Michael J. McHugh and *The Rising of the Moon* by Lady Gregory
Director of Photography	Robert Krasker
Editor	Michael Gordon
Art Director	Ray Simm
Costumes	Jimmy Bourke
Music	Eamonn O'Gallagher
Technical Advisors	Earnan O'Mally, Lennox Robinson, Patrick Scott
Narrator	Tyrone Power

Tyrone Power (*Host*); *The Majesty of the Law*: Noel Purcell (*Dan O'Flaherty*), Cyril Cusack (*Inspector Michael Dillon*), Jack McGowran (*Mickey J., the Poteen Man*), Eric Gorman, Paul Farrell (*Neighbours*), John Cowley (*O'Feeney, the Gombeen Man*); *A Minute's Wait*: Jimmy O'Dea (*Porter*), Tony Quinn (*Station master*), Paul Farrell (*Chauffeur*), J. G. Devlin (*Guard*), Michael Trubshawe (*Col. Frobisher*), Anita Sharp Bolster (*Mrs Frobisher*), Maureen Porter (*Peggy, the barmaid*), Godfrey Quigley (*Christy*), Harold Goldblatt (*Christy's father*), Maureen O'Connell (*May Ann McMahon*), May Craig (*May's aunt*), Michael O'Duffy (*Singer*), Ann Dalton (*Woman with lobsters*), Kevin Casey (*Mr McTigue*); *1921*: Dennis O'Dea (*Sgt Michael O'Hara*), Eileen Crowe (*His wife*), Donal Donnelly (*Sean Curran*), Maurice Good (*P.C. O'Grady*), Frank Lawton (*Major*), Edward Lexy (*R.Q.M.S.*), Joseph O'Dea (*Chief of guards*), Dennis Brennan, David Marlowe, Dennis Franks (*English officers*), Doreen Madden, Maureen Cusack (*False nuns*), Martin Thornton (*Sergeant*), John Horan (*Bill poster*), Joe Hone, John Comeford, Mafra McDonagh (*IRA men*), Maureen Delaney (*Old woman*), and members of the Abbey Theatre Company.
Running time: 81 minutes. Released, 10 August 1957

Sergeant Rutledge (1960)

Production Company	Ford Productions/Warner Brothers
Producers	Patrick Ford, Willis Goldbeck
Director	John Ford
Assistant Directors	Wingate Smith, Russ Saunders
Script	Willis Goldbeck, James Warner Bellah
Director of Photography	Bert Glennon
Colour Process	Technicolor
Editor	Jack Murray
Art Director	Eddie Imazu
Set Decorator	Frank M. Miller
Costumes	Marjorie Best
Music	Howard Jackson

Woody Strode (*1st Sgt Braxton Rutledge*), Jeffrey Hunter (*Lt Tom Cantrell*), Constance Towers (*Mary Beecher*), Willis Bouchey (*Col. Otis Fosgate*), Juano

Hernandez (*Sgt Matthew Luke Skidmore*), Billie Burke (*Mrs Cordelia Fosgate*), Carleton Young (*Capt. Shattuck*), Judson Pratt (*Lt Mulqueen*), Bill Henry (*Capt. Dwyer*), Mae Marsh (*Nellie*), Fred Libby (*Chandler Hubble*), Toby Richards (*Lucy Dabney*), Jan Styne (*Chris Hubble*), Cliff Lyons (*Sam Beecher*), Charles Seel (*Dr C. J. Eckner*), Jack Pennick (*Sergeant*), Hank Worden (*Laredo*), Chuck Roberson (*Juror*), Shug Fisher (*Owens*), Walter Reed (*Capt. MacAfee*), Chuck Hayward (*Officer*), Eva Novak, Estelle Winwood (*Trial spectators*).
Running time: 111 minutes. Released, May 1960

The Man Who Shot Liberty Valance (1962)

Production Company	Ford Productions/Paramount
Producer	Willis Goldbeck
Director	John Ford
Assistant Director	Wingate Smith
Script	Willis Goldbeck, James Warner Bellah, from the story by Dorothy M. Johnson
Director of Photography	William H. Clothier
Editor	Otho Lovering
Art Directors	Hal Pereira, Eddie Imazu
Set Directors	Sam Comer, Darrell Silvera
Costumes	Edith Head
Music	Cyril J. Mockridge, and the Ann Rutledge theme from *Young Mr Lincoln* by Alfred Newman

John Wayne (*Tom Doniphon*), James Stewart (*Ransom Stoddard*), Vera Miles (*Hallie Stoddard*), Lee Marvin (*Liberty Valance*), Edmond O'Brien (*Dutton Peabody*), Andy Devine (*Marshal Linc Appleyard*), John Qualen (*Peter Ericson*), Woody Strode (*Pompey*), Jeanette Nolan (*Nora Ericson*), Strother Martin (*Floyd*), Lee Van Cleef (*Reese*), Ken Murray (*Doc Willoughby*), John Carradine (*Maj. Cassius Starbuckle*), Willis Bouchey (*Jason Tully*), Carleton Young (*Maxwell Scott*), Denver Pyle (*Amos Carruthers*), O. Z. Whitehead (*Ben Carruthers*), Robert F. Simon (*Handy Strong*), Paul Birch (*Mayor Winder*), Joseph Hoover (*Hasbrouck*), Jack Pennick (*Jack, the bartender*), Anna Lee (*Stagecoach passenger*), Charles Seel (*Convention chairman*), Shug Fisher (*Drunk*), Earle Hodgins, Stuart Holmes, Dorothy Phillips, Buddy Roosevelt, Gertrude Astor, Eva Novak, Slim Talbot, Monty Montana, Bill Henry, John B. Whiteford, Helen Gibson, Maj. Sam Harris.
Running time: 122 minutes. Released, April 1962

The Civil War (episode in *How the West Was Won*, 1962)

Production Company	Cinerama/M-G-M
Producer	Bernard Smith
Production Supervisors	Thomas Conroy, Walter Gibbons Fly

Director	John Ford
Assistant Director	Wingate Smith
Script	James R. Webb
Director of Photography	Joseph LaShelle (Cinerama and Ultra Panavision)
Colour Process	Metrocolor
Special Effects	A. Arnold Gillespie, Robert R. Hoag
Music	Alfred Newman, Ken Darby
Costumes	Walter Plunkett
Narrator	Spencer Tracy

George Peppard (*Zeb Rawlings*), Carroll Baker (*Eve Prescott Rawlings*), Harry Morgan (*Gen. Ulysses S. Grant*), John Wayne (*Gen. William Tecumseh Sherman*), Andy Devine (*Corporal Peterson*), Russ Tamblyn (*Confederate deserter*), Willis Bouchey (*Surgeon*), Claude Johnson (*Jeremiah Rawlings*), Raymond Massey (*Abraham Lincoln*).

Running time: 15 minutes. Other episodes of the 162-minute film were directed by Henry Hathaway (*The Rivers, The Plains, The Outlaws*) and George Marshall (*The Railroad*). Released, November 1962

Seven Women (1966)

Production Company	Ford-Smith Productions/M-G-M
Producer	Bernard Smith
Director	John Ford
Assistant Director	Wingate Smith
Script	Janet Green, John McCormick, from the story *Chinese Finale* by Norah Lofts
Director of Photography	Joseph LaShelle (Panavision)
Colour Process	Metrocolor
Editor	Otho Lovering
Art Directors	George W. Davis, Eddie Imazu
Set Decorators	Henry Grace, Jack Mills
Special Effects	J. McMillan Johnson
Costumes	Walter Plunkett
Music	Elmer Bernstein

Anne Bancroft (*Dr D. R. Cartwright*), Margaret Leighton (*Agatha Andrews*), Sue Lyon (*Emma Clark*), Flora Robson (*Miss Binns*), Mildred Dunnock (*Jane Argent*), Betty Field (*Florrie Pether*), Eddie Albert (*Charles Pether*), Anna Lee (*Mrs Russell*), Jane Chang (*Miss Ling*), Mike Mazurki (*Tunga Khan*), Woody Strode (*Lean Warrior*), Hans William Lee (*Kim*), Irene Tsu (*Concubine*), H. W. Gim (*Coolie*).

Running time: 87 minutes. Released, January 1966. Anne Bancroft replaced Patricia Neal, who was taken ill after three days of shooting.

Bibliography

I. Books and Pamphlets

1. William Patrick Wootten, *An Index to the Films of John Ford*, British Film Institute, London, 1948.
2. Jean Mitry, *John Ford* (two volumes), Classiques du Cinéma series, Editions Universitaires, Paris, 1954. Revised and reprinted in one volume, 1964.
3. Tullio Kezich, *John Ford*, Piccola Biblioteca del Cinema series, Guandra Editore, Parma, 1958.
4. Peter Bogdanovich, *John Ford*, Movie Magazine Ltd, London, 1967, and University of California Press, Berkeley, 1968.
5. Philippe Haudiquet, *John Ford*, Cinéma d'Aujourd'hui series, Editions Seghers, Paris, 1968.
6. Per Calum, ed., *John Ford, En Dokumentation*, Danske Filmmuseum, Copenhagen, 1968.
7. Michael Burrows, *John Ford and Andrew V. McLaglen*, Formative Films series, Primestyle, Cornwall, 1970.
8. John Baxter, *The Cinema of John Ford*, International Film Guide series, A. Zwemmer, London, 1971.
9. Warren French, *Filmguide to 'The Grapes of Wrath'*, Filmguide series, Indiana University Press, Bloomington, 1973.

II. Published screenplays

1. *The Informer* (by Dudley Nichols from the novel by Liam O'Flaherty) in *Modern British Dramas*, ed. by Harlan Hatcher, Harcourt, Brace and Co., New York, 1941; in *Modern Dramas*, ed. by Harlan Hatcher, Harcourt, Brace and Co., 1944; in *Theatre Arts*, August 1951; in French, *L'Avant Scène du Cinéma*, February 1, 1965; and excerpts in *The Moving Image* by Robert Gessner, E. P. Dutton, New York, 1968.
2. *Stagecoach* (by Dudley Nichols from a story by Ernest Haycox) in *Twenty Best Film Plays*, ed. by John Gassner and Dudley Nichols, Crown, New York, 1943; in *Great Film Plays*, ed. by John Gassner and Dudley Nichols, Crown, New York, 1959; in French, *L'Avant Scène du Cinéma*, 15 January, 1963; and in Lorrimer and Simon and Schuster editions, ed. by Nicola Hayden, London and New York, 1971, with the Haycox story included.
3. *The Grapes of Wrath* (by Nunnally Johnson from the novel by John Steinbeck) in *Twenty Best Film Plays*; an excerpt, in French, in Haudiquet's *John Ford*; and excerpts in *Filmguide to 'The Grapes of Wrath'*.
4. *How Green Was My Valley* (by Philip Dunne from the novel by Richard Llewellyn) in *Twenty Best Film Plays*, and an excerpt, in French, in Haudiquet's *John Ford*.

5. *Cheyenne Autumn* (by James R. Webb from the book by Mari Sandoz), the text, in French, of a scene cut from the film, in Haudiquet's *John Ford.*

III. Interviews

1. Howard Sharpe, 'The Star Creators of Hollywood', *Photoplay*, October 1936, reprinted in *The Talkies*, Richard Griffith, ed., Dover, New York, 1971.
2. Lindsay Anderson, 'The Quiet Man', *Sequence*, New Year, 1952.
3. Jean de Baroncelli, 'Avec Alfred Hitchcock et John Ford', *Le Monde,* 7 January 1955.
4. Jean Mitry, 'Interview', *Cinémonde*, 14 January 1955; 'Rencontre avec John Ford', *Cahiers du Cinéma*, March 1955, reprinted in *Films in Review*, August–September 1955, and in *Interviews with Film Directors*, Andrew Sarris, ed., Bobbs-Merrill, New York, 1966.
5. Michael Killanin, 'Poet in an Iron Mask', *Films and Filming*, February 1958, reprinted as 'En travaillant avec John Ford', *Cahiers du Cinéma*, July 1958.
6. Colin Young, 'The Old Dependables', *Film Quarterly*, Fall 1959.
7. Jean-Louis Rieupeyrout, 'Rencontre avec John Ford', *Cinéma 61*, February 1961.
8. Bill Libby, 'The Old Wrangler Rides Again', *Cosmopolitan*, March 1964.
9. George J. Marshall, 'Ford on Ford', *Films in Review*, June–July 1964, an account of an appearance by Ford at the University of California, Los Angeles, reprinted in *Présence du Cinéma*, March 1965.
10. Axel Madsen, 'Rencontre avec John Ford', *Cahiers du Cinéma*, July 1965; and 'Cavalier Seul', *Cahiers du Cinéma*, October 1966.
11. Samuel Lachize, 'Brève rencontre avec John Ford', *L'Humanité*, 12 July 1966.
12. Michèle Motte, 'Le vieux John Ford parle du Western', *Paris-Presse*, 12 July 1966.
13. Yvonne Baby, 'John Ford à Paris', *Le Monde*, 16–17 July 1966.
14. Philippe Haudiquet, 'En bavardant avec John Ford', *Les Lettres Francaises*, 21 July 1966.
15. Claude-Jean Philippe, 'John Ford en chair et en os', *Télérama*, 31 July 1966.
16. Bertrand Tavernier, 'John Ford à Paris', *Positif*, March 1967.
17. Burt Kennedy, 'A Talk with John Ford', *Action*, September–October 1968, reprinted in *Films in Review*, January 1969, and *Films and Filming*, October 1969.
18. Claudine Tavernier, 'La 4ème Dimension de la Vieillesse', *Cinéma 69*, June 1969.
19. Anon., 'An Interview with John Ford', *Focus!*, October 1969. An account of an appearance by Ford at the University of Chicago.
20. Philip Jenkinson, 'John Ford talks to Philip Jenkinson about not being interested in movies', *The Listener*, 12 February 1970.
21. Richard Schickel, 'Good days, good years', *Harper's*, October 1970.
22. Joseph McBride, 'County Mayo Gu Bragh ...', *Sight and Sound*, Winter 1970–71.

23. Mark Haggard, 'Ford in Person', *Focus on Film*, Spring 1971. An account of appearances by Ford at the University of Southern California in March 1969 and February 1970.
24. Anon., 'John Ford on *Stagecoach*', *Action*, September–October 1971.
25. Vernon Scott, Associated Press dispatch, 19 November 1971, on Ford's plan to co-direct a film with Frank Capra.
26. Noel Berggren, 'Arsenic and Old Directors', *Esquire*, April 1972.
27. Anon., 'Six Pioneers', *Action*, November–December 1972. An account of an appearance by Ford at the Directors Guild of America theatre in Hollywood.

Material from interviews with Ford also appears in *King Cohn*: The Life and Times of Harry Cohn, by Bob Thomas, Putnam, New York, 1967; *Spencer Tracy*, by Larry Swindell, The World Publishing Co., New York, 1969; *John Steinbeck*, by Richard O'Connor, McGraw-Hill, New York, 1970; and *Don't Say Yes Until I Finish Talking*: A Biography of Darryl F. Zanuck, by Mel Gussow, Doubleday, New York, 1971; and *Starring Miss Barbara Stanwyck*, by Ella Smith, Crown, New York, 1974.

IV. Articles

1. Lindsay Anderson, '*They Were Expendable* and John Ford', *Sequence*, Summer 1950, reprinted as 'The Method of John Ford' in *The Emergence of Film Art*, Lewis Jacobs, ed., Hopkinson and Blake, New York, 1970; 'The Director's Cinema?', *Sequence*, Autumn 1950, on *She Wore a Yellow Ribbon*, reprinted in *Films in Review*, February 1951; '*Wagon Master*' and '*Rio Grande*', *Sequence*, New Year, 1951; '*The Quiet Man*', *Sight and Sound*, July–September 1952; '*What Price Glory?*', *Sight and Sound*, January–March 1953; '*The Sun Shines Bright*', *Sight and Sound*, April–June 1954; '*The Long Gray Line*' and '*Mr Roberts*', *Sight and Sound*, Winter 1955–56; '*The Searchers*', *Sight and Sound*, Summer 1956; 'Éléments pour une biographie', *Cahiers du Cinéma*, August 1958; '*The Last Hurrah*', *Sight and Sound*, Spring 1959; and 'John Ford', *Cinema* (Beverly Hills), Spring 1971 (written in 1955), with an introduction by Gavin Lambert.
2. Jean-Georges Auriol, 'Lettre à John Ford sur *My Darling Clementine*', *La Revue du Cinéma*, Spring 1947.
3. Michael Barkun, 'Notes on the Art of John Ford', *Film Culture*, Summer 1962.
4. John Baxter, '*December 7th*', *Sight and Sound*, Winter 1972–3.
5. James Warner Bellah, 'The Birth of a Story', introduction to his novel *Sergeant Rutledge*, Bantam Books, New York, 1960, based on the script by Bellah and Willis Goldbeck.
6. Bruce Beresford, 'Decline of a Master', *Film*, Autumn 1969.
7. Barbara Bernstein, 'Not Likely', *Focus!*, Spring 1970, on John Wayne. See also *The Films of John Wayne* by Mark Ricci, Boris Zmijewsky and Steve Zmijewsky, The Citadel Press, New York, 1970, and *Duke*: The Story of John Wayne, by Mike Tomkies, Henry Regnery, Chicago, 1971.

8. George Bluestone, *'The Informer'*, and *'The Grapes of Wrath'* in *Novels Into Film*, University of California Press, Berkeley and Los Angeles, 1957.

9. Peter Bogdanovich, 'The Autumn of John Ford', *Esquire*, April 1964, reprinted in *Positif*, No. 64–65, 1964, in French, and in revised form as the introduction to his *John Ford*; and 'Taps for Mr Ford', *New York*, September, 1973.

10. David Bordwell, *'The Man Who Shot Liberty Valance'*, *Film Comment*, Fall 1971.

11. Jean Bouville, *'The Informer'*, *Image et Son*, No. 223, 1968.

12. Stuart Byron, *'The Iron Horse'*, *Film Comment*, November–December 1972.

13. Ernest Callenbach, *'The Man Who Shot Liberty Valance* and *Donovan's Reef'*, *Film Quarterly*, Winter 1963–4.

14. Russell Campbell, *'Fort Apache'*, *The Velvet Light Trap*, Summer 1971.

15. Kingsley Canham, 'Old Master Revisited', *Films and Filming*, July 1970.

16. Samuel Cherniak, 'Toward *Liberty Valance'*, *Moviegoer*, Summer–Autumn 1964, on *The Horse Soldiers*.

17. Collective, *'Young Mr Lincoln* de John Ford', *Cahiers du Cinéma*, August–September 1970, reprinted in translation in *Screen*, Autumn 1972, with an afterword by Peter Wollen.

18. Jean Collett, *'The Fugitive* de John Ford; le mystère de la Passion et le jeu du Western', in *La Passion du Christ comme thème Cinématographique*, Michel Estève, ed., Lettres Modernes, Paris, 1961.

19. Jean-Louis Comolli, 'Signes de piste: *Cheyenne Autumn'*, *Cahiers du Cinéma*, March 1965; and 'Les sept femmes de John Ford', *Cahiers du Cinéma*, September 1966, on *Seven Women*.

20. Bosley Crowther, *'The Informer'* and *'The Grapes of Wrath'* in *The Great Films: Fifty Golden Years of Motion Pictures*, G. P. Putnam's Sons, New York, 1967.

21. Michel Delahaye, 'De John Ford à Sean Feeney', *Cahiers du Cinéma*, October 1966.

22. Daniel Delosne, *'La patrouille perdue (The Lost Patrol)'*, *Image et Son*, No. 223, 1968.

23. Jacques Doniol-Valcroze, *'The Fugitive'*, *La Revue du Cinéma*, March 1948; and 'Paix et tradition', *Cahiers du Cinéma*, November 1952, on *The Quiet Man*.

24. Peter John Dyer, *'Seven Women'*, *Sight and Sound*, Winter 1966–7.

25. David Ehrenstein, 'Ford's Apocalypse', *December*, 1967, on *Seven Women*.

26. Sergei Eisenstein, *'Mr Lincoln* by Mr Ford', *Iskusstvo Kino*, 1960, reprinted in Eisenstein's *Film Essays*, Jay Leyda, ed., Dennis Dobson, London, 1968, and Praeger, New York, 1970.

27. Peter Ericsson, 'John Ford', *Sequence*, Winter 1947, reprinted as 'Les oeuvres récentes de John Ford', in *La Revue du Cinéma*, February 1948.

28. William K. Everson, 'John Ford: A Half-Century of Horse Operas', in *A Pictorial History of the Western Film*, The Citadel Press, New York, 1969; 'Forgotten Ford', *Focus on Film*, Spring 1971; and 'John Ford Goes to War – Against VD', *Film Fan Monthly*, May 1971, on *Sex Hygiene*.

29. Manny Farber, 'Parade Floats', in *Negative Space*, Praeger, New York, 1971,

articles on *The Quiet Man* and *Two Rode Together*, reprinted from *The Nation* and *Artforum*.

30. Charles Ford, 'Un nouveau maître: John Ford', in *Histoire du Western*, Pierre Horay, Paris, 1964.

31. Dan Ford, '*The (American) West of John Ford* and How It Was Made', *Action*, September–October 1971.

32. John Ford, foreword to Frank Capra's *The Name Above the Title*, Macmillan, New York, 1971.

33. Madeleine Garrigou-Lagrange, '*Les deux cavaliers (Two Rode Together)*', *Teléciné*, June–July 1962.

34. René Gieure, 'John Ford', *Image et Son*, February 1961.

35. John Gillett, 'Working with Ford', *Sight and Sound*, Winter 1959–60, an interview with producer Martin Rackin on *The Horse Soldiers*.

36. Woody Guthrie, 'Woody Sez', a review of *The Grapes of Wrath* from *The Daily Worker*, 1940, reprinted in *A Mighty Hard Road* by Henrietta Yurchenco, McGraw-Hill, New York, 1970.

37. Stuart Hall and Paddy Whannel, 'John Ford', in *The Popular Arts*, Hutchinson, London, 1964.

38. Philippe Haudiquet, 'John Ford: hier, aujourd'hui, demain', *Cinématographie Française*, 4 April 1964; and '*Toute la ville en parle (The Whole Town's Talking)*', *Image et Son*, October 1965.

39. J. B. Hoare and M. E. Hoare, '*The Searchers*', in *Screen Education Yearbook*, Roger Mainds, ed., Society for Education in Film and Television, London, 1966.

40. Charlayne Hunter, 'Woody Strode? He Wasn't the Star, But He Stole the Movie', The New York *Times*, 19 September 1971, an interview on *Sergeant Rutledge*.

41. Tim Hunter, 'An Interview with William Clothier', *On Film*, No. 2, 1970.

42. Lewis Jacobs, in *The Rise of the American Film*, Teachers College Press, New York, 1968, pp. 479–86.

43. Albert Johnson, 'The Tenth Muse in San Francisco (2)', *Sight and Sound*, Spring 1955, on *Young Mr Lincoln*.

44. Nunnally Johnson, a letter to Lindsay Anderson about working with Ford, 24 January 1955, printed in Haudiquet's *John Ford*.

45. Abraham Kaplan, 'Realism in the film: a philosopher's viewpoint', *Quarterly of Film, Radio and T.V.*, Summer 1953.

46. Jim Kitses, 'Authorship and Genre: Notes on the Western', in *Horizons West*, Indiana University Press, Bloomington and Thames and Hudson, London, 1969.

47. Hans-Peter Kochenrath, 'Die Welt John Ford', *Filmstudio*, No. 46, 1964.

48. Gavin Lambert, '*She Wore a Yellow Ribbon*', in *The Cinema 1951*, Roger Manvell and R. K. N. Baxter, eds., Penguin Books, London, 1951.

49. Herb Lightman, 'The Filming of *Cheyenne Autumn*', *The American Cinematographer*, November 1964.

50. Blake Lucas, 'John Ford: America's Greatest Gift to Film', The Los Angeles *Free Press*, 14 May 1971.

51. Joseph McBride, 'Stepin Fetchit Talks Back', *Film Quarterly*, Summer 1971;

'Drums Along the Mekong', *Sight and Sound*, Autumn 1972, on *Vietnam! Vietnam!*; and '*Three Godfathers*', *Film Comment*, July–August 1973.

52. Douglas McVay, 'The Five Worlds of John Ford', *Films and Filming*, June 1962.

53. Philippe Maillat, '*Les Cheyennes (Cheyenne Autumn)*', *Teléciné*, January–February 1965.

54. Louis Marcorelles, 'Ford of the Movies', *Cahiers du Cinéma*, August 1958; 'Comment ne plus être Irlandais', *Cahiers du Cinéma*, February 1959, on *The Rising of the Moon* and *The Last Hurrah*; and 'Heureux qui comme Ford', *Cahiers du Cinéma*, November 1959, on *The Horse Soldiers*.

55. Ken Mate, 'How Green Was Your Valley Then, John Ford', *The Velvet Light Trap*, Spring 1973.

56. Arthur C. Miller, 'With Cecil B. DeMille and John Ford' and 'Last Films Before Retirement', in *One Reel a Week* by Miller and Fred J. Balshofer, University of California Press, Berkeley and Los Angeles, 1967; and interviews with Miller in Charles Higham's *Hollywood Cameramen*, Thames and Hudson, London and Indiana University Press, Bloomington, 1970; and Leonard Maltin's *Behind the Camera*, The New American Library, New York, 1971.

57. Jean Mitry, 'Les Premiers Westerns de John Ford', *Positif*, No. 12.

58. Gene Moskowitz, 'John Ford and *The Horse Soldiers*', *Présence du Cinéma*, July–September 1959.

59. Enzo Natta, 'Il grande sentiero', *Cineforum*, March 1965, on *Cheyenne Autumn*.

60. Dudley Nichols, 'The Writer and the Film', in *Twenty Best Film Plays*, Nichols and John Gassner, eds, Crown, New York, 1943; and revised for *Great Film Plays*, Nichols and Gassner, eds, Crown, 1959; and letters to Lindsay Anderson on working with Ford, April–June 1955, printed in Haudiquet's *John Ford*.

61. Frank Nugent, 'Hollywood's Favorite Rebel', *Saturday Evening Post*, 23 July 1949; and a letter to Lindsay Anderson on working with Ford, 3 May 1953, printed in Haudiquet's *John Ford*.

62. Claude Ollier, 'Les saints des derniers jours', *Cahiers du Cinéma*, July 1964, on *Wagon Master*.

63. Richard Patterson, 'Making a Compilation Documentary', *The American Cinematographer*, June 1972, on Peter Bogdanovich's *Directed by John Ford*.

64. William S. Pechter, 'A Persistence of Vision', in *Twenty-Four Times a Second*, Harper and Row, New York and London, 1971, on *The Man Who Shot Liberty Valance*.

65. V. F. Perkins, '*Cheyenne Autumn*', *Movie*, Spring 1965.

66. Claude-Jean Philippe, 'L'Amérique par excellence', *Cahiers du Cinéma*, November 1962, on *The Man Who Shot Liberty Valance*.

67. Rebecca Pulliam, '*The Grapes of Wrath*', *The Velvet Light Trap*, Summer 1971.

68. Mario Quargnolo, 'Ripensando a Ombre Rosse', *Bianco e Nero*, November 1957, on *Stagecoach*.

69. Jeffrey Richards, 'Ford's Lost World', *Focus on Film*, Spring 1971.

70. Jean-Louis Rieupeyrout, in *Le grande aventure du Western: du Far West à Hollywood (1894–1963)*, Editions du Cerf, Paris, 1964, several sections on Ford.

71. David Robinson, '*The Horse Soldiers*', *Sight and Sound*, Winter 1959–60.

72. Andrew Sarris, 'Cactus Rosebud, or *The Man Who Shot Liberty Valance*', *Film Culture*, Summer 1962; '*Seven Women*', *The Village Voice*, 26 May 1966, reprinted in *Confessions of a Cultist*, Simon and Schuster, New York, 1970; 'John Ford' in *The American Cinema*, Dutton, New York, 1969; '*The Searchers*', *Film Comment*, Spring 1971; and '*Stagecoach* in 1939 and in Retrospect', *Action*, September–October 1971.

73. Douglas Slocombe, 'The Work of Gregg Toland', *Sequence*, Summer 1949; see also Robert Parrish, 'Gregg Toland: A Further Note', *Sequence*, Autumn 1949.

74. Alan Stanbrook, '*The Informer*', *Films and Filming*, July 1960.

75. Roger Tailleur, 'Sur trois films légendaires de John Ford', *Positif*, 1964, on *The Iron Horse*, *Young Mr Lincoln*, and *Wagon Master*.

76. Richard Thompson, 'John Ford's *Seven Women*', *Focus!*, May 1967, reprinted as '*Seven Women*' in *Persistence of Vision*, Joseph McBride, ed., Wisconsin Film Society Press, Madison, 1968; and '*Two Rode Together*', *The Velvet Light Trap*, Summer 1971.

77. Frederic Vitoux and Bernard Cohn, 'Deux films de John Ford', *Positif*, March 1967, on *Fort Apache* and *Seven Women*.

78. Eric Warman and Tom Vallance, 'John Ford: Man of the West' in *Westerns*, Golden Pleasure Books, London, 1964.

79. John Wayne *et al.*, 'The Company Remembers *Stagecoach*', *Action*, September–October 1971.

80. Peter Wollen, 'John Ford', *New Left Review*, January–February 1965 (as 'Lee Russell'); and a section on Ford in *Signs and Meaning in the Cinema*, Indiana University Press, Bloomington and Secker and Warburg, London, 1969.

81. Robin Wood, 'Shall We Gather at the River?: The Late Films of John Ford', *Film Comment*, Fall 1971.

82. David Zinman, '*The Informer*' and '*The Grapes of Wrath*' in *50 Classic Motion Pictures*, Crown, New York, 1970.

83. Maurice Zolotow, '*The American West of John Ford* comes to television with the help of an old friend', *TV Guide*, 4 December 1971.

Acknowledgments

Andrew Sarris' writings on Ford provided encouragement and inspiration, and Peter Bogdanovich's invaluable research into Ford's career established a factual groundwork for critical study of the director. Frank Pedi and James Dier of Films Incorporated, Skokie, Ill., generously arranged screenings of Ford films, as did Wayne Merry and Mark Bergman of the Wisconsin Film Society; Sudipta Chatterjee of the Green Lantern Cooperative, Madison; and Audio Films, Chicago. Gerald Peary read the manuscript and suggested some important changes. Linda Detra endured much and kept spirits high. Richard Thompson, Mark Haggard, Robin Wood, Patti Wallace, Fred J. Curran, John Aehl, Robert Gitt, Patrick Murphy, John Belton, Bill Detra Jr, Ken Mate, Alex Ameripoor, Don Schneider, John Baker, Tony Chase, David Shepard, Russell Campbell and Diane Sherman gave advice and assistance. Special thanks are due to John Ford's secretary, Rose Lew.

Sections of this book have appeared previously, some in slightly different form, in *The Velvet Light Trap*, *Film Comment*, *The Silent Picture*, the *AFI Report* and *Sight and Sound*, and the editors' permission to reprint is gratefully acknowledged. Thanks also for stills to the distributors concerned, and to the Wisconsin Centre for Theatre Research and the National Film Archive, London.

We would also like to thank our editor, David Wilson of the British Film Institute, for his unfailing tact and insight.

This book is dedicated to Robin Wood.

J.M., M.W.

Other DACAPO titles of interest